American Nomads

American Nomads

Travels with Lost Conquistadors,
Mountain Men, Cowboys, Indians,
Hoboes, and Bullriders

Richard Grant

GROVE PRESS   NEW YORK

First published in Great Britain in 2003 by Little, Brown, an imprint of Time Warner Books UK, London, England

Printed in the United States of America

Maps by John Gilkes

FIRST AMERICAN EDITION

Library of Congress Cataloging-in-Publication Data on file

ISBN 0-8021-1763-5

Grove Press
841 Broadway
New York, NY 10003

04 05 06 07 08   10 9 8 7 6 5 4 3 2 1

Acknowledgments

Writing this book entailed an ungodly amount of time spent sitting at home behind a desk. This was hard on me and the people around me. Thanks to those who furnished me with other places to go and write: John Catto, George Jackson and the fine people at the Lannan Foundation, who set up their writers with food, money and travel expenses as well.

I also feel indebted to Chuck Bowden and Marcus Boon, both of whom were generous with their knowledge and insights, and offered good advice when it was needed. Thanks to Mike Hatfield for giving me the original idea and to my agent Jonny Geller for helping it along and cutting the deals. Thanks to my parents for their love, support and an emergency loan that kept the book going. Most of all, thanks to Gale for reading, editing, being patient with me and seeing it through.

I take SPACE to be the central fact to man born in America, from Folsom cave to now. I spell it large because it comes large here. Large and without mercy . . . Some men ride on such space, others have to fasten themselves like a tent stake to survive.

Charles Olson, *Call Me Ishmael*

But there are things which you have said to me which I do not like. They were not sweet like sugar, but bitter like gourds. You have said that you want to put us on a reservation, to build us houses and make us medicine lodges [hospitals]. I do not want them. I was born upon the prairie, where the wind blew free and there was nothing to break the light of the sun. I was born where there were no enclosures and everything drew a free breath. I want to die there and not within walls.

Ten Bears (Comanche) at Medicine Lodge, Kansas, 1867

. . . to really tell about this whole extraordinary culture—in Texas and the Southwest, all the way to California—of aimless wandering, this mobile, uprooted life: the seven-mile-long trailer parks, the motorcycles, the campers, the people who have no addresses or even last names.

Truman Capote, *Capote: A Biography*

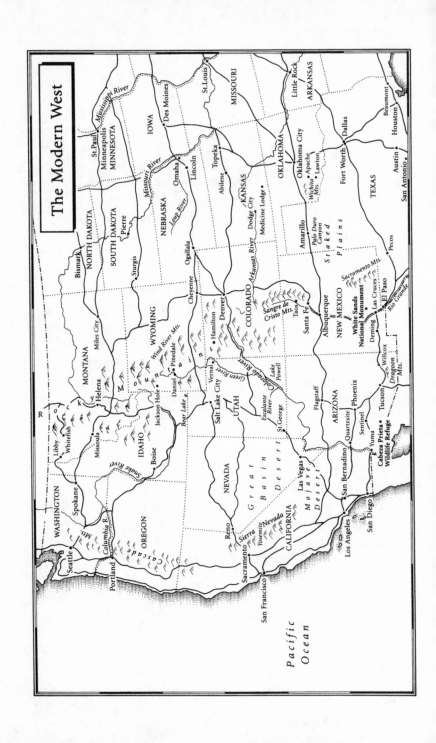

The Modern West

PROLOGUE

Looking back at my own American wanderings, they seem to flow together as one; memories strung out on a single cord of highway, fourteen years long and headed nowhere in particular. I like to think I have tasted freedom, but I also recognize the signs and snares of addiction. After a while, wandering generates its own momentum, its own set of cravings, phobias and justifications. I like to think of it as an adventure, a perpetual seeking out of new horizons and experiences, but like so many endeavors of this kind, it has also been an act of flight—away from a point in space and time, away from routines and responsibilities, away from a state of mind. And when it began, escape was my only concern.

In 1985 I was living in a grim and squalid council estate in east London—broke, unemployed, fresh out of university, hating just about everything English, and hating the weather with a special vehemence. Every winter, when the cold, damp gloom descended and the sky closed over, I felt trapped and claustrophobic, sentenced to another long stretch in a small, dank, overcrowded prison. It's not an uncommon reaction to the English winter. I just had a bad case of it. Maybe it was a childhood spent in Malaysia, Kuwait and other sunny places.

In winter, my drinking increased, and my politics turned fiery and anarchistic, only to mellow with the first good week of summer. Come November and I was ranting in the pub again, denouncing the nanny state and its unbridled police force, railing

against the constrictions of class and accent. By the time February
trudged around, I was ready to behead the Royal Family, or at
the very least pull them off the public teat. It depressed me deeply
that the British paid taxes, and often willingly, toward this symbol
of their subjugation and class inferiority.

The council estate was situated between a gasworks and a six-
lane motorway, in the concrete, high-rise wasteland of Bromley-
by-Bow. Gray mould grew up the wall of my unheated bedroom,
a drunken wife-beater lived in the flat below, Thatcher scolded
from the TV. Weaselly adolescent burglars sheltered from the rain
in the urine-scented stairwells, smirking and cupping their cigarettes, like something out of Dickens, or J. G. Ballard—"Got
robbed didja, mate? Nah, don't know nuffink about it. Prob'ly
one of 'em black cunts, innit? Pakis ain't got the bottle for it,
huh-huh-huh."

I remember walking to the dole office in the pissing rain, head
down and shoulders hunched, and everyone else on the streets
in the same posture. Dead fish in the poisoned canals, a Monday
morning sky the color of rain-darkened concrete. I remember an
old man muttering to himself at a bus stop, losing his words in
the wind. His face was completely caved-in—a physical deform-
ity of some kind, the legacy of a beating perhaps, but I fancied
it was from a lifetime of putting up with England. "Teabags," the
Americans called us, and I could see their point.

I had studied American history, and like so many Londoners I
was well versed in American popular culture, or so I thought. I
read American authors almost exclusively, played American music
as an occasional nightclub DJ, witnessed the inevitable films and
TV shows and advertizing images. I had been to California a
couple of times as a teenager. I had friends in New York and
Philadelphia. America was the obvious escape route. In my mind
it was the antithesis of England: a wide, sunny land, loose and
freewheeling, with no resemblance whatsoever to an old teabag.

I worked as a security guard that winter and hoarded my wages
for a plane ticket. The next summer I left behind a woman I loved,
flew to New York, and spent two months renovating a house for
friends in Philadelphia. At the end of it, I had eight hundred dollars

in my pocket. Where to next? I had read Kerouac at an impressionable age and a cross-country road trip sounded good to me.

We started west in an ageing burgundy sedan, three American friends and me, a twenty-two-year-old Englishman, having the time of his life. I had taken road trips around Europe before, but this was a different feeling. There was a continent ahead, 2700 miles wide, and no border crossings or language barriers to break its flow. There was a stretching-out of possibility, a promise of freedom and adventure, that you don't find on the German autobahn, or the M3 to Basingstoke. Even the place-names ahead had a musical, mythical ring to them: Chattanooga, Memphis, Amarillo, Oklahoma, Santa Fe.

Part of it, of course, was the accumulated weight of all those books, films, songs, TV shows, music videos and commercials. Forget the Statue of Liberty. The road is America's preeminent symbol of freedom, and this is understood by consumers of American culture all over the world. As I write this, a street urchin in Kathmandu, a merchant banker in Bonn and a failed pimp in Caracas are all dreaming about driving across America in a pair of Levi's and a fast car. A factory girl in Liverpool, gutting chickens on a conveyor belt, is dreaming about Thelma and Louise.

We slept the first night in a locust-swarmed campground somewhere in West Virginia, and crunched out of there at dawn, leaving two parallel lines of dead insects in our wake. Then a long day on the mountain backroads of Kentucky and Tennessee: tall, rangy men with beards and baseball caps staring at the out-of-state plates; loaded rifle-racks in the pickup trucks; strange preachers baying on the radio—"Hide ye in the blood of Jesus! Git warshed in the blood of the Lamb!"

We stopped at a liquor store near Black Mountain, Kentucky, bought a bottle of Old Weller 107, and drove on, passing the bottle around the car. Drunk on arrival in Nashville and then a long night rattling around the bars. Children, I wish there was a better way, but where else are you going to mingle with the locals? (Skinny black dealer in the men's room wants ten bucks for a wrap of chewing tobacco—"That's the cold dynamite shit right there, man. That's the shit God smokes.")

We slept by the side of the road, in campgrounds, or not at all, driving through the night and taking turns at the wheel. Oklahoma passed in darkness and dawn rose somewhere over the Texas panhandle. The land had turned from green to brown in the night and lay perfectly flat to the horizon in all directions. There were no more trees and something extraordinary had happened to the sky. I had assumed that all skies in the world were pretty much the same size and I wasn't prepared for this one. It had risen up during the night and spread itself outwards and doubled or tripled its dimensions. I got out of the car and stood in the West for the first time, turning a slow circle and following the unchanging horizon with my eyes, gazing up at the sky, dizzied and awestruck by this stark new world of space and light and wind.

Strange and austere as it appeared, there was also something eerily familiar about the landscape, like a fragment returning from a long-forgotten dream. Maybe it was an echo from my child-hood in the deserts of the Middle East. My favorite place as a boy in Kuwait was an escarpment that overlooked a big, flat, empty expanse of rock and sand. Maybe it was the sense of being dwarfed by the power and immensity of the natural world, contacting some deeper human pulse. Maybe it was just fake Hollywood memories, the high, lonesome, cinematic romance of the Western plains. Whatever the underlying reason, I felt compelled by the landscape and intoxicated by the space in a way I had never experienced before.

Gas pumps like tombstones in a West Texas ghost town, cattle grazing at an abandoned drive-in. A broken windmill. Then twenty miles of nothing. We drove on into New Mexico and the high plains faded into desert. Buttes and volcanic cones and mesas appeared on the horizon, the land turned gold in the afternoon light and the sky expanded even further. In the far west we began to see the faint blue outline of the Sangre de Cristos, the Blood of Christ Mountains, the southernmost range of the Rockies, visible from ninety miles away. "You have to get over the color green," wrote Wallace Stegner about the aesthetics of the Western landscape. "You have to quit associating beauty with gardens and lawns; you have to get used to an inhuman scale." For me, it happened instantaneously. Gazing out of the car window, flowing down the highway through that barren expanse of rock and sky, I felt as if I had found something missing from me.

I could tell you more about that trip—drinking green chartreuse with a black drugstore cowboy in Santa Fe, sunset at the Grand Canyon, a long, grueling, addled night in Las Vegas—but let's move ahead to its conclusion, or lack of one. Arriving in LA, reaching our destination, the other three seemed relieved and elated, but as far as I was concerned we had run out of road. All I wanted to do was turn around and keep driving. I hitched up and down the California coast for a week or so, then found a pickup truck that needed delivering in New Orleans.

Driving back out into the Mojave Desert, leaving behind the smog and the sprawl, the last of the pink-tiled subdivisions and auto dealerships, I felt an overwhelming surge of freedom and release. Leaving London, leaving Philadelphia, Nashville and Santa Fe, I had felt the same way, and I sensed then that this feeling could be habit-forming.

In New Orleans I was befriended by a black street hustler. We spent two days roaming the French Quarter bars, stopping in at his friends' parties, catching up on the latest gossip from the pimps and the whores and the Bourbon Street con men. At the end of it he cold-cocked me with a brick in the doorway of my motel room. I woke up hours later, next to the brick. Everything was gone—the money and traveler's checks under the mattress, all the clothes I wasn't wearing—and the bathtub was ringed with dirt and fur. While I lay unconscious on the floor, my new friend had taken the time to wash his dog.

For two weeks (waiting for the traveler's checks to be reimbursed) I slummed it with the French Quarter winos and street flotsam, who kept me supplied with food and Mad Dog wine, free of charge, and regaled me with conspiracy theories. Cops, ex-girlfriends, space aliens, Nazi bankers, Jewish bankers, organ-harvesting cabals, the CIA—who could fathom the dimensions of the plot against them? I slept in the parking lot of the Marriott

Hotel on Canal Street, and took to spending my mornings at the Marriott pool, posing as a hotel guest and writing long letters about my experiences to friends in England.

People liked those letters, and when I finally made it back to London, they encouraged me to try writing feature stories for British magazines. I managed to sell a few of them, and set up another trip to America with the proceeds. For about six years, that was the shape of my life: I traveled around America until I ran out of money, went back to London and sold stories to raise another stake. Then I started selling more stories and stopped going back to London altogether.

I based myself in Austin, Texas, for a while, then Moab, Utah, then Tucson, Arizona, criss-crossing the country in between, taking long trips into Mexico, but always returning to the wide-open spaces of the American West. I slept in cheap motels, campgrounds, other people's houses, and the back of whatever vehicle I happened to be driving. Twenty-five dollars a day, for food, beer, cigarettes and gasoline, and I was happy. When the funds ran low, there was always a story to be found somewhere.

My plan was to live this way for the rest of my life. Wandering became a manifesto, an obsession, a solution to all problems. Possessions were a pointless encumbrance, ambition was a trap, mortgages were obscene (paying for your own jail cell), and romantic entanglements were something to be wary of. Emotional barriers arose and remained in place for many years: why risk falling in love when you're always leaving town in a week or two? Why not keep it casual and see you next time I'm passing through?

I developed a taste for extended camping trips in the deserts of Arizona and Utah, walking for days until I felt I had reached the middle of nowhere, the back of beyond.

"What's out there?" people wanted to know. Londoners, in particular, were puzzled.

"Nothing," I would say. "Space, silence, rocks. It's very beautiful."

"I see. And what exactly do you do out there?"

"Eat, sleep. Walk around mostly."

Sometimes I went into the deserts with friends. More often, I ended up going alone, for a few nights or a week, sleeping under the stars and finding shelter in a cave on the rare occasions that it rained. I bathed in rivers where I found them, lived on beef jerky and trail mix, gazed into a fire at night. I went feral, you might say, until I tired of my company, or ran out of food or water. Then I would head back into the nearest town, to socialize in the bars, pick up supplies, and move on.

What was I running from? What was I afraid of? These questions never occurred to me. I was young and untroubled by doubt. I woke up grinning in the morning, convinced that I had unlocked the riddle of human freedom. It was simple: never spend more than two weeks in the same place.

Along the way, in campgrounds, truck stops, bus stations and roadhouse bars, in cafés and motels, freight yards and boxcars, and hitchhiking by the side of the road, I met others of a similar bent—Americans who had abandoned sedentary civilization for the nomadic life; men—and they were nearly always men—who looked at the same set of walls for too long and began to climb them. It was rare to run across them in the Northeast, more common in the South and the Midwest. In the West, between Texas and California, between the Missouri River and Seattle, they were everywhere.

For whatever personal reasons—a peripatetic childhood, a well-traveled father and grandfather, a fear and loathing of routine, commitment and responsibility—I found myself adrift in a roadside culture of wandering rootlessness. It was not a community but rather an aggregation of loosely knit subcultures, crossing and recrossing the same ground on parallel lines: oil-field roughnecks, migrant harvest workers, footloose ranch hands and rodeo cowboys, truck drivers and troubadours, itinerant traders and vendors, perpetual tourists, and a legion of drifters, grifters, hoboes and tramps.

I started writing about them, and reading about their historical predecessors, tracing back the lines of connection. What drove a man to spend his life in motion? Was it a natural human impulse, recognized and obeyed, or was it a disease of the soul? Why was the type so prevalent in America, and the American West in particular?

ead, the more I came to see the history of the
act in that ancestral human drama: the conflict
rers and the sedentary, between nomads and the
a conflict that was still embodied in the lives of
erviewed, and often at the forefront of their minds.

It seemed like a useful prism to look through, but it scrambled many of America's most cherished ideas about itself. Reading the diaries and accounts of the frontiersmen, for example, it became impossible to see them as the proud vanguard of civilization, leading its triumphant westward march across the continent. Nine times out of ten, civilization is what the frontiersmen were running away from. They lived more like nomadic Indians than civilized Europeans, as wandering hunters and trappers in the wilderness, wearing buckskins and moccasins, taking Indian wives, learning Indian languages and scalping their enemies. When civilization caught up with them, they moved on, fleeing its confinements all the way to the Pacific.

The cowboys and Indians on the Western plains, from a nomadologist's point of view, were on the same side. For one thing, it was the United States Army, and not the cowboys, who did most of the fighting against the plains tribes. Cowboys and Indians did skirmish from time to time, but they shared a similar philosophy of land use, based on freedom of movement, and the ability to follow the seasonal grazing patterns across the untrammelled space of the plains. Only when sedentary farmers arrived in Kansas and Nebraska and began fencing off the open range and the waterholes did the cowboys reach for their six-guns and go to war.

The war was lost, the range was fenced and divided between private landowners and the government. In the same era, the 1870s and 1880s, the last free-roaming tribes were defeated and penned in reservations. The history of North America, like that of all continents, is one of taming and settling, of nomadic cultures succumbing to the steadily expanding gridwork of civilization and the state. In Europe the process happened gradually, over thousands of years, and was resolved a long time ago. In the American West it happened within a lifetime and you still meet people whose grandparents lived through it.

In the West today there are still huge tracts of land that remain outside the gridwork of fields and cities, and nomadic beliefs and behavior patterns have endured, as a kind of mutant, atavistic strain in the culture, lodged in folk memories and family traditions, and romanticized by popular culture. Who has not driven across the plains and imagined cowboys, Indians and roaming herds of buffalo? How many minds hold the image of John Wayne and a horse's ass, receding into a celluloid sunset?

No conquest is strictly one-sided, especially one which happened in such recent memory. Something of the vanquished always rubs off on the victors. There are always ghosts, and in the American West, the ghosts are nomadic horsemen, riding free and unfettered across the land.

Freedom is a murky concept in this day and age; perhaps it always has been. When Americans start talking about it, the British tend to sneer and chuckle, and mutter something about the freedom to shoot each other with handguns and behave in a gauche manner. The British have been subjugated for so long that they consider American rhetoric about freedom to be naive, windy and deluded. And given the bullying, dictator-friendly record of American foreign policy, and its own internal history of racial oppression, talk of America as the champion of liberty often sounds hypocritical.

Americans certainly love to trumpet and bellow their freedoms to each other and the rest of the world, but it is not always clear what they are referring to, other than myth. With a few exceptions, most notably the right to bear arms, the liberties supposedly guaranteed to them by the Bill of Rights have been either severely truncated or decimated entirely, legislated away over two centuries in the name of national security, public safety, Christian values and patriotism.

The fact that the Bill of Rights has been gutted with so little popular outcry tells us something about how freedom is understood in the American mainstream. Above all, it is a rhetorical construct, a patriotic rallying cry, but it is generally agreed to have something to do with private property rights, unfettered capitalism, low taxation, class mobility and the ability to vote politicians out of office. Free speech is valued highly too, except during wartime, or in the more politically correct universities. In brush-stroke summary we might call it an immigrant's creed of liberty. It addresses the typical immigrant concerns—economic opportunity, social mobility, access to political power—and it is clearly traceable back to the philosophies of the European Enlightenment.

Lurking in the American psyche, however, there exists an entirely different conception of liberty, with no roots in European political philosophy. We might summarize it as a nomad's creed: that freedom is impossible and meaningless within the confines of sedentary society, that the only true freedom is the freedom to roam across the land, beholden to no one. Call it stubborn and anachronistic, doomed, hubristic and naive, but if there is one belief that unites the characters in this book, as they range back and forth across the centuries, this is it.

A Tibetan dignitary, visiting America for the first time, sits by the Green River in Utah, looking out over the mountains and the high windcarved desert plateaus. His name is T. T. Karma Chopel. He has come to America to study the workings of its democracy but that is not in his thoughts now.

Something in the landscape and the great sweep of sky reminds him of his homeland. He thinks of yaks and yak herders, making their endless migrations across the Tibetan plateaus.

He knows there are no yak herders in America but he assumes there must be some equivalent. "Who are your nomads?" he asks.

CHAPTER 1

Notes from an all-night truck stop on the outskirts of Albuquerque. Drinking coffee in a red vinyl booth, gazing out of the window at the gas pumps, I watch the nomads come and go in the night, making their desert crossings: a gang of bikers en route to the rendezvous in Sturgis, South Dakota; six migrant workers in a rattletrap jalopy, following the ripening harvest from Texas to Montana; a vanload of tie-dyed teenagers, headed for the next Phish concert or Rainbow Gathering; truck drivers, traveling salesmen, rambling flea-market vendors; an itinerant preacher in a camper rig nailed together from planks of wood and scrap metal: "Rev. Dale Billings—Traveling Revival—Sinners Welcome."

From the shadowed canyons between the parked Kenworths and Peterbilts (where they drink malt liquor and denounce their enemies), bearded, furrow-faced road tramps and drifters emerge into the sodium glare, shambling across the forecourt to bum cigarettes and spare change.

Across the interstate, parked in neat, orderly rows at an electrified campground, are forty or fifty RVs, Recreational Vehicles, the huge, luxurious motor homes favored by the peripatetic retirees of the Southwest. RV brand names: Wanderer, Sundowner, Sunchaser, Airstream, Nomad.

Through a Western truck-stop window in the early hours of the morning, it seems like half of America is perpetually on the move:

picking up and making a fresh start somewhere else, traveling for a pay cheque, or just traveling to be traveling, moving for the sake of motion. Wanderlust, restlessness, itchy feet, antsy pants, white-line fever. There is more of it here than in Europe, or anywhere else in the industrialized world: the nagging conviction that a better life lies somewhere down the road, or on the road itself. Does it begin on the inside, or filter in from the outside? Is it nature, nurture or disease?

Here's what the sedentary doctors have to say. Dromomania: an abnormal, obsessive desire to roam. Drapetomania: an uncontrollable desire to wander away from home. A nomad, of course, would produce vigorous arguments to the contrary: that being sedentary is a forced, unnatural and oppressive condition for human beings. That the desire to travel is an innate human urge— a genetic legacy perhaps, from the million years we spent as wandering hunter-gatherers. This was Bruce Chatwin's big idea, that humans have similar migratory instincts to certain birds and animals. Why is a human baby calmed by the motion of rocking and swaying? he asked. Because, for 99.9 percent of our evolutionary span, this is what human babies experienced as the natural rhythm of life, strapped to their mothers' bodies in slings or cradleboards, "rocked into contentment by the gentle swaying walk".

The sedentary doctor smiles a patronizing smile: a dromomaniac can always produce a good reason to roam, just as an alcoholic can always find a good reason to take another drink. And, like alcoholism, it is a disease that afflicts a disproportionate number of men. But what does a sedentary doctor know? Has he ever experienced the pure rush of freedom that comes from leaving it all behind—the debts, the ties, the possessions and responsibilities— and launching out into the wild blue yonder? Has he ever been secretly tempted?

"Truck driving is the ultimate fulfillment of the American dream." This is the bold claim of Mike Hatfield, twenty-four, from Reno, Nevada, hauling a load of mattresses across the country, taking time out for a cup of coffee and a bowl of chilli. Slim, bespectacled, well read, cheerful—you would never pick him for a trucker.

"Forget the little house on the prairie," he says. "Forget the white picket fence, the house in the suburbs, the monthly mortgage payment, the two-car garage and the rest of that crap. Americans dream about the road. We dream about burning down the house and saddling up the horse, and it's been that way ever since the plains were knee-deep in buffalo shit."

Mike turns out to be a Western history enthusiast, an amateur scholar of sorts. The cab of his Peterbilt and the sleeper compartment behind are full of books, ranging from pulp gunfighter fiction to the learned, historical tomes of Bernard De Voto and Walter Prescott Webb. The books are well thumbed, dog-eared and coffee-stained, with scrawled comments spidering up the margins and key passages underlined in pencil. The marked passages all address the same theme. "After the Indians came the cowboys and prospectors and railroad men, and they were just about as loose-footed and freedom-loving and prone to rambling. I'm a quarter Cheyenne Indian, and three-quarters Scotch-Irish cowboy. The way I look at it, I was born to roam."

He gives me a ride east into Texas, eating little white pills, chain-smoking Marlboros and talking a blue streak through the night. We are out on the vast tableland emptiness of the Staked Plains, the Llano Estacado, the windswept heartland of the old Comanche country, when the first gray light appears in the east. Mike pulls over to the side of the road and brews up some coffee on a camp stove. He is an aficionado of the dawn and will often stop to watch it rise.

The first rim of sun crests the horizon and a pale apricot light spreads across the blue-gray plain, with the moon still visible in the west, and the coyotes yammering and howling, celebrating the night's hunting perhaps, or the simple fact of being a coyote. Our shadows take form behind us, elongated like figures in a funhouse mirror.

There is a line of telephone poles along the side of the road. The wires hang in loose stitches across the sky. There is a barbed-wire fence clogged with tumbleweeds, and beyond the fence the eye leaps out to the horizon across forty or fifty miles of smooth, pure space.

"Look at this country," Mike says. "It wasn't made for settling down in. It's too big and dry and wide open. The Lord intended man and beast to move about in a country like this. The Comanches knew it, the cowboys knew it, the buffalo knew it. Man, can you imagine? All this covered with buffalo, just black with buffalo all the way to the horizon. That's how big the herds got, as far as you could see."

No one knows how many bison used to roam the Great Plains. The estimates vary between 50 million and 125 million. Whatever the number, it is safe to say that no large wild animal ever grew so numerous, anywhere on Earth, and the key to their success in this environment was mobility. The herds grazed into the wind, which blows almost constantly on the plains. The species evolved with the wind, developing huge shaggy heads and shoulders, for facing down the howling winter blizzards, and small, lean, short-furred, curiously pert hindquarters. In the course of a normal year, the winds on the Great Plains shifted counterclockwise through all four quarters of the compass, so the herd migrations formed a rough circle or ellipse, three or four hundred miles across, passing through cooler locations in summer and warmer ones in winter, always moving toward fresh grazing and water.

Occasionally, the wind blew too long from the southwest and buffalo in their thousands trailed off into the deserts and died of starvation and thirst. The Montana herds sometimes ended up in the far, frozen north of Canada, lured to their deaths by a soft, persistent, northerly breeze in the early part of winter. But these were rare and inconsequential events. Maybe you can grasp the figure of 60 million or 125 million. Mike and I have tried and failed.

It took less than thirty years to bring the herds to the brink of extinction, and most of the killing was done in a single decade, the 1870s. By 1883, only two or three hundred buffalo were left, kept for nostalgia's sake on private ranches. White hide-hunters did most of the killing, working with the approval of the white authorities, and most of the white population, who saw the slaughter of the buffalo as the final solution to the Indian problem. The problem, as always, was how to dispossess the Indians of their land. There was an element of imperialist conspiracy at work, but it was capitalist economics, the emergence of a booming market for buffalo leather in the East and Europe, which accounted for the speed and rapacity of the slaughter, and sent five thousand freelance hide-hunters out onto the plains. Killing and skinning buffalo was exhausting, filthy, dangerous work—up to your shoulders in gore most of the time, and constantly watching for Indians—but for a while the market paid enough to make it worth the risk. Enough, that is, for whiskey and a whore and a gambling spree, when you got back to town and sold your hides.

The meat was left to rot on the prairie, fouling the air for hundreds of miles around. It was a fine, fat, lazy time to be a wolf, or a vulture, or any scavenger of carrion, and a terrible, hungry, world-wrenching time to be an Indian. Not that Indians hadn't contributed to the slaughter. As subsistence hunters, they had barely dented the herds, but by the 1870s they too were entangled in the market economy. They needed more hides than they used to, to trade for guns, ammunition, iron cooking pots, steel knives, needles, awls, cloth, mirrors, coffee, sugar, whiskey and other products of white civilization on which they had become dependent. And contrary to popular belief, Indians did not *always* use every part of the buffalo. If, for example, an Indian was being pursued, or traveling alone, or needing trade goods in a hurry, or craving whiskey, he might take the hide and the tongue, leave the carcass to rot, and think little of it.

Nevertheless, Indians were horrified by the way the hide-men laid waste to the herds, killing relentlessly and methodically until no animals were left, and then moving on to the next herd, wasting unimaginable quantities of meat. Surely this was a sign of sickness or insanity. Indian hunting practices were not always as tidy and thorough as they are remembered, but the plains tribes did feel a deep, religious reverence for the buffalo, which gave up its life in a sacred transaction so that Indians could live.

The great herds had seemed as timeless and elemental as the grass or the wind, and when they disappeared Indians refused to believe it at first, saying the buffalo had gone up to Canada or taken refuge underground. Even the white hide-hunters were astonished that they had killed themselves out of a living in so short a time.

Later, a new market arose, and a rabble army of bone-pickers went out onto the plains. The bones were stacked in immense ricks by the railroad, sixty or seventy feet high, waiting to be shipped east and ground into fertilizer, turned into buttons, combs and glue. Men posed in front of the bone-ricks for photographers, with shabby hats and bristling mustaches, looking like mean, proud, haunted, belligerent dwarfs. If all the bones had been loaded at once, calculated the *Topeka Mail and Breeze*, they would have filled a freight train 7575 miles long, more than twice the distance from San Francisco to New York.

By the end of the great slaughter, in 1883, all the nomadic plains tribes had been corralled into reservations, to be forcibly instructed in the arts of Christian piety, private property ownership and sedentary farming. By 1886 the footloose trail cowboy was gone from the plains too, working on ranches now and sleeping in bunkhouses, fenced off the open range by the settlers he despised. His heyday had lasted only twenty years, and represented the last gasp of mounted nomadism in North America. There were still a few wandering outlaws, recalcitrant Indians and horse thieves left out in the back country and the canyons, but in short order they were hunted down and brought in, and the West was pronounced conquered, tamed and settled.

Traveling around the region today, it doesn't always feel that way. Settlement, and the feeling of settlement, does not occupy the land in the same way that it does back East, or in Europe. It is not just the vast, empty spaces, or all the drifters on the highway, or the ghost towns, being seeded back into prairie by the wind, or the dying family farms, defeated by the harshness of the climate and the machinations of corporate agriculture. The restless, rootless, migratory history of the West is also evident in its cities.

In Albuquerque, Phoenix, Tucson and Las Vegas, urban populations are growing faster than anywhere else in the country, yet these booming, sprawling, modern cities have a flimsy, impermanent presence, at least to an eye trained in Europe. You drive through miles of trailer parks and mobile-home encampments, through brave new suburbs and utopian retirement communities—frame and Sheetrock dream homes, built on a vanishing water supply, designed to make a fast buck for the development company and fall apart in twenty or thirty years: "disposable homes," to borrow a phrase from a friend of mine who builds them for a living. In Phoenix, the most transitory of Western cities, 40 percent of the population have lived there for less than five years, and 50 percent say they plan to leave as soon as they get the chance.

Maybe it's just a matter of time. Maybe in another hundred years the wide open spaces will be gone, or reduced to islands in a sea of concrete, and the inhabitants will come to feel rooted in place. Given time, perhaps, the settlement of the West will be completed, but there remains a formidable obstacle that never existed in the East or in Europe.

Except for a small, soggy corner in the Pacific Northwest, aridity is the dominant characteristic of the American West, the organizing principle of its geography and biology, and the ultimate limit on its ambition of never-ending growth. The underground aquifers, which took millions of years to form, by slow accretion of scant rainfall, are plummeting dramatically. The major river of the Southwest, the Colorado, is already so tapped for irrigation that it no longer reaches the sea. Aridity explains why the grass on this prairie grows in separate bunches, rather than close-packed turf, why there are no trees rooted in the soil, why the rivers and the towns are so far apart. A buffalo seeking water and a truck driver seeking breakfast must travel the same approximate distance to find what they need to move on.

Aridity literally creates space. Where there is no moisture to mist up the air, and no trees to block the view, the human field of vision expands dramatically. From the ramparts of Bryce Canyon in Utah you can see for 180 miles on a clear day—London to Manchester—and still wonder what lies over the horizon. Unless some kind of technological rain dance is devised, it seems likely that the West will remain dominated by big empty spaces, and a certain type of human being will feel compelled to wander across them. First rule of nomadism: open space invites mobility.

"It is geography at bottom, a hell of a wide land from the beginning," wrote Charles Olson in *Call Me Ishmael*, "a stretch of earth—seas on both sides, no barriers to contain as restless a thing as Western man." Asked to define America in a sentence, Gertrude Stein said, "Conceive a space filled with moving."

"I think of myself as a latter-day cowboy," says Mike, driving on for Amarillo. "But it doesn't have anything to do with Western movies, or Marlboro billboards, or any of that bullshit. It's in my blood. My family has been roaming around the West for four generations, and a hell of a lot longer if you count my grand-mother's people."

Mike's great-grandfather crossed these plains on horseback, driving herds of Longhorn cattle from south Texas to the rail-heads at Dodge City and Ogallala, and up to Montana and the Dakotas. When the range was fenced, he went to Wyoming and worked on cattle ranches, between stints as a rustler and spells in jail. At the age of fifty he married a woman in San Francisco and they raised three children on her father's ranch in Nevada.

Mike's grandfather was another roaming ranch hand, moving from one bunkhouse to the next across the northern plains. He married a woman from the Northern Cheyenne reservation in Montana, and they had four children together, raised in six different houses.

Mike's father did a little cowboying in his younger days, got sick of the wages, and became an oil-field roustabout, following the work around Texas, Oklahoma, Wyoming and up into Alaska and the Yukon territory. He married a blackjack dealer in Reno at the age of forty and tried his hand at settling down. Two years later he was gone, back to the oil-fields, and promising to send money for the baby.

"I was raised by my mom," says Mike. "Dad would show up once or twice a year, they would have a fight, and he would leave.

What did they fight about? The usual stuff. He wanted us to come with him up to Fairbanks, or Billings, or the Yukon, or wherever the hell he was working that season, and live in a tent or trailer, depending on how much of his wages he was drinking at the time. Mom wanted to stay in Reno, and keep us fed on that steady pay check."

When he turned twenty-one, Mike enrolled in truck-driving school. He took out a loan to buy a secondhand truck, and he has been on the road for three years now. He gets his mail sent to his mother's house in Reno, but he feels no roots or ties there, or anywhere else, and home is the cab of his Peterbilt. "This is the closest thing you're going to find to freedom in modern America," he says. "There's a lot of bullshit with insurance and regulations and taxes, and I might never get out of debt, but I'm still a free man on the move, and I believe that's how I'm meant to live."

Mike says I'm asking the wrong questions, that I have it all twisted inside-out. "You're asking why there's all these people living on the road, and the real question is why anyone would want to stay put. Why would you want to live in the same damn box all your life, or maybe a bigger box if you work hard enough and kiss enough ass?" Spoken like a true nomad. The same sentiments have been voiced over the centuries by Bedouins, Kazakhs, Mongols, Apaches, Comanches, Crows, Sioux and Mike's own Cheyenne ancestors. Nomads have always scorned the sedentary as weak, craven dupes who have sold out their freedom in exchange for security and comfort. And the sedentary have always stereotyped nomads as unruly, irresponsible and morally reprehensible—a threat to hearth and home, to law and order, and to civilization itself—while simultaneously envying and romanticizing their lives.

I want to know about Mike Hatfield's love life, his capacity for emotional connection. His Cheyenne great-grandparents traveled within a tightly knit mobile community, with wives, children, grandparents, siblings, cousins, in-laws and childhood friends in tow, but that is no longer possible. A commitment to nomadism in modern America usually entails a rejection, or a postponement, or an escape from all of this. "What about wives, kids, raising a family?" I ask him. "What about belonging to a community?"

"I belong to a community," he says, and strikes up a conversation on the CB radio to prove his point. "As far as raising a family goes, hell, raise them on the road. There's a buddy of mine who drives with his wife and daughter in the truck. They're on some kind of home-schooling program and his wife spends four or five hours a day teaching the kid. That kid is eight years old and she's smart as a whip. She can tell you all about Civil War battlefields, and Indian massacre sites, and the Congress and the Senate in DC, because she's been to all those places and seen them with her own eyes. They're not just some old thing she's read about in a schoolbook, or the teacher told her about."

This is where Mike Hatfield sees himself in ten or fifteen years, rolling down the highway, in a bigger truck, with a wife and kid next to him and a mobile connection to an Internet home-schooling program. "In the meantime," he adds, "I'm happy to pick up women where I find them, have a good time and say my farewells. I don't take advantage of women. I'm upfront about it. They know I drive a truck."

For me, the love 'em and leave 'em strategy so common among wandering males started by default. Short of celibacy, it didn't seem like I had a choice, because I could never persuade a woman to quit her job, give up her house or apartment, and live on the road with me. With experience, and a few false unhappy starts, I discovered that the key to making this strategy work was not to fall in love. Love spoiled everything and it wasn't worth the heartache. So I learned to make do with sex and companionship, on a fleeting or intermittent basis, and I usually ended up with women who were cheating on their boyfriends or husbands. Which persuaded me further that love and commitment were a sucker's game.

Recently, I came to the decision that this was unhealthy, that I was missing out on something important. I made a heartfelt and committed decision to curb my wanderings and get serious with a woman in Tucson, who happened to be cheating on her boyfriend. The boyfriend was in France and she wasn't serious about him and I really liked her, so I rented a nice little house in Tucson, bought a bed and a few thrift-store furnishings, and we moved in together. Three weeks later, I was climbing the walls and she left in a rage, putting a motorcycle boot through a glass panel in my front door. My truck was being repaired so I loaded up a backpack with clothes and books and started hitchhiking east.

I wasn't always this way. In London I was a long-term-relationship man: three years, then four years. In London I managed to live under the same roof for four years. It's true that I was often surly and discontented under that roof, and longed to get out of England, but I thought in terms of moving to another city, in another country, and making a permanent home there. In London I would not have reacted to a relationship breakup by walking out to the highway and raising my thumb.

These restless, roaming urges, this ache for the balm of motion: it was something that happened to me in America, something that happened to a persistent minority of all Europeans who crossed the Atlantic, all the way back to the beginning. The internal feelings of restlessness and dislocation, which all emigrants bring with them to some degree, came into contact with all that space and possibility, and a culture of mobility that dated back to the Indians. Much as Europeans tried to re-create their sedentary societies and close-knit, coercive communities under these conditions, they weren't always successful.

"Many crept out through a broken wall," wrote John Winthrop, the first governor of the Massachusetts colony. He was referring to the thin but steady exodus of disaffected Puritans—usually rebellious young men and "disgraced" young women—who ran off into the wilderness and never returned. They became roaming hunters, trappers, wives, mothers, traders, and many of them joined up with Indian tribes. These were the first English-speakers to turn nomadic in America, and there were Frenchmen and Spaniards who pre-dated them. If you dig down to the roots of American wanderlust, it is a process of going native, of Europeans being conquered by America—by the immensity of its geography and the nomadic cultures they found here. And I have come to think of myself as some bastard, postmodern footnote to this tradition.

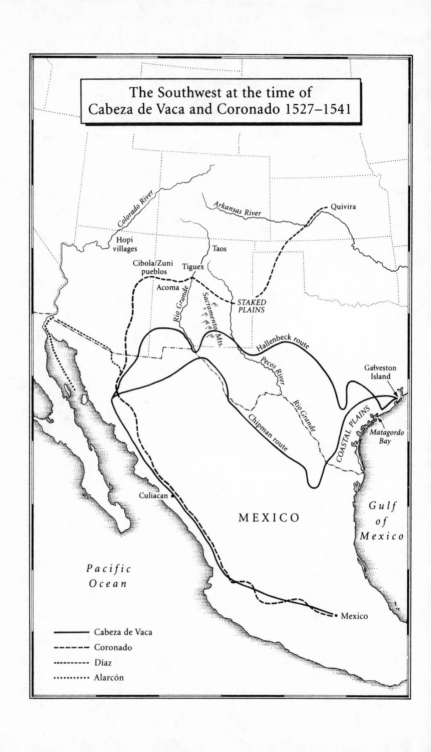

The Southwest at the time of
Cabeza de Vaca and Coronado 1527–1541

Colorado River

Arkansas River

Quivira

Hopi
villages

Taos

Cibola/Zuni
pueblos

Tiguex

Acoma

Rio Grande

Sacramento Mts.

STAKED
PLAINS

Hallenbeck route

Pecos River

Rio Grande

Galveston
Island

Chipman route

COASTAL PLAINS

Matagordo
Bay

Culiacan

MEXICO

Gulf
of
Mexico

Pacific
Ocean

Mexico

———— Cabeza de Vaca
– – – – Coronado
········· Díaz
··········· Alarcón

CHAPTER 2

We ever held it certain that going toward the sunset we
would find what we desired.

Alvar Núñez Cabeza de Vaca,
Adventures in the Unknown Interior of America

L et's pick up the author in 1530, at a low point in his odyssey.
He is naked and emaciated, with long hair and a long, matted
beard, grubbing for cane roots on the shores of Galveston Island
off the Gulf coast of present-day Texas. He has spent the last two
years living with the Han and Capoque Indians—wandering
hunter-gatherers who eke out a hungry existence on roots, shellfish and seasonal blackberry harvests—and for the last year he has
been their slave. His hands are perpetually raw and bleeding from
the cane. His body is covered in lacerations. But it is a miracle
that he is still alive, with so many of his companions dead, and
he holds on to this thought.

He has made it through hurricanes, shipwrecks, mutinies, fevers,
Indian attacks, extended periods of thirst and starvation. He has seen
Spanish noblemen reduced to eating their horses and, later, to eating
each other. Does he recall that hubristic moment when the armada
first made land in Florida? Rations were low, half the horses were
already dead, a series of storms had blown the ships hundreds of
miles off course. The conquistadors raised their flags and banners,
exhibited their written credentials to an empty beach, and declared
a thousand miles of unseen land, and all its inhabitants, to be in

the possession of His Most Sacred Caesarian Catholic Majesty, Emperor Charles V of Spain.

They marched inland, in their medieval armor and plumed helmets, weighed down with lances, swords and harquebuses, and the padres walking alongside in cassocks. Three hundred men and forty horses, propelled into the swamps and jungles of the New World by Europe's hunger for gold and empire. The expedition's commander was Panfilo de Narvaez; vain, arrogant, greedy, red-bearded Narvaez. In a day or two, he assured them, they would come upon a fabulous city filled with gold, another Tenochtitlán, which his rival Cortés had sacked eight years before in Mexico.

Cabeza de Vaca (the name means Head of a Cow) was the expedition's second-in-command and treasurer, charged with collecting the Spanish crown's share of the expected plunder. He came to America as a man of finance and war, thirty-eight years old and steeped since childhood in the ethic of the conquistador. His grandfather Pedro de Vera had led the bloodthirsty conquest of the Canary Islands, and Cabeza de Vaca grew up in a household staffed with the copper-skinned Guanche slaves he had taken.

After five months of wading and hacking their way up the Florida peninsula, fighting off hostile tribes, disease, quicksands and starvation, forty of the men were dead, and all the horses eaten. They had found no golden cities, and they had lost contact with their ships. Soon after they landed Narvaez had sent the fleet up the coast, with a hundred men, and they were never seen again, presumably shipwrecked. In desperation the men cobbled together crude rafts, using their swords and belt-buckles for tools, horsehair and palm fiber for rigging. Hoisting their shirts for sails, they set off on a horror voyage along the Gulf coast. After six or seven weeks at sea—capsizings, drownings, more storms, men dying of hunger, thirst and dysentery—a freak wave washed the survivors ashore on the beaches of Galveston Island. They were too weak to fight, or even to move.

A hundred Han and Capoque warriors came down to the beach, naked and copper-skinned, with joints of cane through their noses and nipples, and armed with flint spears and bows and arrows. The warriors took pity on the shivering, skeletal cast-aways, bringing them food, building fires to keep them warm, and agreeing to shelter them in their huts. Dead Spaniards washed up on the beach, and as the survivors wept for their companions, the Indians wept along with them.

Then the Hans and Capoques discovered that a group of Spaniards on the mainland had been eating each other and their hospitality turned to revulsion and disgust. There were rumors of cannibal tribes further down the coast, but among the Hans and Capoques, who lived with terrible hunger for most of the year, eating human flesh was strictly taboo. To make matters worse, the Indians started dying from disease. It was probably dysentery, from which the Spaniards were dying themselves, but the Hans and Capoques blamed it on the sorcery of these pale, bearded, canni-balistic strangers. Some of the Spaniards were killed or turned out to starve, and the rest were made into slaves.

The King's treasurer grubs for roots in the cane-brakes, beaten and abused, a naked wretch kept alive only for the value of his labor. Does he remember the Guanche slaves from his boyhood, and the way his grandfather treated them? If so, he doesn't mention the irony in his account of his adventures, penned years later as a report to the Spanish King. He consoles himself by remem-bering the suffering of Christ. Despite all that God has done to him and his companions, Cabeza de Vaca's faith has never been stronger. Surely God has spared his life for a special purpose. How else to explain the miraculous events during last season's black-berry harvest?

The Han and Capoque bands were gathered on the mainland coast, where the blackberry plants grew, holding the annual dances and festivities. Cabeza de Vaca met up with two other Spanish captives there, Castillo and Dorantes. Watching these extraordinary-looking men, talking their incomprehensible tongue, the Indians wondered if they also possessed extraordinary spiritual powers. The Spaniards were taken to some huts and instructed to heal the sick.

Cabeza de Vaca and his companions scoffed at the idea, and protested their incompetence, but the Indians refused to give them any food until they tried. Still protesting, "disclaiming any responsibility for our failure or success," the three Spaniards leaned over their patients and blew on them—a technique they had been shown by the native shamans. For good measure, they made the sign of the Cross, recited Ave Marias and Paternosters, and prayed to the Catholic God.

To the joy of the Indians, and the amazement of the Spaniards, the patients all declared themselves healed. "In consequence, the Indians treated us very kindly," writes Cabeza de Vaca, who attributed the miracle to divine intervention. "They deprived themselves of food to give us, and presented us skins and other tokens of gratitude."

It didn't last long. Soon after the healings, Cabeza de Vaca fell ill himself and almost died, which ruined his reputation as a medicine man. Ever since he recovered, a year ago, the Capoques have made his life a torment. Maybe it is religious faith that stops him giving in to despair and resignation. It certainly helps, but he also possesses extraordinary resourcefulness and physical endurance—call it the will to live. Of the four hundred men who sailed with the Narvaez expedition, there are maybe eight or ten still alive, enslaved by various tribal bands on the island and the mainland, and Cabeza de Vaca is the only one to make a successful escape.

Sometime in early 1530 he slipped away from the Capoques and waded across the shallow channel that divides Galveston Island from the mainland. He ran errands for the various tribes he encountered, in exchange for food, and little by little he was able to carve out a niche for himself as a wandering trader. The Indian trade networks had broken down because so many tribes were at war with each other. As a lone, neutral merchant, easily identifiable by his strange, bearded appearance, Cabeza de Vaca was free to trade and travel between dozens of hostile tribes.

My principal wares were cones and other pieces of sea-snail, conches used for cutting, sea-beads, and a fruit like a bean which the Indians value very highly, using it for a medicine and for a ritual beverage in their dances and festivities [probably mesquite beans, possibly peyote]. This is the sort of thing I carried inland. By barter I got and brought back to the coast skins, red ochre which they rub on their faces, hard canes for arrows, flint for arrowheads, with sinews and cement to attach them, and tassels of deer hair which they dye red.

This occupation suited me; I could travel where I wished, was not obliged to work, and was not a slave. Wherever I went, the Indians treated me honourably and gave me food, because they liked my commodities. They were glad to see me when I came and delighted to be brought what they wanted. I became well-known; those who did not know me personally knew me by reputation and sought my acquaintance.

For nearly two years he lived like this, barefoot and naked, toting his wares back and forth over hundreds of miles of present-day Texas, ranging as far north perhaps as Oklahoma. He became as inured to hunger, cold, thirst and exhaustion as the Indians were. Between journeys he stayed in their villages and encampments. He shared their food, learned something of their customs, and by the time his odyssey ended he could speak six of their languages. In the vicinity of present-day Austin, Texas, as near as we can guess, he became the first white man to see buffalo in North America, and mistook them for a species of wild cattle.

They have small horns like the cows of Morocco; their hair is very long and flocky like merinos'. Some are tawny, others black. In my opinion, the meat is finer and fatter than the beef of [Spain]. The Indians make blankets out of the skins of cows not full grown; and shoes and shields from the full-grown. These cattle come from . . . a northerly direction, and range over a tract of more than 400 leagues [1100 miles;

an accurate estimate]. Throughout this whole range, the people who dwell nearby descend and live upon them and distribute an incredible number of hides into the interior.

In the winter of 1532, Cabeza de Vaca met a band of traveling Quevenes, who told him they had seen three "men like himself"— the three other survivors of the Narvaez expedition. They were living as slaves among the Mariames and Yguaces, on the Texas coast, perhaps near present-day Matagorda Bay. When Cabeza de Vaca asked how his colleagues were faring, the Quevenes began slapping and kicking him and jabbing arrowheads into his chest, to demonstrate how the Mariames treated their captives.

Cabeza de Vaca went to the coast to try and persuade them to escape and was made a slave himself. Once again, he was back to the wood and water duties, the endless grubbing after roots, the beatings and the cuffings, all of which were nothing compared to the hunger. Once a year, in the fall, the Mariames and Yguaces went inland and feasted on the prickly pear cactus harvest. For the rest of the year they lived on bitter roots, seafood, a very occasional deer and the reserves of fat built up during the annual feast. Famine was so prevalent among the Yguaces that they would eat absolutely anything to quell their hunger pangs:

> spiders and ant eggs, worms, lizards, salamanders, snakes and poisonous vipers; also earth and wood—anything, including deer dung and other matter I omit. I honestly believe that if there were stones in that country they would eat them. They save the bones of fish they consume, of snakes and other animals, so they can afterwards pulverize and eat them, too.

During his time among the Hans and Capoques, Cabeza de Vaca had been struck by the kind, gentle way in which Indians treated their children, and he was surprised to see that the Mariames and Yguaces had a custom of killing their offspring. They spared a few of the boys, although many were buried alive, and fed all their newborn daughters to the dogs. When they needed a wife, they bought one from the neighboring tribes, for the price of a bow and two arrows.

> They say they do this because all the nations of the region are their enemies, with whom they war ceaselessly; and that if they were to marry off their daughters, the daughters would multiply their enemies until the latter overcame and enslaved the Mariames, who thus preferred to annihilate all daughters than risk their reproduction of a single enemy. We asked why they did not themselves marry these girls. They said marrying relatives would be a disgusting thing; it was far better to kill them than give them to either kin or foe.

In recent decades the idea has become lodged in the cultural mainstream that North America was a peaceful, harmonious Eden before the European conquest, peopled by gentle-hearted, noble-spirited environmentalists. It's an idea which attracts understandable support among modern American Indians, or Native Americans if you prefer, although some find it patronizing—a new twist on the old Noble Savage routine and of no use in solving their current problems. As Vine Deloria, the acerbic Sioux writer, has pointed out, it is white liberals who have led the glorification of the historical Indian, for their own reasons; and, by some quirk, it is often vegetarian pacifists who worship these long-dead, meat-loving warriors most devoutly. How would a white liberal react, I wonder, if thrust back in time to a Mariame camp in the 1540s?

"The men bear no burdens. Anything of weight is borne by women and old men, the people least esteemed."

The idea of preconquest America as a benevolent utopia is interesting on many levels. One could take it as evidence of white guilt, the conquerors' belated sympathy for the conquered. One could use it to show the old human nostalgia for a lost paradise, which is as prevalent among whites as present-day Indians. Perhaps the arrival of the idea in the cultural mainstream reveals more about contemporary society, its spiritual yearnings and its mounting sense of environmental guilt. As a historical theory, however, casting preconquest Amerindians as gentle, New Age saints is as naive and lopsided as a Hollywood Western; another childish search for heroes and villains.

Leaving aside the difficulties of generalizing about so many diverse cultures, you could make a legitimate argument that aboriginal North Americans enjoyed a richer life of the soul than we do, and a closeness to nature that we have lost. But it was a life of incredible hardship and physical suffering, at least to a modern mind, and violence was an integral part of it. Everywhere Cabeza de Vaca traveled, he found war, brutality, famine and slavery, just as he found love, honor, kindness and generosity. By his account, American Indians in their untouched state were neither saints nor devils but human beings much like any other, with the usual proportion of flaws and virtues, and the full range of human emotions.

One might have expected a Spanish nobleman, and especially one who had endured the humiliations of slavery, to rail against the barbarism, savagery and idolatry of the natives, but throughout his narrative Cabeza de Vaca describes Indians in a calm, balanced, tolerant and sometimes admiring tone. He is impressed, among other things, by their skill in war, the acuteness of their senses and their ability to be happy with so little. Of the baby-killing Mariames and Yguaces, he also writes:

> They are a merry people, considering the hunger they suffer . . . Many times while we were among these people and there was nothing to eat for three or four days, they would try and revive our spirits by telling us not to be sad; soon there would be prickly pears in plenty; we would drink the juice, our bellies would get big, and we would be content.

You are never left with the impression that Cabeza de Vaca hated his captors, or any other tribes he encountered in North America. He found some of their customs strange and unsavory, but he tried to understand the function they served, and the reasons behind them. Only one tradition seemed to shock him into moral judgement: the "diabolical practice" of a man living with a eunuch.

Cabeza de Vaca never lost his sense of cultural superiority. He remained an imperialist, convinced that Indians would be better off under a Spanish/Christian civilization, but he included them in the same brotherhood of man as himself, with rights to liberty and fair treatment—"they must be won over by kindness, the only certain way." By modern standards, we would still call him a racist, but for a sixteenth-century European, and a conquistador in particular, he had undergone a radical shift in consciousness. The Spanish term for Indians at the time was *gente sin razón*: people without reason, and therefore on the level of animals. The Catholic Church was trying to determine if they possessed souls.

Cabeza de Vaca was able to empathize with Indians, even as a slave, because he was so deeply immersed in their world. He had lived among them for five years, and learned to shape his thoughts into their languages. In times of famine he starved alongside them, and in times of plenty he joined in their feasts and celebrations. Captors and captives alike shivered in the winter cold.

He still thought of himself as a Spanish gentleman but it had been five years since he had worn clothes or shoes, and six or seven years since he had slept in a permanent building. The thought of one day returning to civilization kept him going, but in the meantime, by necessity, he had adjusted to a different rhythm of life—shelter, fire, water, food—and when the food was gone, or the wares all bartered, moving on to the next camp. He was a new creature on this continent: a European gone partially native, a civilized man living as a wilderness wanderer, a hybrid of Old World and New. In the centuries to come, a similar type would become well established on the North American frontiers.

In September 1534 the Mariame and Yguace bands traveled inland for the prickly pear harvest. Cabeza de Vaca met up again with the three other survivors from Narvaez's expedition and they hatched a plan to escape. On the night of the full moon, they would meet in a certain cactus patch, make a break for it and find their way back to civilization.

Where exactly were they hoping to reach? They had no idea of the continent's size or geography. North America was still widely believed to be a peninsula of mainland Asia. They thought the Spanish settlement of Pánuco in Mexico lay somewhere along the coast to the south, but they wanted to avoid the coastal tribes. To the east was Florida—no Spaniards there—and somewhere to the north, presumably, were China and India. So they went west, placing their hopes in the direction of complete unknown. Somewhere toward the sunset, they told themselves, they would find Spaniards, Christians and civilization, and return to the men they used to be.

Cabeza de Vaca, without dissent, was their leader. Alongside him were Andrés Dorantes and Alonso del Castillo, his partners in the miracle healings five years before. The fourth was a black Arab from Morocco called Estevan, who had joined the Narvaez expedition as Dorantes' slave, and then become the slave of a slave. Even he, presumably, saw some benefit in returning to his former status. Naked and barefoot, skulking and hiding, lacerated by thorns and cactus spines, they made their way through the broken wooded country and out onto the vastness of the plains. Of all the westward treks recorded in American history, this was surely the most epic, the most improbable and surreal, as well as being the first. A betting man would have plunked his money down on death or captivity for the lot of them, but something extraordinary happened, something unforeseen. The news of their miracle cures on the coast had traveled ahead of them, and on the plains they were hailed as holy men.

They acquired a retinue of hundreds and then thousands of adoring Indians. Heralds ran ahead and spread the news: the Children of the Sun were coming, the bearded miracle-workers, coming across the land from the House of Dawn. What began as flight from slavery turned into a kind of triumphant religious procession, a traveling revival show.

At every village or encampment along the way, the tribes held dances and celebrations, and brought out their sick, their wounded and their dying to be healed. Using the same techniques that had worked for them before, the Spaniards blessed the patients and blew on them, and incorporated new methods like passing stones over them and the laying-on of hands. And once again, they worked astonishing miracles—"With no exceptions, every patient told us he had made well." At one point, Cabeza de Vaca states unequivocably that he brought a dead man back to life, by "blessing and breathing on him many times."

Call it what you want: mass delusion, psychosomatic illness, the placebo effect, hallucinations brought on by hunger, exhaustion and religious hysteria. The modern mind does not accept miracles easily, but it is important to realise that for the people who witnessed them, these things happened beyond a doubt. Fifty years later travelers met Indians who were still talking about it: the great procession and the bearded miracle-workers who had brought them the sign of the cross.

The Indians attributed the healings to the power of the sun. Cabeza de Vaca felt the hand of God working through him. Castillo, who started out as their most effective healer, became consumed by self-doubt and gave it up, feeling that his sins made him unworthy to handle such a divine gift. Estevan had little interest in healing. He preferred to spend his time playing with the Indian children, talking geography with the men and sleeping with the women—the gift of a woman for the night was a common courtesy to an honored guest. Estevan (helped by horizontal tutors perhaps) became their most accomplished linguist, able to speak eight or nine Indian languages.

Along the way, perhaps in the far west of Texas, there occurred a "strange new development," as Cabeza de Vaca describes it. His entourage began ransacking the huts of every tribe in their path, and claiming all their belongings as tribute for the Children of the Sun. Having nothing left, and no means of survival, the ransacked tribe would then join the procession and recoup their losses at the next huts along the trail. Cabeza de Vaca tried to put a stop to it, but learned that his authority didn't extend that far.

To keep the procession fed, the women spread out on the flanks, gathering edible plants and insects, and the men ranged ahead for rabbits, deer, quail and other small game; they were south of the buffalo range, in semi-arid desert country. At the end of the day, all the food was brought to the Children of the Sun, and no one would eat until they had blessed it.

> When you consider that we were frequently accompanied by three or four thousand Indians and were obliged to sanctify the food and drink of each one, you can appreciate our inconvenience. The women would bring us prickly pears, spiders, worms . . . strictly forgoing even these until we had made the sign of the Cross over them, though the women might have been starving at the time.

They entered the foothills of mountains in the west, and in one of these ranges Cabeza de Vaca tried his hand at surgery for the first time. He opened up a patient's chest with a flint knife and removed an arrowhead. He stitched up the wound, using sinew and a bone needle, and staunched the bleeding with a hank of animal fur. The next day, he writes, "I cut the stitches and the patient was well . . . He said he felt no pain or sensitivity there at all." After this cure, there was no need for the procession to ransack. The heralds spread the news and the tribes ahead willingly offered up all their food and possessions.

On the Rio Grande, having walked six hundred miles or more, they stayed with a tribe who lived in semipermanent dwellings and raised corn, beans and squash. This was the first evidence of agriculture that Cabeza de Vaca had seen since Florida, although the fields lay barren that year because of drought. At the best guess, these Indians were Jumanos. Once a year, in the autumn, they went north to the buffalo plains for meat and hides, but they had found no way to survive up there year-round. The winters were too fierce, the summers were too dry, and the herds moved too fast for a people traveling on foot.

This semi-sedentary lifestyle, a loose, flexible combination of hunting, gathering and riverbank farming, was common around the Great Plains before later Spaniards introduced the horse to the region. The Pawnees, Wichitas and Osages to the east, the Sioux, Cheyennes and Crows to the north, the Apaches to the west—all these tribes are thought to have practiced some farming at the time of Cabeza de Vaca. Then, when the horse diffused across the plains in the early eighteenth century, they all abandoned their fields, against the supposed grain of human economic development, and became full-time nomadic hunters and raiders. The Jumanos never got the chance. The horse reached their enemies before them and they were wiped out by mounted Comanches and Apaches, probably aided by European diseases.

Somewhere beyond the Rio Grande, the procession crossed what is now the Mexican border. One tribe delivered them into the hands of the next, and then returned home, having recovered their possessions. They were amazed by Cabeza de Vaca's endurance. He walked all day without eating, and was up most of the night blessing babies and food, healing and preaching.

> Through all these nations, the people who were at war quickly made up so they could come meet us with everything they possessed. Thus we left all the land in peace. And we taught all the people by signs, which they understood, that in Heaven was a Man we called God, who had created the heavens and the earth; that all good came from Him and that we worshipped and obeyed Him and called him our Lord; and that if they would do the same, all would be well with them . . . from then on, at sunrise, they would raise their arms to the sky with a glad cry, then run their hands down the length of their bodies. They repeated this ritual at sunset.

When they reached northwestern Mexico, somewhat reduced in numbers, they turned a more southerly course and entered rich agricultural lands. They were among sedentary farmers now, Opatas and Pimas, who lived in permanent villages and raised three crops a year of corn and beans. The Pimas gave the procession six hundred deer hearts, cotton blankets and hides, coral beads, turquoises, and "five emerald arrowheads," which were probably malachite.

In January 1536, after eight years in the wilderness, having crossed the continent from Florida almost to the Pacific, Castillo saw an Indian wearing a Spanish belt-buckle around his neck, with a horseshoe nail woven into it. "We gave thanks to God our Lord. Having almost despaired of finding Christians again, we could hardly restrain our excitement." At first they were worried that the buckle might have been left by a passing explorer, but as they traveled south they came upon more recent evidence of Christians.

> With heavy hearts we looked out over the lavishly watered, fertile, and beautiful land, now abandoned and burned and the people thin and weak, scattering or hiding in fright . . . Those who did receive us could provide hardly anything. They themselves looked as if they would willingly die. They brought us blankets they had concealed from the other Christians and told us how the latter had come through razing their towns and carrying off half the men and all the women and boys; those who had escaped were wandering about as fugitives. We found the survivors too alarmed to stay anywhere very long, unable or unwilling to till [their fields], preferring death to a repetition of their recent horror.

A few days later, traveling ahead of the main procession, Cabeza de Vaca caught up with a party of Spanish slavers. It was a strange, eerie, uncomfortable confrontation, not least because Cabeza de Vaca was facing the type of man he used to be.

The slavers sat on their horses and stared for a long time, dumb-founded by the sight of this naked, bearded, sun-darkened man and his entourage of Indians. They said nothing, so Cabeza de Vaca went forward to introduce himself: "I am the King's trea-surer . . . the Narvaez expedition . . . eight years among the Indians . . . take me to your captain."

For Captain Diego de Alcaraz, the arrival of Cabeza de Vaca's procession looked like a godsend. His slaving expedition had been an ignominious failure. They had caught no Indians, his men were hungry and exhausted, and he was at his wits' end. What provi-dence to have six hundred Indians delivered on a platter!

When Cabeza de Vaca found out that Alcaraz intended to enslave his entourage he was horrified. These Indians were his converts and companions, not chattels to be caged and sold. There was a hot argument, and Cabeza de Vaca stomped off in a rage, taking his procession with him—"to think we had given these Christians . . . cow [buffalo] hides!"

Later, Captain Alcaraz called a conference, and Cabeza de Vaca and his entourage gathered around to hear his words. Speaking through an interpreter, Alcaraz told the Indians that the Children of the Sun were not gods, but men like himself who had been long lost, and were now inconsequential. The Indians were having none of it.

> Conferring among themselves, they replied that the Christians lied: we had come from the sunrise, they from the sunset; we healed the sick, they killed the sound; we came naked and barefoot, they clothed, horsed, and lanced; we coveted nothing but gave whatever we were given, while they robbed whomever they found and bestowed nothing on anyone.

This stands as an eloquent summary of Cabeza de Vaca's odyssey of transformation in North America. The conquistador had become a man of peace, a healer. The grandson of a slaver had become a defender of Indians. In the weeks to come he wrangled with the colonial bureaucracy and managed to put a stop to the slaving, the killing and the stealing of Indian lands (a temporary respite, as it turned out, before even worse abuses).

At the same time, Cabeza de Vaca was going through a personal struggle. For eight years and probably six thousand barefoot miles, as slave, merchant and healer, he had wandered through the wilderness and dreamed of returning to civilization. Now he had finally reached it, this shining destination in his mind, and he felt like an alien. He was shocked by the brutality of his countrymen, but there were more mundane, and perhaps more revealing, examples of how much he had changed.

He couldn't stand the feeling of clothing on his skin, or shoes on his feet, and he was unable to sleep in a bed. He lay down on the floor at night, next to the bed, and wrapped himself in a buffalo hide.

Adventures in the Unknown Interior has never been widely read, and one cannot credit it with influencing later American literature, or habits of mind. Its themes—the epic, searching journey toward the sunset, spiritual transformation in the wilderness, the hope of building a new and better world—seem characteristically American because, in a way, Cabeza de Vaca had become an American by the time he wrote it. He had been through an odyssey that was not possible in Europe, and by the end of it he no longer thought or behaved like a European. In a sense, he had been conquered by America.

Like so many fictional American wanderers after him, Cabeza de Vaca found a measure of brotherhood and understanding across the racial divide, and not just with Indians. The figure of Estevan, the hero's dusky traveling companion, recurs again and again in American literature: Huck and Jim, Ishmael and Queequeg, Natty Bumppo and Chingachgook, all the way to Tonto and the Lone Ranger, and Hunter S. Thompson and his three-hundred-pound Samoan attorney.

How permanent was his transformation? What became of the failed conquistador in the end? In 1537 Cabeza de Vaca returned to Spain and couldn't wait to leave. He felt uneasy and confined in walled cities, court gossip left him cold, and he never did get used to wearing shoes again. His only ambition was to return to the Americas.

In 1540, after three years of lobbying, he managed to get command of an expedition to Paraguay: the beleaguered Spanish outpost at Asunción needed saving. He landed on the coast of Brazil, where ships were waiting to take him on the established sea route via Buenos Aires and up the rivers.

Instead, Cabeza de Vaca took off his shoes and led his men on a thousand-mile walk overland, through a tangled hell of jungle, mountains and cannibal villages that was thought to be impass-able—killing no Indians and losing none of his men along the way. The next year he made another thousand-mile barefoot march, and would have kept going if his men hadn't threatened to mutiny.

In 1543 Cabeza de Vaca was sent back to Spain in chains for trying to prevent the exploitation of Paraguayan Indians. No monument stands to him in either continent.

CHAPTER 3

When the virus of restlessness begins to take possession of a wayward man, and the road from Here seems broad and straight and sweet, the victim must find in himself a good and sufficient reason for going.

John Steinbeck, *Travels with Charley*

Ten miles out from the nearest town, B.J. walks along the side of the highway, following the footprints of other desert travelers: lug-soled boots, a pair of worn-out sneakers, a Mexican in tire-tread sandals, a splay-footed man in cowboy boots. Beneath the asphalt of this West Texas highway lies an Indian trail thousands of years old, which may have been traveled by Cabeza de Vaca and his procession—not that B.J. McHenry knows anything about it, or could give a rat's ass.

His eyes scan the roadside dust and grit, the weeds and the tumbleweeds, the scattered mosaic of tiny bottle shards. A thunderstorm came through here last night, bringing heavy rains and high winds, which means that all four sets of tracks were laid down today. What are all these people doing out here on foot, crowding up the roadside? How far does a man have to walk to find a little solitude these days? It's the same story all over: too many train tramps riding the rails, too many road tramps working the highways, and wetback Mexicans all over the goddamn place.

B.J. doesn't like Mexicans. He calls himself a tramp, but with a few exceptions—experienced professional men like himself—he doesn't like tramps either. Lazy, worthless bums—why don't they get a job? Why don't some of these losers try working for a living, for a change, and get the hell off his road? B.J. doesn't appreciate the company, even in footprint form, and he doesn't need the competition.

As he walks along, grousing over the tracks, he retains a low-level, habitual alertness for rattlesnakes, and objects flung out of car windows. He is amazed at some of the things people throw away: pistols, pocket knives, wedding rings, necklaces, bags of weed, bindles of coke, untouched cheeseburgers, unsmoked packs of cigarettes. Once he came across a tie, a suit jacket, a shirt, a left shoe, then a right shoe, then the suit trousers, strung out along five miles of interstate in the Mojave Desert. He collected the outfit, tried to sell it, and ended up trading it piecemeal to a bunch of train tramps in the Stockton yards.

Sometimes a driver will brake and swerve, perhaps avoiding a deer, and the loose objects on his dashboard will slide out of the open window on the passenger side; snack food, cigarettes and lighters mostly, but occasionally a wallet, or a credit card, or a money clip. B.J. has seen it happen, the wallet falling in his path like a gift from the road. Once he tried to re-create the moment by dragging a roadkilled deer carcass from the verge of the inter-state into the outside lane. Waiting in the weeds, B.J. watched plenty of drivers make the correct brake and swerve maneuver but nothing came flying out of the windows, not even a pack of cigarettes or a stick of gum. He waited there for a couple of hours and then gave up, carving himself off a venison steak and roasting it on a campfire under a bridge. At least he slept on a full belly that night, so no complaints.

The road has its patterns and moods, its runs of good and bad fortune, but they are hard to predict in advance, and seemingly impossible to influence. From what he can remember, casting his mind back across a decade or more, living with a woman is much the same way. For two or three weeks everything rolls along smooth and easy. You get a ride when you want one, meals when you're hungry, tens and twenties for beer and tobacco, without even asking, and sometimes a little gift or trinket as a sweetener.

Then, with little or no warning, the road will withdraw its favors and start acting mean and hostile. You will find yourself stranded on a remote desert highway, waiting two or three days for a ride. You will get caught out in a lightning storm, or a blizzard, or a tornado, with no bridge or culvert for shelter. Over the years, B.J. has been strafed by sandstorms, pelted with giant hailstones, shoved out of moving vehicles, thrown out of moving boxcars, stabbed, robbed, beaten and jailed, and hit in the head by flying beer bottles, which is the one thing that really pisses him off.

Most drivers who throw their empties out of the window do so without looking, or thinking about the consequences, which is aggravating enough when you're on the receiving end. But every now and then, as B.J. is walking along the highway, minding his own business, someone will lean out of the passenger window of a passing vehicle and take deliberate aim at the back of his head. The old American contempt for a man afoot . . . B.J. has got scars and lumps on his skull to prove it, and a half-moon scar on his face, curving down from his temple and around his left cheekbone.

To all you bottle-throwing motorists out there: B.J. wants to know if you understand the velocities involved. If a vehicle is traveling seventy-five miles an hour, he has calculated, an empty beer bottle thrown forward out of that same vehicle is probably doing sixty when it smashes into his skull and maybe more if the guy's got a good throwing arm.

B.J. has been hit in the head three times, not including glancing blows. On all three occasions he was knocked unconscious, woke up needing stitches, and had a hell of a time getting to the nearest hospital. It's a rare driver who'll pick up a big, hairy, wild-looking road tramp when he's covered in blood.

Now he's in the habit of turning his head when he hears a vehicle coming up behind him and checking over his left shoulder for incoming. If you see the bottle as it leaves the window, there's just enough time to duck, or hit the deck, if you need to. Most guys tend to throw a little high and left, especially from pickup trucks, but there are some dead-eye marksmen out on the roads, especially in the South and the Southwest. B.J. has seen them practicing, honing their aim by throwing beer bottles at the highway signs.

B.J. picks the lice from his scalp, his chest hair, his long, graying prophet's beard, and flicks them out of the window of my rental car. He is a tall, broad-shouldered, raw-boned man, tough-looking and ornery. There are fresh scabs and bruises on his scarred, leathery face. His nose is bruised and swollen, and I would guess that it's probably broken, although not for the first time. I picked him up an hour ago, on the arid plains west of Big Spring, Texas, and he's been talking ever since—a gruff, profane, bad-tempered stream of consciousness.

"A lot of guys will shoot out the highway signs, too," he says. "But I've been on the road damn near twenty years and no motherfucker has tried to shoot me yet. If you want to kill me, take a goddamn shot at me! Don't fuck around with these goddamn beer bottles and do it by accident!"

He gives off a stale, sour, smoky smell, redolent of beer, sweat, tobacco and campfires, and a long, hot stretch of road between here and the last shower. He is wearing army-surplus pants, an old denim shirt, a malachite necklace, and a black, sweat-rimmed Harley-Davidson cap, which he lifts from time to time, to scratch at his scalp and hunt up another louse. His hair is a long, greasy, wind-tangled mane, fanning out from the sides of the cap. His eyes are a sun-faded blue, framed into small triangles by his eyelids, and they carry a wary, haunted, feral expression, with no trace of warmth or humor that I can see.

Since Vietnam, he says, he hasn't spent more than ninety consecutive days in the same place. One way and another, that has been his limit. In the late 1970s he spent three months with a woman in Dallas, living off her earnings in the drug trade, until she went nuts and kicked him out (or B.J. drove her crazy). He spent three months with a divorcée in Oklahoma City, drinking up her alimony, until it got so crazy he had to leave. Ninety days in a Texas prison cell, for intent to supply marijuana and resisting arrest: he'd rather be dead, or back in Vietnam, than go through that kind of confinement again.

He grew up in Vermont, New Hampshire and upstate New York, but he stays west of the Appalachians these days, and mostly west of the Mississippi, and his accent has slipped into the characteristic rasping drawl of the Western road tramp. There are too many people back East, he says. Too much law and order, and the winters will freeze your nuts off.

"Where are you headed?" I ask him.

"Phoenix, most probably," he says. "There's a mountain near there where you can buy Indian jewelry real cheap, and sell it for big bucks in California." Then he decides on El Paso, where a veteran's check may, or may not, be retrievable from a long-dormant bank account. Then Albuquerque, then San Diego, or maybe Washington State before the winter rains set in. There's a café in Seattle, 1900 miles from here, which gives out free coffee to the homeless on Sunday mornings.

"Do you ever get lonely?" I ask him. "Do you get lonely for women?"

"Women ain't worth the goddamn trouble," he growls. "I had an old lady a couple of years back. We tramped together on the rails for a while, until the crazy fuckin' bitch tried to stab me one night when she was drunk. I don't even fool with women no more. They ain't worth it."

He's given up riding the rails too, because of the gang violence circulating around the FTRA, the Freight Train Riders of America—the "hobo mafia," as the newspapers call them. The FTRA is probably the most drunken, stoned and shambolic criminal organization in America, and certainly the poorest, but it has been credited with more than a dozen murders in the last five years, and scores of beatings.

Last summer B.J. heard a rumor that the FTRA's "goon squad" was looking for him, and he's been sticking to the roads ever since. He calls himself a rubber tramp now, hitching his rides around the country, and doing a lot of walking in between. Most tramps hate to walk, but B.J. gets antsy and restless, standing there on the same patch of roadside with his thumb out, waiting for the next ride to come along. He'd rather set out on foot and feel like he's making some progress, and some days he'd rather walk than ride. Drivers always want conversation, which is fine when he's in the mood for talking, but some days he doesn't even want to see another human being.

It's been nearly a year since his last sexual encounter (a brief, drunken grappling with a tramp woman in Sturgis, South Dakota), and four or five months since he slept in a bed. Walls, ceilings, doors, beds: they've got them in jails, they've got them in houses and motel rooms. After a few hours in the same building, he starts feeling twitchy and claustrophobic, but he can make four or five days in a homeless shelter, if the weather is bad enough, or a veteran's hospital, if he is too stoved-up to travel. Ninety days in a Texas prison cell . . . it drove his cellmates crazy but B.J. couldn't help himself, pacing up and down the tiny cage at night.

Beds give him "bad dreams," Vietnam dreams. Sleeping sober gives him bad dreams, if he can sleep at all. A bottle, a hand-rolled cigarette and a full belly twice a day, a roof of stars and the road: this is all he wants from the world, this is how he keeps his mind from unraveling.

He knows the roads and rails of the West as well as anyone I've ever met. Name any town on a major highway, and B.J. can tell you which restaurant dumpster to raid for food, the cheapest place to buy beer and Ten High whiskey, the location of the mission and thrift store, the disposition of the local cops and rail-road police, which churches are good for a hand-out and which are likely to call the law, the best place to catch an undisturbed night's sleep, and where to hitch a ride or hop a freight train out of there.

As we drive across the emptiness of West Texas, he points out obscure ranch roads and dirt tracks. This one leads to a railroad switching point, where you can catch out on a slow-moving freight to San Antonio. That one leads to a low hill in the distance, where you can dig up quartz and other saleable minerals, but watch out for the rancher who owns the land, and slow down here, because there's a dip in the road up ahead where the highway patrol cars like to hide. Never take a sip on your beer when you're passing a truck or a truck is passing you. Too many truckers these days are enrolled in highway snitch programs, looking for cash rewards and brownie points by calling in violations to the highway patrol.

If you find yourself hungry in the desert, rattlesnake is the easiest meat to kill. "Find you a big ol' rattler and smash his head in with a fuckin' rock, that's what I say. Snakemeat ain't bad when it's fresh. People say it tastes like chicken, but it tastes like fuckin' snake to me. Hah! Gotta be careful of them poison sacs though. You bet your ass. Cut you a good six, seven inches off the head end, that's my rule, and make sure that snake don't bite hisself when you're killin' him."

B.J. is a mine of useful information, a tough, competent, resourceful man, but there is an air of brooding, unstable violence about him, and it doesn't require a great leap of the imagination to picture him pulling a weapon—his snake-butchering knife, perhaps, or one of those handguns he found by the side of the road. Half the time, he stares out of the window, lost in his stream of consciousness, as if he's talking to himself and has forgotten that I'm sitting next to him. Then something in his thoughts will trip a trigger. He will turn his head and bore his eyes into mine, with a sudden, fierce intensity, as if demanding a show of agreement or respect. I nod along, trying to look sufficiently grave and impressed, and wondering how to get rid of him with the minimum of trouble.

Maybe sensing my thoughts, he pulls out a small, rusty penknife and lays it down on the dashboard. "I found this 'un on the road back there," he says. "I reckon you can keep it, or sell it, or hand it in as lost property, whatever you want. I can't have no weapons on me in case I get stopped and searched by the cops, and they try and pin some bullshit on me. It ain't right but that's the way it is."

The penknife settles me down a little. It would be an odd sequence of events for him to pull a gun now, or a bigger knife. Then he goes off into another angry monologue: police harassment, vagrancy laws, the goddamn federal government, the various beatings he has suffered over the years at the hands of cops and jailers and railroad police, and his small triumphs of vengeance, exacted during fights with other tramps.

I ask him about the scabs and bruises on his face. Was it cops, tramps or flying beer bottles? He turns his head, the eyes zoom in, he bares his teeth in a snarl—"I got rolled by a bunch of fuckin' niggers in Houston! Motherfuckers jumped me, stole my bedroll, stole all my shit, broke my motherfuckin' nose, man! Fuckin' niggers fucked my shit up! If there's one thing I hate in this world, it's a fuckin' nigger, and I hate a fuckin' Texas nigger worst of all."

"Come on," I say, "I was beaten up and robbed by a black guy once. I don't hold it against all the black people who didn't rob me. I've been beaten up by white guys too, and so have you. Assholes come in all colors, so why discriminate?"

That doesn't do any good. I don't *know* niggers like he knows niggers. Until you've been in prison with a nigger, you don't know what he's really like and so on, and so forth. I try to change the subject but that doesn't do any good either. B.J. is locked into his tirade now, venting all his hatred at the world—"Prison's too good for 'em! It's more than a white man should have to bear, to be locked up with those animals."

I try to be a tolerant person. And after twenty minutes of B.J.'s rant, in a flash of temper and a violent desire to slam my elbow into his eye-socket, I find the limit of my tolerance.

"Look," I tell him, slamming on the brakes instead, "I don't want to hear this any more. This is as far as the ride goes."

I turf him out on the edge of Pecos, Texas. Yelling and cursing his defiance, flipping me the finger, B.J. McHenry shrinks and disappears in the rearview mirror.

It's a rueful thought now, but I rented this car with the intention of retracing Cabeza de Vaca's journey across the Southwest. Historical reverie, that was the general idea. By crossing the same ground—watching the landscape broaden and unfurl toward the sunset, camping at some of the same rivers and springs, smelling the same woodsmoke at night, under the same stars—the centuries would dissolve away and the old narrative would come to life in my mind's eye. That was the plan, dreamy and quixotic, and now it lies thoroughly mangled.

In the first place, I had overlooked an unfortunate but fundamental fact of travel in present-day Texas. There are towns now
on many of the old springs and river crossings, and just about all
the land in between—all that big, inviting, wide-open space—is
privately owned. I've been spoiled by the states further west, which
still contain huge tracts of public land. I'm accustomed to finding
an obscure, unfenced dirt road at sunset, leading off into the backcountry, where a traveler can make a fire and sleep next to it
without paying any fees or asking anyone's permission. Try that
in Texas and you run the risk of being woken up by some irate
rancher in the morning, with the legal and God-given right to
shoot any trespassers on his property. If you're on foot and hitchhiking, it's easy enough to duck under a fence and find a secluded
wash somewhere, with deep enough banks to conceal a fire, but
it's hard to trespass incognito in a shiny white rental car.

So I've been sleeping on the backseat at night, parked outside
motels and twenty-four-hour superstores. I've been driving the
interstate corridors most of the way, eating at franchise restaurants, refuelling at franchise gas stations, traveling toward the sunset
in a random, disconnected procession of cars, trucks, motorbikes
and motor homes. There have been a few stretches of historical
reverie, through a windshield at seventy-five miles an hour, but
my thoughts and my notebooks have been preoccupied by the
modern roadscape, and the hitchhikers I've picked up along
the way.

Endless impaling stories . . . Jimmy used to be an oil-field roughneck, a construction worker, a truck driver, a hunting guide, a
fishing guide, a movie stuntman, or so he says. Now he has prospects
in San Antonio, working construction for a friend's uncle. He tells
the stories with a kind of appalled glee. A guy falls from a high
platform at an oil refinery in Beaumont, Texas, and impales himself
on a scaffolding pole. How about that? In New Orleans, he sees
a man run through with a sword-cane in a bar. Story after story:
birds impaled on cactus spines after a windstorm, hunting accidents with crossbows, a harpooning accident off the coast of
Florida. He tells a story about a skewered truck driver that I've

heard before—a highway legend, I suspect—but Jimmy says he saw it up close and personal.

"A few years back, I was hauling a load west on I-10, about twenty miles out from Tucson, and I come up on this big old wreck in the highway. There was two smashed-up cars and a semi gone off the road and a load of twenty-foot steel pipe all over the highway. The cops weren't there yet so I got out of my rig and went up to the semi to check on the driver. He was a black guy and I saw right away what must have happened. One of those twenty-foot pipes he was hauling must have come loose, when he slammed on the brakes most probably. It had gone right through the back of the cab, speared him through his back, come out his chest, and the end of it was sticking into the dashboard. And get this: he was still *alive*. He was alive but there was no way he could move! The poor bastard was just *pinned* there! So I says to him, 'Oh man, oh buddy, I'm sorry. I'm sorry buddy but you're fucked.' That's what I told him and it was the last thing he heard before he died."

It's always difficult to assess the level of truth, if any, in a story told by a chance acquaintance on the road. I've heard the one about the impaled truck driver six or seven times now. The location varies—Arizona, New Mexico, California—the date varies from yesterday to eight or ten years ago, but the core details remain the same: steel pipe, black trucker, pinned to the dashboard but still alive. And the narrator, or the narrator's close friend, is always there to offer a few brusque, consoling words at the moment of death. Is it rooted in some original factual incident, or is it pure legend? Damned if I know, and I'm not about to check back through ten years of highway accident reports, in three different states, to find out.*

So what about B.J. McHenry? Why treat him as a reliable

---

* A report in the *New York Times*, October 1999, refers to a stretch of I-95 in Florida as the "impalement capital" of America, and cites three incidents in which unsecured metal rods flew off trucks and skewered passing motorists, pinning them to the inside of their cars. Amazingly, none of the motorists died from their injuries.

narrator? Well, I can offer no proof to back up anything he said, but leaving aside the part about blacks being subhuman, I believed most of it. The flying beer bottles, the snake-eating, the intimate knowledge of roadside America, his troubles with women and the law—it all seemed to jibe with his battered, scarred, feral appearance, and what I've seen and heard in my own experiences on the roads and rails.

I've had bottles and beer cans thrown at me several times (all of them Bud Light drinkers, no hits so far), and I've heard numerous other tramps complaining about the practice. Eating roadkill is so commonplace that there are state and federal laws regulating the ownership of the meat. In some parts of the country you are free to take whatever cow, moose, deer, elk, antelope or smaller animal that you collided with, or found already dead on the road. In other areas the practice is illegal, or levied with fees. Eating rattlesnake is less common, but I've heard the same butchering tips before, and I've eaten it myself, fixed up into a chilli and served as a gimmick item in a south Texas restaurant.

In San Antonio I stopped off at the university library. The vicinity of San Antonio, according to my edition of Cabeza de Vaca's narrative (University of New Mexico Press, 1997), was where he traveled with the Mariames for the prickly pear harvest, escaped with his companions, and began the long sunset leg of his journey. That was one of the things I liked about the University of New Mexico edition. Interspliced with the text is a detailed geographical description of Cabeza de Vaca's route, matched against modern place-names. It's a fine, understated translation too, and I loved the name of the translator and editor: Cyclone Covey.

Some of the geographical references in the text seemed a little vague—"a river which ran between mountains," and so on—but Cyclone Covey put my doubts to rest in his preface. Cabeza de Vaca's route was discovered in the 1930s by Carl Sauer and Cleve Hallenbeck, the two leading Southwestern trail historians of their era. Working independently of each other, they found that the procession had traveled, for the most part, on the established Indian trails across the Southwest—trails that were still traceable in the

1930s. "The thorough work of these two distinguished professors," wrote Covey, "plus that of innumerable others in such disciplines as archaeology, anthropology, cartography, geology, climatology, botany, zoology and history, has given surprisingly sharp definition to much of the old narrative . . . Hallenbeck, in fact, incorporates and supersedes all previous scholarship on the subject."

That sold me on the route, but I was still curious to know how the experts had mapped it out so precisely. At the San Antonio library, I found Hallenbeck's book. It was a simple process of deduction, he argued. There were only a few practicable trails by which a procession of thousands could have crossed the plains and deserts without dying of thirst. Hallenbeck had driven, walked and camped out on all of these trails, and there was only one that matched the geographical and botanical references in Cabeza de Vaca's narrative, and the joint narrative he wrote with Dorantes and Castillo. Like most Indian trails, it was originally worn by migrating game, and it made the best possible use of the far-flung rivers and springs.

Then I found two more books, and a number of journal articles, which suggested that Hallenbeck's route is now regarded as something of a joke among Cabeza de Vaca scholars. Hallenbeck keeps the procession north of the present-day Mexican border, all the way across Texas, New Mexico and into Arizona, turning them south into Mexico at the last geographically conceivable moment. The suspicion in some quarters is that Hallenbeck's patriotism, his eagerness to claim Cabeza de Vaca as an American hero, got the better of his scholarship. The leading modern Cabeza de Vaca scholar, Donald Chipman, places the route further south in the Rio Grande country, looping in and out of Texas and present-day Mexico, and probably never setting foot in New Mexico or Arizona.

I spent a long, irksome afternoon reading through the debate, getting bogged down in the arcane minutiae—the relative thickness of piñon nut shells in different mountain ranges, the effect of climate shifts on the latitude of prickly pear harvests, and so on. In all, six different routes have been proposed, with Hallenbeck at the northern limit and Chipman at the southern, and each route has attracted its own camp of supporters and detractors. Ultimately, like the University of New Mexico Press, I decided to ignore the whole controversy. I got back behind the wheel and set out west on a vague approximation of Hallenbeck's route, mainly because it had already brought me to San Antonio, 180 miles north of the Rio Grande, and because it's illegal to drive this rental car across the Mexican border—a border put in place three hundred years after Cabeza de Vaca.

The trail historians will never agree on the route, I suspect, because all of them are extrapolating from the same vague, ambiguous set of references, and besides, I'm more interested in the mental geography of Cabeza de Vaca's trek, his eight-year journey out of the European mind. It left him a better man by our culture's reckoning, if not his own, but why did it leave him so restless?

I also read about his adventures in Paraguay—the epic barefoot journeys into the wilderness, undertaken against the advice of his superiors, the pleas of his men and all prevailing wisdom—as though Cabeza de Vaca had developed a driving psychological need to go on thousand-mile treks among the Indians. Was this a sign of damage and derangement wrought by his experiences in North America? Some of his colleagues in Paraguay thought so—why else, for example, would he prohibit them from looting, raping and enslaving the Indians along the way?

I prefer to think that Cabeza de Vaca had found his calling in life, and decided to follow it.

The highway crosses the Pecos River and arrows across the desert toward the Rio Grande; isolated mountain ranges on the horizon now, dappled with shadows by the late afternoon sun, and the wide desert valleys turning gold. Here at least, in the southwestern corner of Texas, the trail historians have reached a broad consensus. This was the country of the Jumanos, the seminomadic hunters and riverbank farmers who gave Cabeza de Vaca the buffalo hides he became so attached to.

> They are the best looking people we saw, the strongest and
> most energetic, and who most readily understood us and
> answered our questions. We called them the "Cow People,"
> because more cattle are killed in their vicinity than anywhere;
> for more than fifty leagues up that river they prey on the
> cows.

The river might have been the Rio Grande, but there were many
more buffalo fifty leagues up the Pecos, which flows along the
western edge of the Llano Estacado, the staked plains, the vast,
uplifted, surreally flat plateau where buffalo once roamed in their
millions and mounted Comanches later established the purest
nomadic warrior culture in North America.

It's mostly irrigation farming up there today—wheat, cotton,
pastured cattle—but sedentary agriculture has been a dubious
experiment on the Llano, and it has an uncertain future. In the
1930s, the Llano Estacado formed the southern rim of the Dust
Bowl. In the 1950s it was hit by another drought, and now the
land is ploughed up and overgrazed again. The wind is as relent-
less as ever, and the climate patterns suggest that another long
drought is overdue. From the Jumanos onward, people trying
to raise crops in West Texas have run into the same cyclical
problem.

> We asked [the Jumanos] how it happened that they did not
> plant corn. So they would not lose what they planted was
> the answer: no rain two years in a row; moles got the seed;
> must have plenty rain before planting again. They begged
> us to tell the sky to rain.

The current generation of farmers on the Llano use well-water
to grow their crops, water their cattle and keep the topsoil in
place, but the wells are starting to come up dry. The farmers put
their faith in the existence of an underground river flowing down
from the north, which will keep replenishing the aquifer, but most
hydrologists regard this notion as fantasy, and predict that irrigation farming on the Llano has a practical future of twenty or

thirty years; maybe less if another drought kicks in, or the bankers lose patience.

Like the buffalo herds, or the gold deposits which sparked the stampede to California, the aquifers of the Southwest are finite, nonrenewable resources that accumulated over millions of years. To put it another way, the aquifers are being mined, and when the mine is no longer producing it will be time to abandon it and move on.

I drive on into a huge purple and red sunset, given extra color and vibrancy by the cloud of dust and pollution hanging over the border conurbation of El Paso and Ciudad Juárez—three million people living on another plummeting aquifer. The highway bends to the north, leaving the sprawl behind, and after seven hundred miles of Texas crosses into New Mexico. I start thinking about my campfire in the wilds again. Up in the Gila National Forest maybe, or the Sacramento Mountains, where Hallenbeck has Cabeza de Vaca performing his miracle surgery with a flint knife and a deer bone. Or for a small fee, and no campfire, in the moonlit gypsum dunes of White Sands National Monument. Then it occurs to me that it's only three hundred miles to Tucson, and that nice little house I rented on the edge of town, the one that is supposed to feel like home.

I stop in Las Cruces, pick up a microwaved burrito, coffee to go and a fresh pack of smokes, and drive on, letting my mind unspool behind the wheel. I trace out looping, tangled connections between Cabeza de Vaca and B.J. McHenry, the two dominant influences on this journey. Somewhere between them, I decide, there is a narrative to be teased out, which tells the history of wanderlust in North America. It's possible to look back and see a chain of developments that Cabeza de Vaca's journey set in motion. The stories he brought back inspired other Spanish expeditions into the Southwest, which introduced the horse to the region, which led to the great nomadic efflorescence among the plains Indians, which left such an indelible impression of freedom on the American mind.

Maybe there is some truth in that line of reasoning, but the history of human behavior seldom moves in such orderly progressions. It proceeds more by accident and confusion. It turns back on itself and takes triumphant detours up blind alleys. What appears, with hindsight, to be a straightforward process of cause and effect is always fraught with exceptions, paradoxes and strange offshoots. The present is gone before we can make sense of it, and the future is made up of distorted echoes from the past.

Maybe it's more helpful to think of wanderlust on this continent as a recurring condition of mind, a psychological syndrome with Cabeza de Vaca as one manifestation and B.J. McHenry as another. The first white man to cross this ground became wiser and more enlightened during his travels, with an enlarged understanding of humanity, himself and the world. He also developed a compulsion to keep traveling, and who can blame him? For all the pain and hardship he suffered, a sense of wonder and fascination shines out of his North American narrative—his "sojourn to the sunset," as he described it. It seems reasonable to assume that his treks across Paraguay were motivated by a desire to recapture these feelings, and that court life in Spain seemed unbearably drab and constricted by comparison.

I hesitate to offer up B.J. McHenry as an archetype of the modern American wanderer, because no such archetype exists, but there are plenty of men like him on the roads today: troubled loners and oblivion-chasers, who want as little contact with humanity as possible. They were familiar figures west of the settlements in the nineteenth century—"many succumbed to the violence and solitude of the frontier, which abounded with shiftless drifters and strange, broken characters"*—and they seemed to resurface again, en masse, when the soldiers came home from Vietnam.

Not all of them are racists. Not all of them are claustrophobes, or feral snake-eaters for that matter, but they are engaged in the same basic process of retreat and withdrawal, from the damage within themselves and human relationships in general. These are the parameters of the condition. The best of us find a measure

---

* Frank Thistlethwaite, *The Great Experiment.*

of wisdom, enlightenment and self-fulfilment through constant travel. The worst of us are fleeing from ourselves, and most of us strike a wavering course somewhere in between.

Strange things happen to the mind when you've been driving for fourteen hours. There comes a point beyond simple fatigue, beyond sleepiness, when the mind empties and the body seems to melt away, and it becomes easier to keep on driving than to stop.

Standing by a gas pump in Deming, New Mexico, I feel wobbly and disoriented, like a sailor returning to dry land. It's a relief to get behind the wheel again and slip back into the trance of motion. No music, no radio, just the hum of rubber on asphalt, the rhythm of the pistons, and the warm night air blowing through the windows. I drive on through the yucca flats in the moon-light, and sixty miles slip by like nothing.

Then the tiredness returns, the ache in the muscles and the eyeballs, and the giant jackrabbits start to appear. What you see is a rapid, bounding, luminescent shape, yellowish white or bluish gray, streaking along the roadside in your peripheral vision. I've heard truckers and friends of mine refer to them with an easy familiarity—"when you start seeing the giant jackrabbits . . ." In other parts of the country they manifest as deer, horses or ghost elk, but in the desert Southwest bone-tired drivers hallucinate giant jackrabbits. I know from experience that you can drive through them and reach a trance of motion on the other side, but it requires serious determination, and most highway safety experts would probably advise against it.

I make it across the Arizona border, feeling a vague sense of homecoming. This is the state listed on my driver's license. This is the state where I file taxes and keep an address and telephone number, and it has come to feel more like home than anywhere else. I have begun to entertain fantasies of owning property in Arizona, at least ten square miles of virgin desert in which I will build absolutely nothing except a campfire from time to time.

I find a remote exit leading off toward a mountain range where no lights are visible, a two-lane blacktop which soon turns to dirt. I pull over by the side of it, climb in the backseat, wake up at dawn. Here's an odd thing about road fatigue: it will collapse you into a heap of utter exhaustion, but it doesn't take much sleep to recover from it.

Willcox, Arizona. Over weak coffee and slimy eggs at a truck-stop diner I break out the Cabeza de Vaca book again. There is a passage in the afterword, by William T. Pilkington, that I woke up thinking about.

> The American journey of discovery ends in one of two ways: in hope or in bleak despair. In recent times, as the world has grown progressively darker, it has usually concluded with the latter, with its course leading nowhere. What the modern wanderer normally discovers is a blank, the spiritual equivalent of the nihilistic landscape through which he has trekked.

To hell with William T. Pilkington and his airy pronouncements. This journey of discovery has a happy ending. When I get back to my rented house in Tucson there is no girlfriend, very little furniture and mouse shit all over the kitchen, but good news is blinking on the anwering machine. The London media are craving Americana—white supremacists in northern Idaho, a vicious greedy religious cult in Tennessee, lowrider car clubs in east Los Angeles—and a German magazine wants me to cover a horse roundup in Colorado. That adds up to a good six weeks on the road, and probably five thousand miles, with all expenses paid.

CHAPTER 4

We had no word for the strange animal we got from the
white man—the horse. So we called it *sunka wakan*, "holy
dog." For bringing us the horse, we could almost forgive
you for bringing us whiskey.

> John Fire Lame Deer (Sioux),
> *Lame Deer, Seeker of Visions*

The weather station in Yuma, Arizona, is recording 108 degrees
in the shade but there is no shade out here. No trees, no
rock overhangs, no bushes to crouch under. The desert floor is a
tightly packed pavement of black and dark gray pebbles, polished
to a dull sheen by the wind, and it holds and radiates the heat
of the sun, much like the wall of an oven.

Walking beside me, delivering an impassioned monologue on
American Indian rock art, is a government archaeologist named
Boma Johnson. He is a tall, loping, amiable man in his late fifties,
with splayed front teeth and thick glasses, wearing a brown checked
Western shirt and an old, sweat-stained canvas hat.

"What do you think the temperature is out here?" I interrupt,
stopping to pour another pint of water down my parched throat.
"How hot is this air we're breathing?"

"Oh, around one-thirty, one-thirty-five, maybe."

I offer him my canteen and again he turns it down. He has
brought no water of his own. "This kind of weather doesn't bother
me," he says. "I've been walking around these deserts for twenty-

five years. It's actually pretty mild today, for an afternoon in late June. It gets a good fifteen or twenty degrees hotter than this. On a hot day, this desert pavement will melt the soles off your boots if you're not careful."

With his loping camel's gait he leads me up an old Indian trail to a series of flat, barren terraces, fanning out from the base of a small hill and commanding a view of the surrounding desert. Away to the west there are sand dunes, blinding white in the early afternoon sun and melting into mirage. To the south is a channel of the Colorado River, which marks the Mexican border, with a shantytown on the other side, and another shimmering expanse of desert beyond it.

Yuman Indian tribes—Cocopas or maybe Quechuans—once held their dances and ceremonies on these terraces, and you can see faint rings tamped into the desert pavement by generations of dancing, circling feet. You can see shards of quartz, chipped away as they made their amulets, and two circular depressions, about six feet in diameter, where Boma thinks the huts of the tribal shaman and his apprentice once stood.

In places, the surface covering of pebbles has been scraped away entirely, leaving large designs and animal figures exposed in the pale sand underneath. Like the Nazca lines in Peru, which were made in the same way, on a much grander scale, these intaglios, or geoglyphs, show up most clearly in aerial photographs, but they have a more visceral impact up close, walking among them and seeing where the artist's hand touched the earth, or perhaps scraped it with an abalone shell, three or four hundred years ago.

Boma takes me to a lizard, twenty-six feet long, with its feet tramped out by sightseers, and the head and tail very faint. Then a crude human figure with no legs. "If they don't have legs, or the legs are just tamped in lightly, it means that they're spirit figures, traveling through the spirit world," he says. "They don't need legs where they're going. At least, that's what the tribal elders have told me. In our tradition we paint wings on people to symbolize the same thing, which the elders think is hilarious."

Then he takes me to the horse, the most impressive of the

intaglios, and the one I've come here to see. Twenty-three feet from nose to tail, with a long arching neck and an open mouth, standing sixteen feet tall on lightly tamped-in legs, it may be the earliest surviving image of the horse in North America.

Earth intaglios are notoriously difficult to date, but we know that mounted Spaniards passed this way in 1540 as part of Francisco de Coronado's expedition, and that these were the first horses that the Yuman tribes had seen. "I can't prove it," says Boma, "but my best guess is that a Cocopa shaman made this intaglio, during or soon after that first encounter."

Coronado was marching north out of Mexico, chasing a rumor of gold. To be precise, he was looking for seven cities of gold, founded by seven exiled Catholic bishops, who had left Europe long ago and sailed toward the sunset. It was an old Spanish legend, dating back to the eighth century, but it had become fresh and urgent with the return of Cabeza de Vaca's party. Indians had told them about permanent settlements to the north, in present-day New Mexico, with houses four storeys high and great stores of wealth, and it was no leap for the sixteenth-century Spanish mind to translate this into seven cities of gold.

Do you recall Estevan? The Moor who had been a slave, the slave of a slave, a fugitive slave, and then a god? And then a slave again, when Cabeza de Vaca's procession reached the Spanish colonies in Mexico. In 1539, a year before Coronado, he was released to travel with an expedition of explorers, led by an ambitious Franciscan friar known as Fray Marcos. Estevan was to be their guide and interpreter, and lead them north to the seven cities of gold.

Adorned with bells and feathers, carrying a sacred medicine rattle he had been given on Cabeza de Vaca's procession, Estevan traveled well ahead of the rest of the expedition. He returned to the northern tribes as a Child of the Sun, with an escort of Christianized Indians, and he reaped the same tribute in gifts, women and adoration. The friars fretted that Estevan was taking on blasphemous airs, and they disapproved of his womanizing, which is one reason why he traveled so far ahead of them.

When Estevan reached the Zuni pueblos in New Mexico, his luck ran out. The Zunis saw that the sacred rattle he was carrying belonged to an enemy tribe. They were suspicious of his claims to godhood, and they resented his demands for their turquoises and women. So they took Estevan prisoner and killed him. The rest of his party escaped and made it back to Mexico with Fray Marcos, who reported that they had reached the very portals of the golden cities, in a place called Cíbola.

So Coronado marches north with 300 conquistadors, 1000 Indian servants, 500 head of cattle and mules, a huge flock of sheep and close to 1000 Spanish horses. His mind is unclouded by doubt. The Seven Cities of Cíbola are there for the taking. And somewhere beyond them are China and India.

The Yuman tribes never encountered the main column of Coronado's army. It traveled up through the mountains of southeast Arizona into New Mexico, far to the east of their farming villages on the Colorado River. The first Spaniards they saw belonged to a supply arm of the expedition, commanded by a Captain Alarcón, and they came up the river in ships.

As meetings between conquistadors and Indians go, it was a happy occasion. Alarcón handed out gifts and announced himself as a Child of the Sun. By sign language, he told the Indians on the riverbank that he had come to put an end to their wars and teach them about a new, all-powerful god who lived in the sky. The Yuman tribes were delighted by this news, and they begged Alarcón to stay and rule over them. They were fascinated by his long, flowing beard, of which the chroniclers tell us he was inordinately vain.

Alarcón liked the Yuman tribes—farmers, hunter-gatherers, scalp-taking warriors. They were huge, muscular people with big heads and prodigious strength; even today some of the men reach seven feet. Alarcón made no attempt to take their lands or steal their possessions, and they had no gold to tempt his avarice. He stayed and preached awhile, explored further upriver, hoping to find Coronado's army, and then gave up and returned to Mexico, leaving the Indians mourning his departure on the riverbanks.

Boma Johnson thinks that Alarcón might have had horses with him, because it would have been unusual for a party of conquistadors to travel without them, even by ship, but there is no mention of horses in the Spanish chronicles of Alarcón's voyage. The first confirmed account of horses in the Yuman country is from later that year, with the arrival of Melchior Díaz's party on the Colorado River.

They had just ridden four hundred miles across the desert, looking for the ships—twenty-five Spanish horsemen, accompanied by Indian servants on foot, a flock of sheep for food and a greyhound. When they reached the river, they found a note left under a tree by Alarcón: gone back to Mexico; California is not an island but a peninsula of the mainland.

The encounter between Díaz and the Yuman tribes was more typical. Mutual suspicion led to a fight, during which the Spaniards rode down and lanced a quantity of Indians. The rest of the warriors scattered and fled, and the musketeers picked off more of them as they ran.

Díaz's party crossed the Colorado River on rafts, with the horses swimming alongside, and explored the desert on the California side, looking for the coast. Desert thirst and sand dunes turned them around, and soon afterwards their captain died from a bizarre impaling accident. The greyhound had been bothering the sheep again and Díaz galloped toward it in a rage and hurled his lance. The lance missed the dog and stuck in the ground. Díaz was unable to swerve his galloping horse and rode onto the butt end of the lance, impaling himself in the groin, puncturing his bladder, and dying a long, painful, twenty-one-day death.

Perhaps, as Boma Johnson suspects, the first horses came here on Alarcón's ships. More likely, they came with Díaz. The oral histories of the Yuman tribes, which Boma collects assiduously, contain no dates or verifiable details about their initial encounter with the horse, but they do record the emotions of the experience. Like so many tribes in Mexico and South America, they looked at a horse and rider for the first time and saw a huge, supernatural beast with two heads. When one of the heads detached itself and walked toward them like a man—a man-shaped monster encased in shiny metal—they fell on the ground shaking with terror.

"I put more faith in Indian oral histories than most archaeologists," says Boma, "but this one in particular has a ring of truth to it. Indians don't like telling stories to white people which make them look foolish, even if it was hundreds of years ago."

When Coronado reached Cíbola he discovered that the seven cities of gold were the six pueblo villages of the Zuni. Their houses were built of dried mud and their wealth was in corn, beans, turquoise and pottery. There was a brief skirmish, a desultory pillaging, then the expedition went on to the Hopi villages, and were disappointed again.

Wintering among the pueblo tribes on the Rio Grande, near the site of present-day Albuquerque, the Spaniards met a traveling Pawnee Indian, whom they nicknamed "the Turk" because they thought he looked like one. He told them that the cities of gold were out on the plains to the east, in a province called Quivira, and he offered to show them the way.

The Turk, as he later admitted, was part of a ruse engineered by the pueblo tribes. The same ruse was employed to good effect by other tribes who wanted to get rid of conquistadors: the thing you crave is not here but down that trail, a few days' journey away, in the country of our enemies. It worked on Coronado's expedition because their minds were so primed and ready to find the seven cities. People had been talking about them for eight centuries, and now they had fresh confirmation from Cabeza de Vaca and Fray Marcos. They had the examples of Cortés in Mexico, and Pizarro in Peru, who had sacked cities richer and more magnificent than any Spanish fantasy. And let us not discount the magical power of gold itself, and the greed and delusions it produces in the European mind—"the shiny metal for which the whites go crazy," as later Indians called it. Or, as Cortés had put it to Montezuma's envoy, "I and my companions suffer from a disease of the heart which can be cured only with gold."

So Coronado led his army out onto the plains: if the seven cities were not in Cíbola, they must be somewhere else. The Turk traveled with them as a guide, spinning ever more extravagant tales about the riches of Quivira, and leading the army deeper and deeper into the endless sea of grass.

Cabeza de Vaca's party had skirted the southern edge of the Great Plains, where buffalo were occasional winter visitors, but Coronado went into the heart of their range on the Llano Estacado, and his scribe recorded buffalo "in such large numbers that nobody could count them."

> I do not know what to compare them to, except with the fish in the sea . . . many times when we started to pass through the midst of them and wanted to go through to the other side of them, we were not able to, because the country was covered in them . . .
>
> The bulls are large and brave, although they do not attack much; but they have wicked horns, & in a fight use them well, attacking fiercely; they killed several of our horses & wounded many. We found the pike to be the best weapon to use against them, & the musket for use when this misses.
>
> Pedro de Castañeda et al., *The Journey of Coronado*

They felt swallowed by space, disoriented by flatness. Mounted on horseback, a man could see for thirty or forty miles in any direction, eighty miles if he could find a knoll, but if he sat on the ground, the rim of the world closed in to the distance of a musket shot. Occasionally, they would reach an abrupt break in the tablelands and find themselves at the edge of a cliff overlooking a river canyon, with willows and cottonwoods growing alongside it, but for most of the journey they rode through dead-level, unchanging grasslands, rippling and undulating in the wind—a landscape more maritime than terrestrial, where the horizon was bounded only by the curvature of the earth. Like the surface of the ocean, the grass parted briefly to let them through, then sealed up behind them, recording no sign of their passage.

Who could believe that 1000 horses and 500 of our cows and more than 5000 rams and ewes and more than 1500 friendly Indians and servants, in traveling over those plains, would leave no more trace where they had passed them than if nothing had been there—nothing—so that it was necessary to make piles of bones and cow dung now and then, so that the rear guard could follow the army. The grass never failed to become erect after it had been trodden down, and, although it was short, it was as fresh and straight as before.

They encountered a friendly tribe called the Querechos, who "lived like Arabs," in conical tents made of buffalo hide—tepees, as they would later be known. These Indians hung buffalo paunches full of blood around their necks, to quench their thirst between rivers, and they ate their meat raw, or lightly seared over buffalo-dung fires.

Historians are undecided as to their identity—possibly they were forerunners of the plains Apaches—but from the accounts we have, the Querechos were more committed to the wandering, buffalo-hunting life than most of the plains tribes before the horse. By sign language, they told the Spaniards that they raised no crops, unlike the neighboring tribes who farmed along the rivers and came out on the plains once a year to hunt. The Querechos wintered on a river to the west (the Rio Grande), where they traded their buffalo hides for corn and beans, but they spent the rest of the year traveling the plains and transporting their belongings by dog travois.

They load these dogs like beasts of burden, and make saddles for them like our pack-saddles, and they fasten them with leather thongs, and these make their backs sore on the withers like pack animals. When they go hunting, they load these with their necessities, & when they move—for these Indians are not settled in one place, since they travel wherever the cows [buffalo] move, to support themselves—these dogs carry their houses, and they have the sticks of their houses dragging along tied on to the pack-saddles, besides the load which they carry on top, and the load may be, according to the dog, from thirty-five to fifty pounds.

After a month of plains travel, the Turk confessed that he had been lying and the Spaniards strangled him. Coronado sent the bulk of his army back to Mexico, but he was unable to abandon his quest entirely—even though El Turco had been lying, the seven cities might still be out there somewhere. Maybe the Turk's confession, at this point in the journey, was designed to throw them off the scent, just as they were getting close. Maybe the seven cities really *were* in Quivira, as he had said originally.

Coronado went on with thirty men. After forty-two days they reached the place called Quivira and found a semi-agricultural tribe living in grass huts on a riverbank, with supplies of dried corn laid in but a singular absence of gold and emeralds. They were Wichita Indians, and Coronado had reached the Arkansas River in central Kansas. The Wichitas said that what he was looking for was further on, but his supplies were running low and so, finally, was Coronado's faith in the seven cities of gold. He turned around and made the long march back to Mexico and disgrace, traveling an Indian trade route that later became famous as the Santa Fe Trail.

Coronado had no way of knowing it, but another Spanish expedition, led out of Florida by de Soto, had reached the lower drainage of the Arkansas River at the same time, and this coincidence has given rise to a persistent myth about the introduction of the horse in North America. One of Coronado's stallions ran off south and caught the scent of a mare which had strayed north from de Soto's herd: so began the lineage of the North American mustang, and the plains Indian horse culture. It's a nice story but the muster records indicate that neither Coronado nor de Soto had any mares with them at the time. It was the preference of conquistadors to ride stallions.

Historians are now agreed that horses were permanently introduced to North America in 1598, by Juan de Oñate's expedition of settlers into New Mexico. They brought stallions and mares with them, and transplanted the Spanish/Mexican horse culture into colonial towns, villages and ranches along the Rio Grande Valley. During the first half of the seventeenth century—gradually, with many false starts—horses and the knowledge of horsemanship spread out of the colonies into the surrounding tribes. Navajos and Apaches began stealing horses, eating them at first, but later learning how to ride them. The Spanish, against their better judgement, began trading horses to these and other tribes in exchange for hides. And there were almost certainly runaway horses during this era, which escaped from the Spanish herds and went feral.

The first written accounts of mounted Indians in North America are from the 1650s, more than a century after Coronado, when marauding bands of Apaches began riding into the settlements around Santa Fe. These were not plains Apaches. They came from the deserts and mountains to the west, and until recently had lived in semipermanent villages and experimented with raising crops. Now they were in the process of abandoning their fields and becoming full-time raiders, reveling in their new-found power and mobility. Here, for the first time on this continent, an old human drama was replayed: the conflict between sedentary farmers and mounted, nomadic warriors.

Out on the plains to the east of Santa Fe, the horse–buffalo culture seems to have begun later, in the 1680s, and then diffused slowly eastwards and northwards. In 1738, French travelers found horseless tribes on the northern plains, still using dog travois to make seasonal hunts, and the horse did not reach the Canadian border until the 1780s.

The dominant image of the American Indian in the modern imagination—the mounted Sioux warrior, with his flowing warbonnet of eagle feathers—was a sight unseen until the late eighteenth century. In 1750, the Siouan tribes were still living in the Minnesota woodlands, gathering wild rice, hunting and fishing, and traveling on foot or by canoe. They were forcibly ejected on to the plains by their enemies, the Ojibwas, also known as the Chippewas, who had acquired muskets from French and British traders. The Sioux backed out onto the plains reluctantly, but once they learned how to ride, hunt buffalo and make war on horseback they became the grand imperialists of the northern plains, displacing the Kiowa, the Crows and the Pawnees, and claiming a territory that encompassed all of South Dakota, most of Nebraska, and a good chunk of North Dakota, Wyoming, Montana, Minnesota and Iowa. Mounted on their "holy dogs," they ranged even further to hunt, make war and steal more horses, deep into Canada and as far south as Texas—distances unimaginable to a people on foot.

The charming fable of Coronado's stallion and de Soto's mare mating in the 1540s does not survive scrutiny, but there is an appealing, romantic aspect to the horse's later diffusion across the North American plains. In a sense, the horse had traveled full circle around the world and come home, because its ancestors had evolved on these same plains.

The prototype for the horse was a small, three-toed rodent, no bigger than a rabbit, called *Hyracotherium*, which lived in the American West some sixty million years ago. Then came the terrier-sized *Eohippus*, and the Labrador-sized *Mesohippus*, whose fossils are concentrated in South Dakota and the Colorado plains. Then, over tens of millions of years, through *Mesohippus*, *Parahippus*, *Merychippus* and *Pliohippus*, there appeared *Equus*, the horse of the Pleistocene, which was the size of a small modern pony. Some of the earlier versions had made the migration west across the Bering Strait into Siberia, but *Equus* was the only horse which survived these journeys, and it spread its progeny west across Asia and Europe, and into Arabia and North Africa.

In North America, however, *Equus* became extinct, about eleven thousand years before the Spaniards arrived, and nobody is certain why. Perhaps it was drought, cold or disease. Perhaps *Equus* was hunted to extinction by prehistoric Indians. Perhaps the buffalo, which came east across the Bering Strait, monopolized the grazing. These are the theories proposed and none of them convincingly explain the disappearance of the horse from the American fossil record. It remains a puzzle for archaeologists and a subject of heated contention.

But let us celebrate the return of *Equus* to the North American plains, its westward journey around the circumference of the globe. Along the way, it had been domesticated by humans and bred into many different varieties, and by pure coincidence the Spanish horse turned out to be the best suited of all the breeds to the lean, arid environment of the American West.

Unlike the northern European horse, a large and stately beast that required plenty of grain and frequent water to survive, the Spanish horse could survive on the sparsest of forage, endure annual periods of starvation and long stretches without water. In the language of horse-breeders it was a Barb. It had been bred by desert-dwellers—Arab nomads, and then the Moors of North Africa, who introduced it to Spain over seven centuries of invasions.

To the eyes of an Englishman, a Frenchman or a German, it was not a handsome animal, being small, shaggy-maned and long-tailed, not to mention "hammer-headed, ram-nosed, ewe-necked, goat-withered, cat-hammed, sore-backed, hard-mounted, mean-tempered."* But it was incredibly tough and hardy, and once it escaped onto the plains, its population exploded. By 1800 there were probably two million horses in the American West: a million in the possession of the nomadic tribes and another million running wild and free.

I should mention that Boma Johnson harbors deep suspicions about this circular version of the horse's history in North America. Despite the complete lack of fossil evidence, despite the total absence of supporting Indian art and to hoots of derision from his peers, Boma doesn't believe that the Pleistocene horse ever became extinct in North America, and this is mainly because Boma is a Mormon.

Mormonism is a fundamentalist faith and its sacred text, the Book of Mormon, states that America at the time of Christ was populated by two lost tribes of Israel, who possessed horses, sheep, goats, pigs, oxen, elephants, wheeled chariots and metal swords—none of which have turned up in the archaeological record. One

---

* J. Frank Dobie, *The Mustangs.*

of these tribes was the Nephites, described as "white and delightsome." The other was the Lamanites, who were cursed by the Lord with dark, "filthy" skins and were the ancestors of the American Indians. The story gets a lot weirder and more improbable than this (and maintains the same level of racism), but there is no room for all of that here.

One more detail: Jesus came to the Americas, traveling from Israel and crossing the Atlantic in some unspecified conveyance. Some Mormon scholars assert that it was a wooden submarine, but Boma Johnson suspects that Jesus came to the New World in a spaceship. How else to explain the widespread Indian legends about sky people and pale-skinned bearded gods who visited long ago?

It is late in the afternoon when Boma begins to talk about the Book of Mormon. I have drunk three-quarters of a gallon of water and I have yet to urinate. My body's cooling system uses it all up before it reaches my bladder. It is 130 degrees Fahrenheit in the sun and the air is so dry that neither of us is sweating. The moisture evaporates right out of our pores before it gets a chance to form as sweat.

Boma still hasn't taken his first sip of water. He is on a roll—ebullient, impassioned, unflagging—oblivious to everything but the ideas coursing through his brain, leaping from one conclusion to the next with long and agile strides. What about the circular designs pecked into these rocks over here? Is that not the shape of a flying saucer, viewed from underneath?

Mormonism is perhaps the most awkward of all the world's religions for an archaeologist to believe in. Its founding prophet, Joseph Smith, who came to his revelation in upstate New York in 1830, was an enthusiastic amateur archaeologist himself, and his archaeological/historical pronouncements, as recorded in the Book of Mormon, are at the core of the faith. Proving the existence of the horse in the Americas before the Spaniards and concurrent to the time of Christ has become something of a Holy Grail for Mormon archaeologists, because there are so many references to horses in the Book of Mormon. Some have gone so far as to suggest that the horsemen Joseph Smith describes were riding

South American tapirs—three-toed, rubbery-snouted animals no bigger than a large pig.

This is not a theory to which Boma Johnson subscribes. He takes the horse references in the Book of Mormon as evidence that the Pleistocene horse never became extinct in North America.

"But there are no fossils," I protest. "No depictions in Indian art. No evidence whatsoever."

"Maybe we just haven't found it yet," he replies. "We're making new archaeological discoveries all the time. The old orthodoxies are falling one after another. I think it's entirely possible that the Pleistocene horse survived in small pockets and later bred with the Spanish horse. It would certainly explain a lot of references in the Book of Mormon."

Boma the Mormon would love to date the horse intaglio back to the time of Christ, but Boma the archaeologist is sure that this is a depiction of a Spanish horse—from the long, flowing tail and from the Indian oral histories about the intaglio. Was it created after Díaz's visit in 1540? Or during Juan de Oñate's trip through this country in 1605? Or later still? In 1701 an intrepid Jesuit missionary named Padre Kino rode through this country, and the Quechuans challenged his horses to a foot race, which suggests that they knew either little about the horse or had forgotten what they had learned from earlier horse encounters.

Whoever made this intaglio, and whenever he made it, we can say with certainty that he was an artist. By the crudest technique imaginable, scraping on the surface of the earth, he was able to give a stance and character to the horse, a grace of presence. Its lines are smooth and flowing. The muscles in its haunches and shoulders are represented by low, bunched mounds of pebbles. The arching neck and the open mouth suggest anger—bared teeth—and the tail flares out behind.

The artistic skill evident in the horse intaglio has led some observers to conclude that it was the work of later white men. Boma doesn't agree, and on this point at least I think he is right. "Look at the legs. It's hard to imagine a white artist going to the trouble of scraping out the head, the body and the tail, doing it all so beautifully, and then not following through with the legs. The legs are just lightly tamped in, which is the distinguishing characteristic of Indian art in this area."

We walk back to Boma's truck and he gives me a ride to his office in Yuma, where he shows me an aerial photograph of the horse. We shake hands and I thank him for his help and an interesting afternoon. I stop off at a convenience store on the edge of town, buy a six-pack of beer and a fresh gallon of water, and drive back out toward the horse.

Walking up the trail it's still hot, but the ferocity has left the sun, and there are living things on the desert pavement now: a roadrunner that sprints off at high speed when it sees me, a few lizards and ants, and the occasional raven or turkey vulture overhead. I notice plant life that I had missed before: isolated, desiccated tufts of sage, a few spiny wands of ocotillo on the ridges.

I get to the horse just before the sun hits the horizon. I sit down at its feet, facing the sunset, crack open a beer, and immediately become transfixed. There is a low, uneven bank of pebbles around the top of the horse's neck and in the slanting light it throws a shadow that falls exactly like a mane—surely this was the artist's intention. The mane grows longer and longer, and the rest of the horse fills with shadow. Then, for a long minute, everything turns purple: the sand dunes to the west, the sheen on top of the desert pavement, the skin on the back of my hands and the outline of raised pebbles around the horse. Bats appear, diving and chittering overhead, and a peculiar-looking fluffy white ant (Thistledown Velvet Ant, as I later determine) crawls out of a small hole it has excavated in the horse's belly.

I think of Melchior Díaz and his impaling, of lost Israelites riding tapirs, of the pueblo tribes in New Mexico who anointed themselves with the sweat of Coronado's holy dogs. I think of the famous Quechuan runners, men who could follow a deer until it collapsed from exhaustion, challenging one of the Padre Kino's horses to a race, and the look on their faces as horse and rider galloped effortlessly past them and streaked away into the distance.

As the stars come out, my thoughts wander eastwards and I

imagine the wild exuberance of an Indian galloping a horse across the plains for the first time, like a teenage boy with the keys to his father's sports car, and realizing this was the only way to travel. There was no going back to the riverside fields, no more grubbing after roots and spiders, no more traveling on foot. The Comanches, they say, would mount their horses to travel 150 yards, just as a modern American will get in his car to drive the same distance across a shopping mall parking lot.

The horse never made much of a difference to the Yuman tribes, because there was nothing in this desert for horses to graze on, but out on the sea of grass it brought on a revolution of space and distance and velocity. Suddenly it was possible to travel at the same speed as the buffalo, to pick out a choice animal and gallop alongside it neck for neck, holding on with the knees, and aiming the arrow just behind the ribs. It was possible for the tribe to follow the endless migratory circles and loops that the buffalo made, instead of hoping and praying that a herd would come by, with the wind in the right direction for a fire surround or a stealthy belly-crawl, or a hidden cliff nearby to drive the buffalo over. Seated on the back of a horse, as Castañeda noted, the human eye commanded a wider stretch of the land, and that alone was enough to give a new feeling of power and confidence.

Some historians (Hubert Howe Bancroft, T. R. Fehrenbach) have argued that the arrival of the horse doomed the plains tribes by luring them off the sedentary farming track toward civilization and locking them into the primitive, nomadic hunting life. As far as I can see, they were doomed anyway. The Aztecs and the Incas had cities, farms, tax collectors, totalitarian governments, huge standing armies, and it didn't do them any good. Indeed, it's hard to think of any primitive peoples, whether sedentary farmers, nomadic hunters or city-dwellers, in the Americas or anywhere else in the world, who were able to withstand the full onslaught of European imperialism and technology.

Certainly, the horse was a barbed, Trojan gift, because disease, whiskey and millions of well-armed, ferociously determined, genocidally inclined invaders came along in its wake. But at least the horse tribes, for 150 years or so, were able to experience the life of a mounted nomad, and it is clear from the way they talked about it, and mourned its departure, that it was a life they loved with a fierce passion. "The life of my people is a life of freedom," said Sitting Bull, echoing the speeches of nomad leaders the world over. "I have seen nothing that a white man has, houses or railways or clothing or food, that is as good as the right to move in the open country, and live in our fashion."

The word "nomad" is derived from the Greek *nomos*, meaning pasture, and, strictly speaking, it refers only to pastoral herding peoples. The more pedantic scholars, such as the Russian authority A. M. Khazanov, maintain that true nomadism has never existed in North America, with the arguable exception of the Navajo Indians, who commandeered domesticated European sheep, as well as horses, from the New Mexican settlements. Khazanov discounts the wandering buffalo tribes because they hunted their meat, instead of domesticating it and raising it on the hoof. Similarly, he discounts the mounted Apache raiders, who lived perpetually on the move, and often drove stolen herds of cattle and horses across the Southwest and northern Mexico, because they looked at livestock as the spoils of war, to be eaten or sold, and had no interest in nurturing, breeding and increasing the size of the herds.

Outside scholarly circles, however, the word nomad has a broader, more metaphorical meaning—"Any of a people who have no permanent home, but moving about constantly, as if in search of pasture," to quote *Webster's New World Dictionary*. To put it another way, forms of nomadism emerged in North America that don't correspond to the model set up by European historians.

In Europe and Asia, and later in Africa, it seems probable that pastoral herding developed as an offshoot of sedentary agriculture, rather than as a continuation of the mobile hunting and gathering life. Khazanov dates the first mounted nomads at around 2000 BC, emerging in the Near East and the Eurasian steppes, two or three thousand years after the first permanent farming villages were established in the Fertile Crescent. Presumably it was easier to domesticate livestock and experiment with animal husbandry in a sedentary environment, with fences, corrals and surplus grains. Presumably the area around the village became overgrazed and the herders began roaming further afield to find fresh grass, until they severed the ties entirely and founded a rival culture. All is guesswork, there are no facts. Maybe, in light of the strikingly egalitarian cultures that nomads developed, they wanted to get away from the social hierarchies and governmental systems that agricultural societies were developing, in order to administer the food surpluses, build irrigation projects and enforce the division of labor. Or maybe some deeper yearning was pulling at those early horsemen, for the act of travel itself.

On the North American plains there were echoes of the same historical process, but it did not happen by spontaneous, indigenous development. The American form of nomadism, which reached its apogee in the horse–buffalo culture on the plains, was the inadvertent creation of European invaders. It arose out of contact with a sedentary agricultural civilization an ocean away.

With the exception of the Navajo, the North American horse tribes remained hunters—food extractors, not food producers—but once mounted they developed the same attitudes and prejudices as nomads the world over: contempt for sedentary farmers, the equation of freedom with space and mobility, and the horror and hatred of everything linear, rectangular and confining.

Sitting by the horse intaglio, watching it fill with moonlight, I recall the words of Satanta the Kiowa chief, as he realized his people's way of life was coming to an end: "I have heard that you intend to settle us on a reservation near the mountains. I don't want to settle. I love to roam over the prairies. There I feel free and happy, but when we settle we grow pale and die."

When the beer is gone, I roll out my sleeping bag on the desert pavement. It makes a hard bed, but it's worth it for the view of the stars, the moonlit sand dunes to the west and the dreams of running horses. In my dreams, at least, I am a superb horseman, galloping effortlessly across the plains and mesas, living out an urbane, civilized fantasy that Franz Kafka once described:

If one were only an Indian, instantly alert, and on a racing horse, leaning against the wind, kept on quivering jerkily over the quivering ground, until one shed one's spurs, for there needed no spurs, threw away the reins, for there needed no reins, and hardly saw that the land before one was smoothly shorn heath when horse's neck and head would be already gone.

CHAPTER 5

The space of nomad thought is qualitatively different from
State space. Air against earth. State space is "striated," or
gridded. Movement within it is confined . . . to preset paths
between fixed and identifiable points. Nomad space is
"smooth" or open-ended. One can rise up at any point and
move to any other.
                    Translator's introduction to Deleuze and Guattari,
                                                A Thousand Plateaus

T he next morning I get up before dawn and drive east, across
    the Colorado River and into the sprawl and billboard land-
scape of Yuma ("Foxy Vegetables Welcomes You!," "Visit The
Yuma Territorial Prison"). The motel parking lots are empty. The
trailer parks and RV camps are deserted, all three hundred of
them. In summertime the population of Yuma shrinks by 50
percent, from 120,000 to about 60,000.

I was here in January and the city, if that is the right word for
it, was clogged and seething with nomadic retirees in motor
homes—"snowbirds," as the locals call them, a term that describes
their southerly migration in winter and hints at their white plumage.
There were vibrant encampments on these abandoned lots, a chirpy,
wholesome, neighborly, Eisenhower-generation feeling in the air—
golf clothes and cocktail parties, bridge tournaments and shuffleboard contests, coffee klatches and quilting bees—and it is strange
and eerie to see all of it gone, all of it evaporated by the heat.

Toward the end of March, as the temperature climbs into the nineties, the spirit of migration moves through the flock. They pack up their satellite dishes and cocktail shakers, roll up their Astroturf lawns, and point the RVs north, chasing the perfect 80-degree day up and down the continent. The Mexican fruit and vegetable pickers, who work the irrigated farms around Yuma, have gone north too, chasing the harvest, and so perhaps have the troubadours and low-rent prostitutes who used to appear at their camps on payday.

At the edge of the farms there is a line of transition. The bright, garish, incongruous swath of green ends at the last irrigation canal, and the native buffs, duns, tans, grays, khakis and pinks take over. Linear, rectangular space gives way to smooth, untrammeled space—nomad space—wide flat desert valleys and isolated, sawtoothed mountain ranges, with stands of tall, armed saguaro cactus growing on their flanks and foothills. The valleys measure twenty or thirty miles across, and out in the middle of them there are whirling columns of dust, raised up by the wind, spinning counterclockwise like miniature tornadoes. They twirl and undulate and skid across the valley floors, gathering speed, until they blow apart and disappear, and another dust devil forms somewhere else.

Nomad space: too far from the river to irrigate, too dry for crops or cities to take root. Like the deserts of the Bedouin, the Mongol steppes, the Tibetan plateaus or the buffalo plains, this is a harsh, marginal, wide-open landscape, with long horizons and a paucity of water. This was the homeland of the Sand Papago, or Hiaced O'Oodham as they called themselves, the last free-roaming hunter-gatherers in the lower forty-eight states to be brought to heel, at the close of the nineteenth century. Fifty years earlier this had been the westernmost range for the Western Apache raiding parties, attracted by the emigrant caravans traveling to the California goldfields. This, on the evidence of dust devils, is a place where the earth itself feels compelled to rise up and move.

Even today, with the richest, most powerful, and most technologically advanced nation-state in history behind it, sedentary civilization has gained little more than a toehold on this stretch of desert. Every thirty miles or so, the interstate will reach a flyblown gas station, with a noisy air conditioner and a few ramshackle trailers parked around it—a settlement dependent for its existence on passing travelers. I get stranded in one of them (Sentinel, Arizona) for two and a half hours, because the proprietor is sleeping off a hangover and my tank is close to empty. I consider waking him up and reconsider when I see the National Rifle Association stickers on the door, the scrawled promises in red ink to shoot all intruders and the scrawled boasts about intruders already shot.

"Why would anyone want to live out here?" wonders a Californian truck driver, stranded in the same predicament. Apart from a few surly outcasts, huddled around their air conditioners and beer coolers, modern Americans, like Sand Papagos or Apaches, treat this desert as a place to be traveled across, a place where it feels wrong to be stationary. At ten-fifteen, when the grizzled, wincing proprietor finally appears, driving the fifty yards between his trailer and the gas station, the temperature is already 100 degrees in the shade and rising steadily.

Further east, as the interstate approaches Tucson, the mountain ranges grow taller and more impressive, rising up out of the desert to eight or nine thousand feet now, with a dark green mantle of pine forest around their summits. When storm systems track across southern Arizona, these "sky island" mountain ranges capture most of the precipitation, leaving the deserts around in a rain shadow. The mountains release water to the deserts as snowmelt and run-off, encased within the banks of unreliable rivers and streams.

The same process has shaped the geography of the American West as a whole: the Great Plains might also be described as the rain shadow of the Rocky Mountains. The Mojave and the Great Basin Desert in Nevada and Utah lie in the rain shadow of the Sierra Nevada. The arid plains of eastern Washington and Oregon are created by the rain-hogging Cascades.

When it does rain on the deserts or the plains, it tends to be dramatic and unpredictable: a thunderstorm boiling up and dumping its contents on a small, localized area of land, rather than blanketing the whole region in rain. Grazing springs up in one place and shrivels away in another. Dry gulches roar into flash flood, then return to dust and sand. Capricious rainfall patterns, temporary shifting zones of vegetation, seasonal temperature extremes, far-flung and unreliable water sources, what Pierre Hubac calls "diva-gation of local climates"*—these too are characteristics shared by nomad lands all over the world. Historically, these were the lands ceded to the nomads by the emerging sedentary states, and nomadism was the logical way to stay alive on them.

I think this type of landscape still activates the human desire for travel and mobility on some deep instinctual level, but I don't know how to prove it, and there are certainly exceptions. I think that's what happened to me in the American West, but I'm aware of other factors and more plausible explanations.

A fascination with deserts and wandering tribes, for example, has been a recurrent phenomenon among the misfits of European civilization, and among a certain class of well-educated Englishmen in particular. "A part of their brain reflects the desert perfectly," writes Michael Ondaatje in *The English Patient*. "The English have a great hunger for desolate places," says Alec Guinness, playing a Bedouin chief in *Lawrence of Arabia*. I'm not about to compare my ramblings around the American West with the epic feats of T. E. Lawrence, or Doughty, Philby or Wilfred Thesiger, but I think I understand the compulsion that drove the English Arabists out into the deserts and the company of nomads. I think I know why they felt so restless and claustrophobic in England.

Travel was in my family too. I come from imperialist stock: the Britons who wanted to get the hell out of Britain. My father, my paternal grandfather and his father before him were Scottish by blood but born in India, Anglicized by the Raj, and they probably encountered some of my mother's English relatives at colonial func-tions and banquets. I was born in Malaysia, where my father made a good show of settling down after traveling across most of the world in his twenties. Then we moved to Kuwait, made extended visits around the Middle East before "coming back" to England, a

---

*Pierre Hubac, *Les Nomades*, quoted in Deleuze and Guattari, *A Thousand Plateaus*.

country that was entirely foreign to me and reluctant to give me citizenship. My nationality was filed under "Miscellaneous" at the British Passport Office.

It is a dreary, commonplace adage among the sedentary and stay-at-homes that people travel to escape from themselves. There is some truth in the old cliché, as there is in most, but if you spent your childhood on the move—and with the big proviso that you and your family had a happy time doing it—then moving on feels the right and natural state of affairs, and assumes an air of inevitability. It's when you get stranded in one place for too long, at least in my case, that you start to feel divorced from yourself. Setting out on a journey, almost invariably, I have a sense of becoming whole again, of doubts and confusions lifting, and my self slotting back into place.

I remember my childhood as a happy time, but my father started suffering from periodic depressions after we "came back" to England, and as I recall they usually coincided with the onset of winter. I knew about the English winter—the damp cold in your bones, the afternoon dark, the driving rain in your face, as if the elements had singled you out for persecution—but through the shielding efforts of my parents I knew very little about the downturns and redundancies at the office and the steady decline of the British shipbroking business, to which my father had attached his fortunes.

I did notice that my father was restored to his old self, at least temporarily, by going on a trip to some sunny foreign country or other. He returned from abroad in fine spirits, with presents and stories to tell, and old reminiscences sparked—his time as a lumberjack in British Columbia in the 1940s, his heiress-hunting escapades in San Francisco in the 1950s, the old gambling, golfing, cocktail-swilling days in Kuala Lumpur and Singapore, the anecdotes and adventures from Spain, Italy, Mexico, Montreal, Vancouver, Cape Town, Burma, India, Ceylon, Thailand, the Philippines. Listening and watching, as the rain lashed the windowpanes, and my father told his stories and twirled his Scotch-and-water, it was clear to me that everything vivid and exciting in life happened in other countries. At no stage in my upbringing did it occur to me that I would live in England once I was old enough to leave.

My urge to travel, and travel toward the sun, was foursquare in the family tradition, but the style of my travels, I suspect, included an element of rebellion against my background. I wasn't hunting tigers in India with a troop of native bearers and telling the story over a gin-and-quinine cocktail at the governor's mansion, like my grandfather. I wasn't chasing debutantes and craving a life in high society, like my father. I was slumming it around the redneck hinterlands in grubby jeans, hitchhiking and riding freight trains, drinking in roadhouses and dive bars, sleeping in cars and flopping in the dirt. Growing up in houses filled with nice *objets* (Persian rugs, Chinese altar tables, antique silverware), and bombarded by consumerist advertizing in Thatcher's London, I took pride in being able to carry my worldly possessions and replace them for less than two hundred dollars if necessary.

To wake up by the side of the road somewhere, light a cigarette, and start pondering the decision of whether to set off north, south, east or west . . . To be sitting in a New York bar and fall prey to a sudden urge to go to Texas, Montana or Mexico, and be able to leave in the morning without a care—this was my idea of freedom, this was my definition of success in life.

Turning off the interstate, approaching my sun-baked rental house in Tucson, I feel an ache of nostalgia for those loose, freewheeling days, a sense that something has gone wrong with my life, a suspicion that I have been duped. Call me spoiled, lazy, naive, or immature, but I resent the fact that I have to work a lot harder than I used to, and yet I have less spending money and less time in which to spend it.

The house is pleasant enough and cheap to rent, and there are undeniable practical advantages in having a home base, but when you're used to living on the road the whole set-up looks like an outrageous swindle, a blatant and egregious con-job. Tramps and hoboes will tell you the same. Rent, phone, electricity, gas, water, state and federal income tax, monthly payments on the truck, vehicle insurance, credit card payments—how do people put up with it? The beds, tables, chairs, desks, window coverings, lamps and shelving units that houses cry out for; the pots, pans, knives, spatulas, plates, mugs, bowls, coffee-makers, towels, cleaning prod- ucts—I lived happily without owning these things and now they have become necessities.

I turn the key and get the Tucson oven-door treatment: a blast of superheated air in the face. I look around at the betrayal of my nomadic principles, the end of the nomadic experiment that was my life. Well, maybe it doesn't look like much to you: a few articles of thrift-shop furniture, a lumpy, worthless futon bed, from Peace-a-Shit Hippie Futons, the absence of TV and VCR and the bare walls. But observe the sleek, black, dust-covered nine- hundred-dollar stereo system and the stack of CDs next to it. For some reason, I can drive happily for days without listening to music, but back here at home base I need it constantly. Something about the rhythm and the passage of songs helps to break the feeling of dead, calm, empty stasis.

Observe also the computer, printer and fax/answering machine, which I once made a living without, and which have now plunged me into debt. ("Debt: an ingenious substitute for the chain and whip of the slave driver," as Ambrose Bierce defined it.) Observe the burgeoning book collection and the new shelving unit to accommodate the overflow. I don't want to give up the books, because they give me pleasure and the satisfaction of ownership. I don't want to give up the house (although I fanta- size constantly about it), because I've grown dependent on its practical conveniences—a telephone number, an address for mail, a bank account, a reliable desk to work at, a filing cabinet for notebooks and newspaper clippings. And I tell myself that a fixed home base will make it easier to form lasting relationships. No progress so far. My last serious attempt is marked by a square of cardboard nailed over a missing glass panel in the front door. She is back in France now and I keep the cardboard there as a memento.

I make myself a cup of coffee, in my new Italian espresso pot, and drink it on the front porch. My gaze travels out across the city, warped and shimmering in the heat, and up into the mountains that loom above Tucson. Much as I enjoy the intensity of desert heat, and respect it as a worthy adversary, the mountains look like an inviting prospect, compared with the sweltering desk inside. Up there the air is cool and pine-scented, the shade is deep and green, and there will be water in some of the swimming holes. An inviting prospect perhaps, but I have too much work to do, too many debts to pay, deadlines pressing in on all sides. And besides, it's a Saturday. The campgrounds and swimming holes will be packed with Tucsonans escaping the heat, cranking up their boom boxes, guzzling beer, whooping and bellowing exuberantly. These are fine activities when you're with a group of friends, but they are not much fun to be around when you're alone and looking for a little peace and quiet.

Then I start thinking about the ranges further east, which have no roads and fewer visitors. The Rincons or the Santa Ritas, or, better yet, the Dragoons. I picture myself leaning against a pine tree, collecting my thoughts in silence and solitude, drafting magazine stories with a pen and paper. Only a fool would try to work down here in the desert, in the dog days of summer, with no air-conditioning, a worthless old evaporative cooler and a nineteen-dollar fan. There was a lesson to be learned from the Chiricahua Apaches here, who had an eminently sensible approach to the task of living in southeastern Arizona. They spent their summers camped up high in the mountains and descended periodically into the desert settlements to trade or plunder.

The camping supplies are still in the truck. I get back on the interstate, leaving the gridwork of Tucson behind, driving east into the old stomping grounds of Cochise and Geronimo. I pass a sign for the Cochise Terrace RV Resort, stop for a "peanut buster parfait" at a nearby Dairy Queen and buy a postcard of Geronimo at the gift shop next door. It's a famous photograph, taken in 1884 during one of Geronimo's temporary stays on the reservation, two years before his final surrender. He is down on one knee, clutching his rifle, his mouth like a downward-curving knife-slash across his face, staring at the camera with a fierce, angry, embittered and slightly crazed look in his eyes. He looks like he's thinking about killing someone, or possibly every white person in Arizona, beginning with Frank Randall of the *New York Herald* on the other side of the camera.

Sitting in armchairs and libraries, at a comfortable remove, it is easy to feel admiration and respect for the way the Apaches lived, and sadness or outrage at the way they were tricked, swindled and hunted down into submission. In the final denouement Geronimo and his band of thirty-three Chiricahuas held off five thousand US Army troops and three thousand Mexican soldiers for five months— running, dodging, hiding and skirmishing through these deserts and mountains, and down into Mexico. It was traitors from his own people, working as scouts for the US Army, who finally tracked down Geronimo and persuaded him it was hopeless. "Once I moved about like the wind," Geronimo said to General Crook at the final capitulation. "Now I surrender to you and that is all."

Given my predilections and prejudices, I find it impossible to read the history of the Chiricahua Apaches without rooting for them and sympathizing with their tragedy, but if I was traveling through southeast Arizona when they were at large, I"m sure I would have a very different perspective. I would be conjuring up hallucinations behind every rock and bush, gripped by the feeling of being watched and hunted, nerves peeled raw, guns loaded and cocked.

You seldom saw Apache warriors until it was too late. They were masters of stealth and concealment, ambush and illusion. Their enemies were consistently amazed by their ability to melt away into the landscape, to whirl up out of nowhere like a desert dust devil and then disappear again. Some Apache warriors, like the great war chief One-Who-Yawns, who was named Geronimo by the Mexicans, believed they had the magical power to become invisible, but they used tried and tested practical techniques, too.

They studied the ways of light and shadow and mirage on the desert, the distortions of visibility created by different light at different times of day, and planned their ambushes and escapes accordingly. Alongside this interstate, which was once the main trail and stagecoach line through Chiricahua country, they were known to dig shallow pits and lie down in them, pulling earth and debris over themselves, and then rise up, seemingly out of nowhere, with a volley of arrows or bullets and a blood-curdling war cry.

From an early age, Apaches were trained in the skill of immobility. Knowing that the human eye is drawn, above all, by movement, they learned to hold their bodies in the same position, sometimes contorting themselves into the shapes of rocks, and stay that way, without moving a muscle, for hours at a time. Another part of their stealth training was to rub themselves with sage or other plants, to disguise their scent, and stalk up to an animal, moving as slowly and silently as possible, like a gently swaying branch or a creeping afternoon shadow, and touch the animal before it sensed their presence. Preferably, they would touch the animal as lightly as an insect or a leaf and then melt away undetected. The wolf had the keenest senses and was the most difficult to stalk. The grizzly bear was the most dangerous and thrilling. After their final defeat, bored and cooped up on the reservations, a brief craze developed among young Apache men for "bear slapping." The idea was to stalk a grizzly bear, slap it across the ass as hard as you could, and then run up a stout tree before it killed you.

Endurance was another major part of a warrior's upbringing. In winter, boys were required to take a pre-dawn dip in icy mountain rivers and lakes. As a rite of passage, adolescent boys made a two-day run across the desert with no food, sleep or water, and at the end of it they were supposed to refuse water when it was offered to them. Later, when they went out with raiding or war parties, they might need to run for a hundred miles, at a steady dog-trot, on a handful of food and a few swallows of water. Apaches embraced the horse when it came, but when they needed to do some serious traveling they left the horses behind, or rode them to death, ate them and continued on foot. Simply put, a horse needed more water, food and rest to cover a hundred miles of this country than an Apache on foot.

The ability to endure physical pain was an integral part of their lives, a key to their survival, and this led to what a modern mind might term a sado-masochistic obsession or at least a deep abiding interest in pain. Young boys were required to set twig fires on their skin and watch them burn down to ash without flinching. From early childhood, boys and girls were brought animals and birds to torture, and as they grew older they were allowed to practice on human captives. Torture was probably less prevalent among the Apaches than the Comanches, the Kiowas, or the Huron and Iroquois tribes to the east, to say nothing of the Spanish Inquisition, but the Apaches had a reputation among their enemies as particularly inventive torturers.

Travelers passing this way in the mid- and late nineteenth century sometimes came across gruesome no trespassing signs: men staked out naked on anthills with their stomachs cut open, being eaten alive from the inside out; or facing the desert sun with peeled eyelids; or lashed to cactus bushes with wet rawhide, which contracts as it dries for a slow impaling; or hanging upside down from a tree limb, having been roasted over a slow fire; or with their genitals cut off and stuffed into their mouths and the skin flayed off their bodies in long strips. It was generally agreed that the worst fate was to be turned over to the women, who had more patience than the men, and had often lost their husbands, brothers and children to these same enemies and invariably concentrated their efforts on the tenderest parts of the male anatomy.

Modern revisionist historians, with some exceptions, tend to gloss over the prevalence of torture, not just in Apache society but in most Amerindian cultures, or argue that it was a response to Spanish and Anglo-American cruelty. There was definitely an escalation of violence when the Europeans arrived—a rippling, continent-wide upheaval of disease and territorial displacement, traveling in advance of the military conquest—but tribal warfare was already endemic, and so was rough treatment, if not outright torture, of captives. By the mid-seventeenth century, tribes all over North America, including some who had never seen a white man before, were torturing their tribal enemies with fire and cutting, and mutilating their bodies. There is some evidence that the practice of taking scalps and parading them on poles, which, contrary to popular belief, the Apaches performed only occasionally, came across the Bering Strait from Asia ten or twenty thousand years ago.

I agree with David Roberts, who wrote a history of the Apache Wars called *Once They Moved Like the Wind*. The grim truth is that North American Indians would have been an anomaly in the human family if they had *not* practiced torture. Amnesty International's researchers have come to the depressing conclusion that "Every nation has practiced torture at one time or another in its history," and a glance at the organization's current reports show that torture is alive and well in the modern world, and more fiendishly inventive than ever.

Still, if I was trespassing in this valley in the nineteenth century, cultural relativism would not be on my mind. I would have felt, presumably, the same way that almost all whites felt about Apaches at the time. Gruesome stories, images and stereotypes would have paraded through my mind, and fear, as it usually does, would turn to hatred. Call in the army! Exterminate the brutes!

At Texas Canyon, a surreal arrangement of giant boulders and weird rock formations, I turn south and take a dirt road along the base of the Dragoon Mountains—a favorite range of the Chiricahuas. Cochise was born here around 1815 and he died here, free and undefeated, in 1872. His body was lowered into a crevice somewhere in the tangle of rocks now known as Cochise Stronghold.

Looking up at the Stronghold, a memory surfaces, a story told by a traveling Irishman that I dismissed when I heard it. I met him a few months ago in a diner in downtown Tucson—a disheveled, long-haired Dubliner in his late forties with a hemp-bound crystal dangling from his neck. He had just come from the Dragoons, he said, where he had spent two weeks with a group of Apaches who were living up there in a remote cave, illegally and undetected. They had left the reservation to get away from their drinking problems, he said, and were trying to get back to their roots and live in the old, traditional way, minus the raiding and warfare. The cave was deep in the north-central interior of the range, well away from the Forest Service trails. They had horses there, he said, and poached venison drying on racks. They made buckskin pouches, moccasins and turquoise amulets, and periodically they would come down into Tucson or Bisbee, sell their handicrafts, and stock up with corn, beans, rice, tortillas and tobacco. He produced a clumsily sewn buckskin pouch, with lightning designs burned into it, and tried to sell it to me for thirty bucks.

I didn't believe a word of it. It was a dreamy imagining, or an inventive sales pitch, or a tall tale he had heard somewhere and insinuated himself into. Ever since Geronimo surrendered for the last time, stories of "lost Apaches" and "wild Apaches" have circulated around the Southwest and they persist to this day. Somewhere in the rugged heights of the Sierra Madre in Mexico, I have heard, there is a beautiful, hidden mountain valley where a band of Apaches—Chiricahuas or Lipans—have been living undisturbed since the 1880s. They have given up the gun and the steel knife and gone back to the bow and arrow and stone blades. I've spent some time in the Sierra Madre, with Tarahumara Indians (some of whom do live in caves; were they the basis for the Irishman's embellishment?) and Mexican farmers and ranchers four generations deep, and they all scoffed at the gringo story of the lost Apaches and their hidden Shangri-la.

The Irishman's story, with its details of alcoholism and involvement in the Indian handicraft economy, was a little more convincing, but I took it as a variation on the same romantic, primitivist fantasy. Still, here I am, looking up at the Dragoons with no particular destination in mind. Why not follow the Irishman's directions, as well as I can remember them, and see what happens?

I park the truck, strap on the backpack and start walking up a dry streambed into a likely looking canyon. I see what looks to be a game trail, leading up and out of the canyon, near its head, which should take me up to the interior peaks. There are no human tracks in the streambed, which always changes the feel of things. I startle a few lizards, rouse a few birds, but the mammals are all hidden away, in shady nooks, crannies, thickets and burrows, doing the sensible thing and taking a siesta. Only the mad-dog

Englishman, shaded by his sweat-stained cowboy hat, is out plodding in the afternoon sun.

The dry streambed dead-ends into the cliff of a dry waterfall. The game trail turns out to be a band of exposed, light-colored rock. This is why I usually stick to Forest Service trails in the mountains: I'm a lousy bushwhacker. I start backtracking down the canyon until I find a place where it's possible to scramble up the side.

I make it up onto a ridge, but it disppears into the base of a steep, rocky slope, pitched at about 40 degrees, with plenty of loose scree, shindagger cactus, impenetrable manzanita thickets and tangled rocky outcroppings that look like textbook illustrations of rattlesnake habitat. Looking back down at the thin, precipitous rock ledge that I climbed up is an even more daunting prospect. Bad planning is the mother of adventure, I tell myself, and start hauling myself up the slope, grabbing at bushes to stop myself sliding back, incurring various stabbings and lacerations from the cactus spines (mistaking them in wild panic for rattlesnake bites), gushing sweat and panting obscenely, coming to a firm decision to give up smoking, once and for all, very soon indeed. I see a few caves here and there, but I don't have the energy to investigate them, and there's no way you could get a horse through this country.

By late afternoon, having exhausted my second, third and fourth winds, I reach the base of a broad, domed, rocky peak, protruding from the pines. I take off the backpack (which has correspondingly doubled, tripled and quadrupled its weight) and make the final, wheezing scramble up to the peak, rewarding myself with a well-earned cigarette at the top, and a modest nip of whiskey from my hip flask.

It's not as cool as I had imagined, still 85 degrees or so, but the views are spectacular. Hawks, ravens and vultures are wheeling over the foothills, there are dust devils out on the dry lake beds to the east, and beyond them range after range of blue mountains, extending away into New Mexico. To give you an idea of scale: I can see five separate and distinct storm systems, each of them flashing lightning and trailing a veil of rain. And yet here, and for twenty miles around, it is bright and sunny, and within my field of vision there are a dozen sunlit patches of a similar size, grouped around the storms, so the land has a mottled look, a camouflage pattern of light and cloud shadow.

Cochise and Geronimo used to position their sharpest-eyed scouts on these peaks. I can't help wondering what went through their minds as they sat and smoked and looked out over this view. The scale and appearance of the land, presumably, would have looked entirely normal and unremarkable, and I don't think it will ever look that way to me. As desert-dwellers, the sight of thunderstorms must have pleased them, but they weren't up here for reasons of aesthetic contemplation.

Way off in the distance, at the far limit of his sight, a Chiricahua scout sees three ravens rise up off the desert. Then the faint smudge of dust, signaling the approach of enemy invaders, coming to steal and desecrate his people's land, or US troops looking for Apaches. The scout notifies the camp and the band packs up swiftly and moves on. They were a wandering, predatory people, but for the last twenty-five years, Chiricahua nomadism was shaped primarily by the need to run and hide from soldiers.

By 1870, most, if not all, Chiricahuas would have lost close family members to the Mexicans, or the "White Eyes" as they called Anglo-Americans (in Apaches the sclera of the eye is naturally bloodshot). They too had seen their loved ones raped, scalped, mutilated and tortured—violence and cruelty had escalated on all sides. Geronimo's children, as babies, were thrown in the air by Mexican soldiers and speared on their rifle bayonets. Later in life he used to mete out the same treatment to white and Mexican babies, tossing them in the air, until they gurgled with delight, and then catching them on the blade of his knife. In his old age they came back to haunt his dreams, and he would wake up groaning with sadness and regret for the helpless, smiling babies he had killed.

There was one form of torture, practiced exclusively by the Mexicans and the White Eyes, that held a particular horror for the Apaches: imprisonment. Pain was one thing. It was an integral part of life, and the physical pain of being flayed or burned alive, for example, offered a man the chance to die with courage and honor, if he could stifle his screams. But for the nomadic Apaches, to lock up a human being in a cage, sometimes for years, was a cold and inhuman form of sadism.

There were many good reasons for the Apaches to hate their invaders, and vice versa, and underlying it all was a very basic, fundamental conflict over land. The whites justified their conquest by saying the land in Apache territory was going to waste. There were no farms, no cattle grazing on the grasslands, no villages, towns or cities. There was gold and silver in the mountains that these wandering savages were too lazy or ignorant to mine. Apacheria looked like no-man's-land because, like all nomadic peoples, the Apaches had left no permanent signs of occupation—just the occasional abandoned rancheria, with its crude, temporary huts and fire-pits.

From the Apache perspective the White Eyes were bent not only on conquering their land, but on destroying it and desecrating its spirit. Why else would people gouge through the skin and into the flesh of Mother Earth, to dig up and sell the metals in her veins? Why would they push out the deer and antelope, in order to graze their dull-witted, slow-moving cattle, which fouled the streams and trampled the riverbanks, and presented absolutely no challenge in the hunt? The White Eyes announced their presence on the land with destruction and regimentation, imposing straight lines and rectangles on its natural, flowing contours—corrals, fences, fields, railroads, telegraph wires, four-cornered houses and boxy little churches, in which people shut themselves away from everything sacred in the world.

The ancestral conflict of nomad and settler is inbuilt and unavoidable, and founded in these two colliding philosophies of land use. The first settlements began on riverbanks, and as they divided their labor, and formed into hierarchies and states, they yearned to expand their power and take control of the nomad spaces gnawing at their fringes. The free flow of goods and people is a natural affront to a strong state. It calls for the establishment of fixed borders, the building of roads, the imposition of taxes, tariffs and systems of land ownership, the establishment of police agencies and bureaucracies to enforce the new order. The state can't help itself, any more than a cancer cell expanding its territory in a human body. This is what states do.

For a tribal nomad, everything depends on free, uninhibited movement. This is how nomads harvest the resources of their land and ensure their survival. This is how they raid and make war. State armies prefer to advance in a linear column, with supply lines back to the settlements, and clash with the enemy on a predetermined battlefield, or besiege his city. Nomad warriors fight according to a different model: striking and withdrawing, disappearing and reappearing from unexpected directions, dispersing and re-forming like a desert dust devil, "occupying an open space with a vortical movement that can rise up at any point," as Deleuze and Guattari put it in *Nomadology: The War Machine*.

Much as they hated sedentary settlements and all they stood for, the Apaches also became dependent on the products of those settlements. They would raid one settlement and trade their plunder at another, for guns, ammunition, steel knives, liquor, corn, beans, squash, melons, cloth, needles, awls, blankets, trinkets, beads. Genghis Khan used a similar strategy, raiding and trading to get the products and weapons that he needed from the settlements. The towns that failed to pay him tribute were usually obliterated. His horsemen would burn down the buildings, trample the fields and sow grass seeds from the steppe in the ruins to restore the grazing and bring back the smooth space.

"Raids are our agriculture" was an adage of the Bedouin tribes in Arabia, and the Chiricahua Apache used to make a similar boast. Traveling through this country in 1863, the adventurer John Ross Brown reported, "These vagabond Indians have a saying, no less sarcastic than true, that the Mexicans are their vaqueros [cowboys] upon whom they depend for their horses and cattle; and that the Americans are their teamsters and mechanics, who haul goods for them and supply them with arms."

Settlements fuel the avarice and ambitions of nomads, and for a while the two opposing cultures can coexist in an uneasy, bullying symbiosis, but in the end the settlements always expand, become more technically advanced and grow stronger militarily. Cochise died free and undefeated, but Geronimo's Apaches knew their time was coming to an end. Whether they fought or surrendered to the reservations, the whites kept coming and the buildings, towns, cities, railroads and telegraphs multiplied across their land. Geronimo's argument in favor of war was essentially one of honor: it was better to die fighting than to submit to the inevitable. And with hindsight, we can say that he was wrong.

Of all the Apache bands, Geronimo's Chiricahuas fared worst. The government broke General Crook's promise of a reservation in Arizona and put them on a locked train, with all the windows sealed, to a prison camp in Florida, where they died in droves from malaria. And then to Oklahoma, where Geronimo posed for tourist pictures, dressed up in plains Indian garb and sporting a ridiculous, twin-horned jester cap. The Chiricahuas, as a people, went to the brink of extinction. In 1913, their numbers were down to 213 and they were still not permitted to return to their Arizona homeland.

The other Arizonan bands—San Carlos, White Mountain, Tonto—who gave up the fight earlier, at least got their own reservations. God knows those reservations have had their problems, and now the language is dying out, and those Apaches who want to learn their traditions must do so by reading about them in the white man's history books, but at least they are living on their own land, with tribal sovereignty over the same mountain ranges where their ancestors lived and died. Here in the Dragoons, which hold Cochise's bones, the Apaches are notable by their absence. Unless the Irishman's story is true and a few of them are hiding out in a cave somewhere.

The window of sunlight is closing. A large and malevolent storm is coming this way, the seconds are reducing between lightning flashes and thunderclaps, and the land behind the storm is obscured by a sheet of rain. I get down from the peak, put on the backpack and start descending by the easiest route available, which turns into a bona fide game trail, marked with coyote and deer tracks. The storm pushes a cool wind ahead of it, which smells of rain, and then the rain itself comes, falling in fat droplets that splatter on the rocks and drum on my hat brim, and send up little puffs of dust on the trail. I take off my hat, letting the rain run in rivulets down my face and chest, and down the back of my neck. This is the first rain I've felt on my skin for three months, and I crave it in a way I never thought possible. Then a huge, rending explosion of thunder, the feel of electricity in the air. I see what looks like a cave, partially obscured by boulders and a stand of juniper trees, and I start running for it.

I come to an abrupt halt thirty yards short because the cave is occupied. A white man with a long beard is sitting cross-legged in its entrance, sheltered from the rain by an overhanging lip of rock. He is wearing a filthy green sweatshirt, an old, red, sleeveless ski jacket, with the padding erupting from one of the shoulders, and a black-and-orange Harley-Davidson bandanna tied around his forehead. I look for the gun but don't see one. He beckons me into his camp.

"Welcome home, brother. I've been expecting you," he says.

"You've been expecting me?"

"Yup. Knew you was coming. Me and all my brothers knew you was coming."

I look around. No sign of anyone else.

"Could I trouble you for one of them cigarettes?" he asks, pointing with his chin at the pack of Camels protruding from my shirt pocket. He breaks off the filter and lifts up the cigarette as a symbolic offering to the mountain peaks, or maybe the storm. He pulls out a pinch of tobacco and scatters it on the ground, and then he lights what's left of the cigarette and sucks down a deep, luxurious lungful.

He sits by the embers of an old fire, smoldering in a blackened circle of stones. Scattered around him are buckskin pouches, bundles of dried plants and roots, plastic bags full of nuts and berries, empty cans of beans, pieces of bone and antler, piles of colored rocks and minerals. At the back of the cave is a rolled-up sleeping bag and a canvas army-surplus duffel bag.

"They call me Medicine Man, and this here's my medicine cave," he says. "I come up here to purify myself and get straight with the spirits. To learn the wisdom of the plant and animal nations, the four-leggeds and the winged brothers of the air. Look around, brother: this is my home, my church, my schoolhouse, my grocery store, my pharmacy. See here? This is yucca root. Mash it up, boil it up in water and you've got soap. This here's greasewood. Good for aching joints and snakebites, and it'll help out women with the menstrual cramps."

I tell him the Irishman's story and ask him if he's seen any Apaches. "I'm Apache," he says. I look at his blue eyes, his long, gaunt face, the reddish cast to his graying beard. He sees my look and nods. "I'm Apache, I'm Navajo, I'm Sioux, Cheyenne and Cherokee. I'm an African, a Chinaman, an Aborigine from Australia, an Irishman, you name it. My tribe is all families and all races, and my territory is as far as I can travel."

He has a beautiful pipe, elaborately carved out of purple wood and red stone, with a long, tapering stem. He fills it with marijuana from one of his pouches, takes a puff, and raises the pipe to the mountain peaks as he exhales. I offer him my hip flask, and he waves it away, saying he doesn't need the energy and that whiskey is "Babylon poison."

"I've seen the planet on fire, everybody barbecued," he says a few minutes later. "I was up there with *them*, you know, looking down, so I asked them straight out, 'What the hell is going on down there?' They were real casual about it: 'Oh, the humans blew up their planet again. They do it all the time.' Well, that's the kind of insanity we've got to checkmate. Big time. What people need to do is just turn everything off—the computers, the TVs, the lights, the electricity, the nuclear generators—just turn all that shit off and see if there's still a brain inside your skull. We've got to wake up the people before it's too late."

He doesn't like questions or straight answers. He prefers to speak in esoteric riddles and rambling pronouncements, with the air of a slightly addled guru or preacher. Gradually, through clues, hints and asides, I glean a few details about his life, which may or may not be facts. He started hitchhiking at the age of twelve, as a boy named Michael in California's Central Valley—his parents were Dust Bowl migrants from Oklahoma—and he has been traveling ever since he dropped out of high school. For twelve years he was a merchant seaman and sailed around most of the world. His career at sea was ended by a back injury in the mid-1970s, and he went back to California and started hitchhiking again.

He counts himself as one of the Rainbow Family now, a loose, anarchic confederation of hippies, New Agers, Deadheads, tramps, weekend potheads, ravers—a kind of blanket organization for the counterculture which holds a big annual gathering every Fourth of July weekend. It is hard to make any generalizations about the Rainbow Family because so many different types and groups are included within it, but its broad tendency is anti-materialistic, communitarian, utopian, primitivist, vegetarian and nomadic, and it offers a kind of garbled, all-inclusive spirituality, drawing on American Indian religions, Buddhism, Hinduism, Christianity, Taoism, New Age holisticism and Rastafarianism. Rainbows use the Rasta pejorative "Babylon" to describe Western capitalist society.

The storm blows over, the rain stops. He extracts some seeds from his marijuana pouch and walks over to the banks of a dry streambed. He buries the seeds in the damp earth and slops some water from his canteen over them. "I'm a seed man," he says. "Wherever I go, I plant seeds. Not just herb. I'm talking about food for the Family. If the birds or the animals eat them up, that's all right, because they're family too. But sometimes I'll go back, and there's a whole bunch of healthy-looking plants waiting for me. I'm trying to wake up the Family and get everybody doing it. Wherever you go, plant a seed. Then, when the shit comes down, there'll be food to eat, out in the wild places, and herb to smoke."

There are long periods of silence while he blisses out on the birdsong, the wind in the trees and the departing smell of rain, and I feel my own senses open up, becoming aware of sounds and patterns to the sounds that I was oblivious to before. Bird alarm calls, for example, travel in concentric rings away from the point of disturbance in the normal ebb and flow of the forest. A thousand feet below on the Forest Service trail, a hiker clatters a rock and the nearest blue jays start cawing to announce the alarm. Birds further away hear them and set off their own alarm calls.

A raven rises up into the sky to see what all the commotion is about. A ground squirrel, hearing the bird calls, stops in its tracks and listens for further signs of danger. This, I realize, is how he knew I was coming.

"Do you know what a coyote gourd is?" he asks. "It's a kind of gourd that grows around here. We used to keep water inside 'em and bury them around the desert. I've got hundreds of them gourds buried all over this desert. It don't matter where I'm at, I ain't dying of thirst."

Ten minutes go by in silence. Then a lecture on the intelligence of squirrels. "If it's a cold night coming, you'll see 'em running around, picking up all kinds of dried grass and leaves and stuffing them into their nests. The squirrel is your brother and he communicates his intelligence by example. I've got a cheap, piece-of-shit sleeping bag, but if I stuff it with dry grass and leaves it'll keep me warm to ten below. We're all in this together: you, me, Brother Squirrel, the President. All of us live by the grace of the same earth. One earth, one world, one love. Praise be to the Great Spirit, Jah Rastafari, I don't give a damn what you call him."

"How long have you been here, in these mountains?" I ask him.

He shakes his head and sighs wearily. "See, now you're getting into time. Babylon time. Time turns in a circle, like a wheel, so why keep track of it since it always ends up in the same place? Answer me that, brother? I pay attention to the seasons, and the storms. As far as whether it's Tuesday the 9th or Wednesday the 27th, I couldn't give a flying fuck, because it don't matter."

Dusk is invading the mountains now, and it's been a long day. I make a date for breakfast, hoist my pack and walk off. My feet carry me half a mile or so and then I flop down on the damp ground and pull out my sleeping bag. This is the secret to a calm and restful night's sleep in rattlesnake and scorpion country: total exhaustion.

I have a bag of coffee, a can of beans and a fresh pack of cigarettes. He has a tin of Quaker oats, some dried cactus fruit, some de-spined prickly pear pads and roasted piñon pine nuts. He rises from his cross-legged position to get more wood for the fire and gets stuck halfway to vertical in some terrible back spasm. It takes him two or three minutes of puffing and blowing, groaning and grimacing, but he manages to work his way out of it. I offer to get the wood, which he accepts. I offer him some ibuprofen, which he refuses as "Babylon medicine" and fills his pipe instead.

"Man, I got to get back to my hot tub," he says, stirring the fruit and nuts into the oats. "Got me a hot springs in Idaho, way out in the backwoods. Nobody knows where it's at unless I tell them about it. Got me some plants that should be budding out pretty soon and a hollowed-out cedar tree where I stay at. When I get to my hot tub, I'm *home*, brother."

He was going to spend the summer up there, but got lured down to Arizona by the prospect of a woman. He met her at the Rainbow Gathering last summer, took down her address in Tucson, promised to take her out into the woods and teach her how to live off the land and prepare medicinal plants. She was happy to see him, if a little surprised, when he turned up on her doorstep a year later. But she had a live-in boyfriend, and after a few nights of sleeping on their floor Medicine Man took off for the Dragoons on his own.

There are three basic types of lone, heterosexual wandering males, in my experience: those who hate women, those who have grudgingly resolved to do without them, and those who yearn for them. Medicine Man falls into the third category. Once he gets going on the subject there is no stopping him. For years now he has been looking for a woman who wants to live as he does, camped out in the backwoods, planting seeds, living off the land and communing with nature. In the past there were a few women who thought that was what they wanted, but after a few weeks or months they tired of the life, or Medicine Man's company. They missed taking showers, he says, they missed talking to other people. It's getting harder to find likely prospects now. He's not as young as he used to be and it seems that the women are different nowadays.

"I can't figure 'em out no more," he says. "You'll be getting along fine and grooving on each other's trips, and it looks like something is going to happen, and then, all of sudden, they just nut up on you. All you can do is just stand there and try to protect yourself, because you can't be hitting a woman. I despise a man who hits a woman. So what you do is put up one arm like this to cover your face and use the other hand like this to protect your balls."

God knows what the background to that speech is. It's not a problem I've been running into, but maybe I'm meeting a different class of woman. When you're broke, unwashed and the wrong side of fifty, drifting around the backwoods with a bad back and a hacking, wheezing cough, the field of available women is drastically reduced, and it may well be possible that some of them are violently insane.

It's hard not to take him as an augury, a warning sign of what happens to a man after a life on the road, a man for whom wandering turns out to be more than a youthful phase. Medicine Man sailed under foreign flags and has never held down a regular job in America. He has no health insurance, no pension or social security checks coming, no disability payments, and he's no longer equipped, physically or psychologically, to work a real job. His only alternative to the road, the backwoods and the Rainbow Gatherings is some city skid-row or homeless shelter, and he hates cities. He believes they are about to go down in apocalyptic flames.

Given the parameters his life has set for him, he's doing the best he can. It might look aimless from the outside, but he feels a deep sense of purpose. He is setting an example for the rest of us, showing us there is a better way, gathering the knowledge that will save us. It's easy to dismiss what he says as stoned gibberish, but understand that it is integral to his sense of self-worth. He is not looking for sympathy. He is looking for recruits, disciples and converts; he wants us all to live as he does. A good woman, he says, is all it would take to complete his happiness.

He's got spiritual fulfilment covered. He's got his survival needs taken care of. He grows his own weed, sells or trades it for money and food at Rainbow Gatherings and biker festivals, and supplements his diet with nuts, fruits, berries and roots harvested from the land. He carves pipes, digs out turquoises and quartz crystals, bundles up sage to sell, collects animal skulls and deer hooves. He makes pouches and moccasins from deer hide, trading for the skins, because he won't kill an animal or eat its meat. Did the Irishman meet Medicine Man up here, I wonder, and embellish him into a group of carnivorous Apaches?

The hot tub is calling him. It's the only thing that eases his back when it gets this bad. The hot tub is eighteen hundred miles away, but this doesn't seem to bother him. He collects up his belongings and starts stuffing them into his duffel bag. "Hell, I'll hitch into New Mexico, get up to Colorado, catch a freight up to Montana and hitch across into Idaho. I'll be there in a week." I agree to give him a ride to the interstate to get him started.

It takes him most of the morning to get down the mountain. Every two hundred yards or so, he has to stop and rest, and stretch out his back. I offer to go down, leave my pack at the bottom and come back up for his duffel bag. "Nope," he says. "A man can't hump his own gear, it's time for that brother to get off the road, and I ain't ready to quit. I'm just taking her easy. Ain't no hurry. I got all the time in the world."

I get impatient but have to admit that he paces himself nicely down the mountain. When finally we reach my truck he doesn't look much worse than when he started. I drive east into the town of Sunsites, where he buys a tin of Tops tobacco, some rolling papers and a root beer. Then north to bisect the interstate. I drop him off at the rest area in Texas Canyon, intending to turn around and go back into the Dragoons to get some work done. Then it strikes me that that is a hopelessly quixotic idea, a blatant strategy of procrastination, and that work requires a desk, a chair and a computer. I point the truck toward home base in Tucson and leave him to make the long journey north to his equivalent.

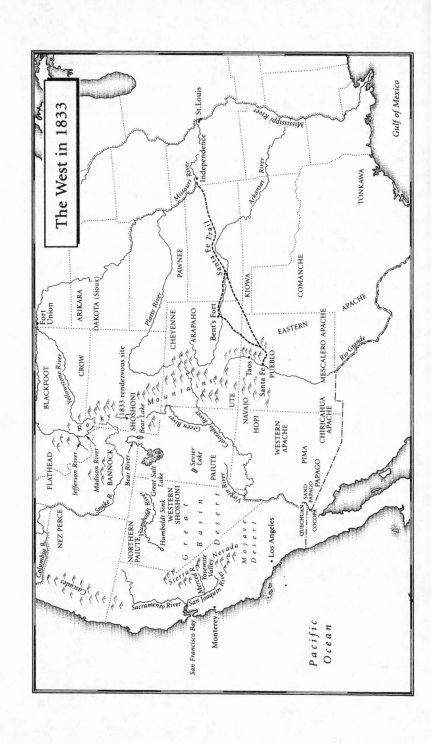

CHAPTER 6

This afternoon Mr. Walker, whom we met at Independence Rock, visited our camp; he has picked up a small party at Fort Laramie; and wild-looking creatures they are—white and red. This man has abandoned civilization,—married a squaw or squaws, and prefers to pass his life wandering in these deserts; carrying on, perhaps, an almost nominal business of hunting, trapping and trading—but quite sufficient to the wants of a chief of savages. He is a man of much natural ability, and apparently of prowess and ready resource.

Captain Philip St. George Crook, *Scenes and Adventures in the Army*, 1856, quoted in Bil Gilbert, *Westering Man: The Life of Joseph Walker*

In the summer of 1833 Joe Walker was thirty-four years old, already a highly respected man among the trappers, fur traders and Indian tribes of the Far West and already traveling in the style of a nomadic chieftain. See him riding into the fur-trade rendezvous in early June, with six of his trappers and a band of two hundred Shoshoni, or Snake Indians, for an escort. Picture the long, winding, dusty caravan of horses and riders, coming down out of the Salt Mountains and into the wide, flat valley of the upper Green River, with the wolfish, long-muzzled Indian dogs trotting alongside, the horses painted and hung with bells, beads and ribbons, and the Snake women ornamented in a similar fashion; the warriors making their horses prance and curvet, some wearing buffalo-horn headdresses and wolf's-head caps, carrying trade muskets and lances decorated with human scalps; the shamans juggling as they ride; the infants, the elderly and the band's possessions dragging along behind the packhorses on buffalo-hide travois platforms tied across the tepee poles. And Joe Walker riding at the head of the procession with a long rifle across his saddle.

He was a huge man, six feet four and heavily muscled, with a full beard and curly reddish-brown hair that fell below his shoulders. He had a ruddy, weathered complexion, a hawkish nose, and the requisite "piercing blue eyes," which all frontier heroes seemed to come equipped with. If the two portraits painted of him are accurate, Walker projected an air of alertness, strength and complete self-assurance: pride without arrogance, fearlessness without aggression. If he arrived in his usual style, he was riding a big, fast stud horse, on which he expected to win money at the rendezvous horse races, and the horse was extravagantly decorated in the Indian style.

Joe Walker was something of a dandy among the trappers and fur traders of the Far West—"mountain men," they called themselves, and there were few dandies among them. They were a ragged, sour-smelling breed for the most part, usually seen in the literature with matted hair and beards, wearing buckskins turned black and shiny from the season's accumulation of buffalo grease, beaver fat, dried blood, campfire soot and their own secretions— the type, as the old Western joke goes, who takes a bath every springtime, whether he needs it or not.

Walker was known for his stylish, feather-plumed slouch hats, the fine cut and quality of his fringed buckskin leggings and hunting shirts, and his unusual attention to personal hygiene and grooming. He stood out among the mountain men like Beau Brummell strutting through a crowd of shabby office clerks. Brummell was the famous London dandy of the 1810s and 1820s who popularized a new style of beaver-felt hat, which spread to Paris, Milan, Cologne, Vienna, St. Petersburg, New York, Boston and all over the civilized world, which decimated beaver populations in Europe and raised the price of beaver pelts, and so enabled the Rocky Mountain fur trade, the mountain men and their annual rendezvous to come into existence. This was the reach of the global economy in the early nineteenth century. Here was a line of dominoes set in motion by a fashion coup in Mayfair, reaching deep into the half-explored wilderness of the American West, leading from one dandy to another.

Walker's tailors were Indian women, skilled in the patient art of rubbing a deer's brains into its hide until the hide achieved a buttery softness, and wonderfully dextrous at sewing, fringing, beading and porcupine-quill embroidery. Highest in Walker's estimation were the young women of the Shoshoni tribe, and not just for their tailoring skills. Snake girls were generally agreed by the mountain men (although there were many heated arguments on the subject) to be the great belles of the Far West: the best looking, the lightest skinned, the most artful with makeup and perfumes (fashioned from wild plants and flowers, later augmented with trade goods). They were also hardworking cooks and seamstresses, engaging storytellers and gossips (with the usual graphic, bawdy sense of humor that prevailed among Indian women in the West), and skillful, enthusiastic sexual partners. In return, and especially at rendezvous, they expected to be showered with jewelry and finery, and given gorgeous, high-performance horses to ride, so they could outshine their feminine rivals. Like so many mountain men, Joe Walker ended up marrying a Snake girl (she was probably fifteen or sixteen, the standard age for marriage in the tribe) and dressing her up like a Christmas tree.

Fast horses, Snake beauties, fine clothes, tobacco for his pipe, a moderate amount of drinking and gambling: these were Joe Walker's pleasures, as far as we can determine, but secondary and peripheral to his grand passion for travel and exploration. He had no way of knowing it in 1833 (although maybe he suspected) but it was to keep him on the move, over enormous distances, for nearly fifty years. By my guesswork, Joe Walker covered more miles on horseback than any white American, before him or since, and probably more than any Indian.

The rendezvous that year was held where Horse Creek flows into the Green River, on and around the site of present-day

Daniel, Wyoming. At its height, there were about 350 mountain men and 500 Indians—Snakes, Bannocks, Crows, Flatheads, Nez Perces—come together for the annual trade fair and grand debauch of the Rocky Mountain West. The mountain men were a mixed group of French-Canadians, half-Indian French Creoles, displaced Delawares from the East, a few Swedes, Mexicans and Irishmen, very few black Americans (Jim Beckwourth, who became a blood brother and war chief of the Crow tribe, was the most famous), but by 1833 their ranks were dominated by men of Joe Walker's background: white Americans born on the trans-Appalachian frontiers. The French had opened up the Great Plains and Rocky Mountain fur trade as early as 1700, but now its dominant language was English, spoken in a heavy drawl.

Years later, some of the participants judged 1833 as the greatest rendezvous of them all—the wildest, the purest, the last one before tourists, missionaries and white Christian ladies started showing up and spoiling the fun. What a spectacle of nomadic pageantry it must have been: the tents and tepees extending for ten miles along the riverbanks, immense herds of horses turned out to graze on the surrounding plains, and mountain ranges rising up to the north, west and east. There was an excitable, carnival atmosphere in the encampments. Impromptu horse races broke out, attracting big crowds and heavy betting. There were marksmanship contests, mock battles, Indian dances and ceremonies, mounted parades and exhibitions of trick-riding.

And what a noisy, uncouth, depraved spectacle it must have been, up close and in the firelight: the staggering and roaring of drunken trappers and drunken Indians, many of them drunk for the first time since last year's rendezvous, firing their guns into the air and screaming out their war cries. Indian prostitutes were available for a handful of beads or an awl—some lay drunk on the ground with their dresses hiked up, offering themselves to any man who would buy them another drink—and many a trapper left rendezvous with venereal disease or a "weeping in the pants," as they called it. There were more romantic couplings too, trappers taking squaws as their temporary girlfriends, and sometimes as their brides, although all forms of sexual activity with Indian women, excepting rape, required an outlay of goods. Sometimes there was a kind of after-the-fact pimping operation at work among the tribes. Your new girlfriend's father or brothers would show up and demand payment, in horses, beaver pelts or whatever else you had, for the services she had rendered.

The mountain men, like the Indian warriors, were tremendous boasters and braggarts, forever thumping their chests and recounting the coups of bravery they had struck in battle, showing off their collection of scalps and recounting how each one was taken, promoting their prodigious skills as hunters, trackers, horse thieves, lovers, gamblers, fighters. The mountain men in particular would issue bellowing challenges to each other, which sometimes led to bragging and lying contests, and sometimes to brawls, fistfights, stabbings, shootings and wrestling matches that turned into eye-gouging contests.

It was de rigueur to drink until you collapsed and sleep where you fell, and this in itself was a demonstration of the courage and devil-may-care recklessness they admired, because rabid wolves were skulking into the encampments at night. Twelve people were bitten during the 1833 rendezvous and subsequently died of rabies, which had little effect on the drinking and collapsing habits of the rest. A wild young trapper called Joe Meek claimed to have so much alcohol in his blood that it was bound to kill or cure any rabid wolf.

Rendezvous was an institution devised and operated by the fur companies, dating back to 1825. Its basic purpose was to part the trappers and the Indians from their beaver pelts for as little money as possible, and then get the money back by selling them overpriced goods from civilization—overpriced booze in particular. They called it "whiskey" at rendezvous, but in reality it was raw grain alcohol, diluted with river water, progressively diluted as the customers grew less discerning, and in 1833 it sold for five dollars a pint—the same price as a pint of bad whiskey today.

In St. Louis, where the fur companies outfitted their traders, raw alcohol sold for less than thirty cents a gallon, but give them a little credit for transportation. Between St. Louis and the upper Green River lay fifteen hundred miles of wilderness, with its full complement of warlike tribes, grizzly bears, quicksands and a hundred other lesser dangers and difficulties. Under the very best of conditions, with no Indian attacks or horse thievery, with easy river crossings, good grazing for the pack animals, and plenty of game to eat along the way, the journey took seven weeks. And then seven weeks back again with the furs.

The mark-up on goods at rendezvous, however, ranged between 1000 and 2000 percent, and for the trappers and the tribes there was little choice but to pay. Both groups were horse nomads who roamed the wilderness after meat, furs and hides, and like all mounted nomads in recorded history they needed and craved certain products manufactured in the settlements: superior weapons, tools, clothing, intoxicants, cultivated foods like flour, coffee and sugar—we have seen the same kind of list before.

The mountain men, if not the Indians, knew they were being gouged unmercifully, but they refused to let it spoil their annual party. If you drank enough overpriced alcohol, it was easy to forget how much it was costing you. You became cavalier and expansive, inspired to blow the rest of your beaver pelts (or credit for beaver pelts) on more of this fine whiskey and an extravagant shopping spree at the company store. Indian women were often the main beneficiaries of this extravagance. It became a matter of honor and competitive pride among the mountain men to dress up their wives and girlfriends in as much imported finery as possible: beads from Venice and Prague, vermilion from China, blankets from Lancashire, lace from France or Belgium, bangles, ribbons, garters, mirrors—the feminine accoutrements that Indian women adored and which the mountain men called "foofaraw."

Gambling was another good way to bankrupt yourself at rendezvous, playing the Indian game of "hand." A small, carved piece of bone was palmed in one hand, and rapidly passed to the other, back and forth, with feints and double-bluffs. When the movement stopped, and the closed hands were held apart, the watchers had to guess which one contained the bone. The Indians played in teams, facing each other across a blanket, and put their faith in spells, incantations, prayers and visions. The mountain men played as individuals, employed flourishing sleight-of-hand maneuvers, and kept up a running commentary like carnival barkers.

Nine out of ten trappers left the rendezvous flat broke and in debt to the fur company, for their traps, powder, ammunition, horses, pack mules and everything else they needed to survive and carry on. They rode off into the mountains with monumental hangovers, and perhaps a weeping in the pants, facing another year of fighting off Indians, grizzly bears, starvation, thirst and disease, wading into icy streams and beaver ponds to set their traps, plunging back in at dawn to retrieve the drowned beavers (early rheumatism in the legs was the trappers' health scourge), with a grand blowout at next year's rendezvous as the inducement and reward, assuming they lived that long. The attrition rate was horrendous. In 1856 a veteran furman called Antoine Robidoux could account for only three survivors for the three hundred mountain men he had known in the 1820s.

Joe Walker was atypical for a mountain man. For one thing, he came to the rendezvous as the "partisan," or field commander, of a trapping brigade—a member of the small elite in the fur trade that had managed to rise above the annual cycle of debt and spree. For another, his personality was unusual. Walker, despite the flashiness of his dress, was a quiet, prudent, self-contained man, a moderate tippler in the midst of an alcoholic binge. We will allow him a few horse races, perhaps a Snake girl and a shopping spree, but Joe Walker seems to have spent most of his time at the 1833 rendezvous assembling recruits for his next expedition. Captain Benjamin Bonneville of the US Army, who was looking into the prospects for American expansion under cover of fur trading, had asked him to explore the country west of the Great Salt Lake, which was blank space or fiction on the maps of the day, and go all the way to the Mexican province of California if possible. Joe Walker had tried and failed to go there in 1820. Jedediah Smith, a pious, priggish Puritan from New England stock, the most atypical mountain man of them all, became the first explorer to reach California overland in 1826, and he went back in 1827. A handful of others—Ewing Young's trappers out of Taos, the British furman Peter Skene Ogden—had been there since and stories had filtered back.

The journey was known to be horrendous, across hundreds of miles of desert with little or no game or water, and then over an immense wall of perennially snowcapped mountains: the Sierra Nevada. Of the thirty-two men who had gone with Jed Smith on the two expeditions, twenty-six had died and two had deserted. For some of the men who signed up with Joe Walker, the danger and hardship were positive inducements, fitting challenges to their courage, skill and toughness. To survive such a journey, and live to tell the yarns, would be "a feather in a man's cap," as Joe Meek put it.

They had also heard stories about the warm winter sunshine in California, the willing Mexican girls, mission wineries that never ran dry and vast, uncountable herds of horses and cattle, ineptly guarded by docile Catholicized Indians—a fortune on the hoof that could be bought cheaply or easily stolen. California was already established in the American imagination as a mellow, easy-living, golden land, with beautiful girls, a bountiful economy and plenty of suckers for the taking.

There was also the simple inducement of the Pacific, the end of the continent, as far west as you could go. Joe Walker, like so many mountain men, was born on the frontier, into a culture that faced west. His family had been moving west for three genera-tions, from Scotland to Ulster, to Pennsylvania, Virginia, Tennessee and then Missouri, sitting outside their log cabins with a pipeful of tobacco and a jug of homemade whiskey, watching the sun go down and wondering what was out there and convincing them-selves it was better than here.

We'll rejoin the historic expedition to California, but first I want to delve deeper into Joe Walker's family history, because it's the best single explanation of his wandering, restless spirit that we have. And here I must blow the trumpets for his biographer Bil Gilbert, who has managed to trace Walker's family tree back to Wigton in the southern Lowlands of Scotland in the 1690s and his ethnic background to the English Midlands in the Dark Ages.

Walker's people: originally they were a disparate group of Danes, Angles and Saxons, pushed north out of England by a series of violent upheavals, culminating in the Norman invasion of 1066. They took up an uncertain tenure in the Scottish Lowlands and border country, started marrying into each other's families and forming into armed clans for self-protection. They were caught between the Celts to the north and the English to the south, whose kings and warlords used this country as a battleground in a recurrent conflict that lasted for seven hundred years.

The border clans were slaughtered, robbed, raped, tortured and chased out of their hovels by Scots and English alike. They were starved out by rackrenting landlords and tax-collectors, forcibly recruited into their oppressors' armies, harried and shunted across the moors until they lost all attachment to a sense of home ground—if indeed they had one to begin with. Their architecture reflected their rootlessness, as well as their poverty: hastily erected cabins of stone and mud, with ferns strewn on the floor, that were no loss to leave behind. When their descendants reached the Appalachian forests they built similar structures out of hardwood logs and clay: small, low-roofed, rectangular and temporary, like a modern-day American trailer home.

In the mid-sixteenth century the Lowland Scots acquired a cultural leader and figurehead, John Knox, who had been to Reformation Europe and brought back Presbyterianism. The clanfolk grafted its grim certainties onto an older creed of blood and vengeance, loyalty and honor. For as long as they could remember, their lives had been shaped by war and violence, and its codes were deeply embedded in their culture. Maybe it was only their belligerence, their sheer ferocity, that saved them from extinction, but it developed into something more than a survival mechanism. In the brief periods of respite between Anglo-Scottish wars and invasions, the Lowlanders took to robbing, raping, torturing and killing each other, in a series of bloody clan feuds, raiding sprees and vigilante reprisals.

In 1605 James I decided to settle the Lowland Scots on plantations in the Ulster colony. His intention was to kill two birds with one stone: to sap the influence of these wild, ungovernable

Presbyterians on the mainland and use them to counterbalance the power of the Catholic rebels in Ireland, who were proving almost as troublesome. It must have seemed like an elegant solution at the time, but like generations of American leaders after him, both white and Indian, King James underestimated the determination, land-hunger and ruthlessness of the Lowland Scots, and the consequences of his decision are still felt today in Ireland.

When they got to Ulster, the Scots began seizing Irish lands and killing Irishmen, plunging the colony into a protracted guerrilla war, such as they were accustomed to as normal life in the Scottish borders. At the end of it, fifteen thousand Irish dissenters were dead and the Ulster Scots were harvesting crops in the stolen fields. With the help of French Calvinists they set up a thriving textile industry, prospered economically for the first time in their history and began to threaten the power of the Anglican elite.

The elite clamped down firmly, raising taxes and rents, banning the Ulster Scots from holding political office, crippling their textile industry with trade tariffs, outlawing all of their religious ceremonies, marriage included, and taking away their right to bear arms (a decision with long consequences in American history). Terrible famines ensued and by the end of the seventeenth century the clanfolk were back in the old, familiar station of surly, downtrodden wretchedness. Except that now, more than ever, they were an uprooted people in an alien land.

When they began to arrive en masse in Pennsylvania in the 1720s, the Ulster Scots aroused widespread disgust and consternation among the predominantly Quaker citizenry. Most of the Ulster immigrants were poor, some had indentured themselves to make the passage, but they carried themselves with a fierce, bristling pride and were quick to take offense—natural-born troublemakers. The men tended to be tall, lean and tough-looking, with stern, dour faces, loutish manners and a look of brooding violence. The Quakers were appalled by their thirst for whiskey and their "rough and tumble" wrestling contests, in which the object was to gouge out the opponent's eyeballs with your thumbs, bite off his nose or ears, rip the testicles off his body or whatever it would take to make him call a halt and admit defeat. The Quakers usually described the women as "slatternly" and surrounded by hordes of grubby, "insolent" children. Benjamin Franklin, looking over the newcomers in Philadelphia, pronounced them "white savages."

Within their clan structures the Ulster Scots had strict, patriarchal lines of command but their history had left them with a deep hatred and suspicion for all external, institutional forms of authority—governments, armies, laws, courts, judges, tax-collectors, state Churches—and indeed for anyone to whom they weren't related. In northern Britain, before they got to Ireland, the border Presbyterians had been known as "crackers" (loutish braggarts) and "rednecks" (fiery religious dissenters). These pejorative terms crossed the Atlantic with them and are still used to describe their present-day descendants.*

The Pennsylvania authorities encouraged the Ulster refugees to settle in the Appalachian Mountains. There, in the wolf and Indian-haunted wilderness to the west, these ungovernable white savages would at least be out of the way, and it was hoped they would establish a stable buffer zone between colonial civilization and the warlike Appalachian tribes—an echo of King James' disastrous Ulster experiment.

Joe Walker's great-grandparents John and Katherine Walker left the economically depressed hellhole of Wigton in about 1700, tried and failed to prosper in Northern Ireland and arrived in Pennsylvania in 1728 with eight children, two nephews and a son-in-law. Fifty thousand Ulster Scots crossed the Atlantic that decade, along with about ten thousand of their kinfolk from the Scottish Lowlands. (Between 1713 and 1775 more than a quarter of a million of these people migrated to America, and became known as the Scotch-Irish.) The Walkers were among their social betters, which is to say that they were failed tenant farmers but

---

*The original derivations of these words have been obscured in popular American usage. "Cracker" is widely believed to refer to slave overseers, cracking their whips, who were mostly poor Southern whites of Scotch-Irish descent. And "redneck" is generally thought to derive from the strip of sunburned skin between the collar and the hat, common among bigoted rural whites in the South and the West—a region largely pioneered and settled by the Scotch-Irish.

closely affiliated with the Church and therefore literate and better educated than most.

In 1732, unable to find affordable land in Pennsylvania, the Walkers followed the usual pattern and set out for the frontier, strengthening their party with several other Ulster families they met on the trail. They passed the last trading forts and cabin settlements on the Shenandoah River in Virginia, which marked the extreme edge of the frontier, and kept going. The further away they could get from government jurisdiction, the better they liked it.

On the Maury River they met up with an Ulsterman called Jack Hayes, a lone hunter, trapper and trader who ranged up and down the Appalachians in buckskins and moccasins. Hayes' descendants claim that he was the model for the Natty Bumppo character (aka Hawkeye, Leatherstocking, Deerslayer) in James Fenimore Cooper's novels, but there were others like him on the frontier, and their numbers were growing—white wilderness roamers who lived more like Indians than Europeans. Daniel Boone, who is usually cited as Fenimore Cooper's model, was a later, less extreme example, born in 1734.

Jack Hayes showed the Walker party to a river valley below Jump Mountain in Virginia, where they hacked into the virgin forest, built a fortified log compound, cleared some land for corn and founded a notable frontier settlement known as the Creek Nation. In its early years it was the westernmost English-speaking settlement in North America.

Over the next generation, the Walkers and the other families at the Creek Nation transformed themselves from European tenant farmers, mill hands, cattle drovers and blacksmiths into a large and formidable clan of American frontiersmen. They multiplied prodigiously, mastered an entirely new set of skills—hunting, trapping, woodcraft, axemanship, Indian fighting—then began pushing the line of settlement deeper into the wilderness. Other Scotch-Irish clans were engaged in the same process up and down the Appalachian frontier but Walkers were consistently at their western vanguard.

Once a new log compound was established, groups of men would go off on extended hunting and trapping expeditions into the western wilderness, partly for the sake of exploration and adventure, partly because they needed furs and hides to buy manufactured goods (one deerskin bought a dollar's worth of store goods, hence the word "buck" for a dollar) and partly to find suitable locations for the next log compound, for when the neighbors got too close or the game too scarce. In 1771 Walkers were among a party of Long Hunters, as these groups became known, who set out from Natural Bridge, Virginia, and returned nine months later with a big haul of furs and hides.

The Long Hunters of Appalachia were the forerunners of the mountain men—figuratively, and in Joe Walker's case biologically—but they were not yet fully nomadic. Their wanderings returned them to a log building and a patch of corn, where a sedentary wife raised their children. The Long Hunters lived a semi-nomadic lifestyle, much like the Indian tribes of the Appalachian forests. The Creek, Shawnee and Cherokee also based themselves in fortified log settlements and raised corn in the forest clearings. Indian men went off on long seasonal journeys to hunt and make war, and left the women behind to tend the crops, haul the water, collect the firewood, tan the hides, sew the clothing, look after the children, the elderly and everything else. White women on the frontier were doing much the same, although more of them were left alone to cope with the domestic and agricultural responsibilities. Indian women performed these tasks communally and considered the isolation of white women to be a great cruelty.

In Europe, hunting had been a rich man's privilege and like most immigrant groups the Ulster Scots arrived in America with no tradition of it. So they did the logical thing and studied the Indian hunters, borrowing many of their techniques: the imitation of animal calls, the use of stealth and disguise, fire hunts and surrounds. White hunters used long rifles in preference to the bow and arrow (as did Indians when they could get their hands on them), but otherwise the two groups hunted in similar ways and used their furs and hides to trade for the same goods.

Many white hunters and backwoodsmen started dressing like

Indians. They let their hair grow long, greased it with bear tallow and wove it into braids. They wore deerskin moccasins, stitched with European awls, long, baggy hunting shirts of linen, wool or buckskin, deerskin leggings tied above the knee, and an Indian breechclout, which left their upper thighs, hips and a portion of their buttocks uncovered. Samuel Kercheval, a frontier preacher, observed that the white backwoodsman was "proud of his Indian-like dress" and would wear his breechclout into church ("It did not add much to the devotion of the young ladies").

> The Americans and Indians who lived in these backwoods hunting communities also shared a set of general social values. Both groups were geographically mobile, in part because hunting constantly led them further into less exploited territory, in part because the growing coastal populations pressed on them from the East, in part because that was the way they liked it. Both emphasized personal freedom and independence while at the same time adhering to the loyalties of family and clan … Both were warlike and violent, believers in honor and vengeance, adherents to the ancient law of blood, and for both cultures the bloodshed was made worse by alcohol. By the eighteenth century these two groups were fully acculturated into each other's ways.
>
> John Mack Faragher, *Daniel Boone*

Encounters between white and Indian hunters were friendly more often than not, at least in the first half of the eighteenth century. They met on forest trails, shared their bear meat and tobacco, conversed by hand signs and a few shared words, carved out maps and pictures on pieces of bark. There were violent encounters too, but nothing like the full-scale warfare that broke out along the Appalachian frontier in the 1750s and raged for the next fifty years. It was the bloodiest white–Indian conflict in American history, with women and children considered legitimate targets by both sides—evidence perhaps that both sides were fighting with genocidal intent. Measured by death tolls, massacres or atrocities, the forest wars far outstripped the later, better-publicized Indian wars on the Western plains and deserts, but they flowed from the same cause: white invasion of Indian land.

Indians had been able to tolerate the early white hunting parties, which came and left, and generally tried to avoid trouble, but now thousands of settlers were pouring into their ancestral lands, establishing permanent dwellings and permanently decimating the game.

Walkers were in the thick of the forest wars. They were Long Hunters, probing into Indian lands, a target for any war party who found their tracks, unless they had a trading relationship, or a personal friendship, with the chief. Walkers are listed in the companies of "rangers," who patrolled the woods on a semiper-manent basis, looking for Indians to kill and scalp—another habit they had picked up in America. Walkers were isolated settlers, doggedly defending their log cabins, with granny reloading the rifles, and sometimes being butchered and burned out. Thirteen Walkers, as far as we know, were killed in the forest wars, and two were taken as captives.

William Walker, aged eleven, was taken by the Delawares in 1781 and sold to the Wyandot. He grew up hunting with them in the woods around Detroit, learned their customs and language, and was accepted as a full tribal member—Indians having no prej-udice against skin color and a long-standing custom of using captives to replenish the tribe's numbers. When he reached the age of manhood William Walker was free to return to white civi-lization, but he chose not to, taking a half-Indian wife and raising their children within the tribe.

This was not unusual. If white captives were taken as adults, they usually, though not always, tried to escape. If they were taken as children or adolescents, it was more likely that they would assimilate into the tribe and live out their lives as Indians. The reverse was seldom true. Indians had little or no desire to join white society, with its laws, punishments and jails, its sexual taboos and its rabid prejudice against Indians. On the Muskingum River in 1764 a captive exchange took place that illustrates the point nicely. The Indian prisoners ran back to their tribe with signs of great joy. The white captives had to be bound hand and foot,

kicking and screaming, and forcibly dragged back to the emis-
saries of civilization. Later, many of them escaped from their
rescuers and went back to live with the Indians.

Another group who went native were the runaways, who
voluntarily abandoned colonial civilization and joined up with
the nearest Indian tribe. Draconian laws were passed to try to
curb the practice, which suggests how common it was. By the
eighteenth century runaways tended to fall into four groups:
indentured servants, escaped slaves, "disgraced" women and adolescent farmboys who were sick of doing the chores. Sam Houston,
a Scotch-Irish frontier boy who went on to become a US senator,
fell into the fourth category, running off to join the Cherokee as
a teenager. "The wild liberty of the Red Man," he said, was prefer-
able to the "tyranny" of his older brothers, who headed the father-
less family. Later in life, after he had been governor of Tennessee
and taken his position in the Congress, Houston went back to
live with the Cherokee, although this time it was for an extended
bout of alcoholism, brought on by an unhappy marriage. He
pulled out of it and went on to become the president of Texas.

"Thousands of Europeans are Indians," noted Hector St. John
de Crevecoeur, a strait-laced farmer who harbored a secret envy
for their free and easy lives, "and we have no examples of even
one of these aborigines having from choice become Europeans!"

It is an undertold story in American history, because it runs
contrary to the dominant theme of the conquest, and because it
strikes at the European ideas of racial and cultural superiority that
were used to justify the conquest, in particular the notion that
sedentary Christian civilization is the pinnacle of human progress,
and God's plan for North America. The Long Hunters, the
roaming buckskinned traders like Jack Hayes, the captives who
refused to come back, the runaways and later the mountain men:
all these groups, to some extent, rejected civilization as too
constrictive and went native. As Bil Gilbert writes:

> It is small wonder that some white frontiersmen found this
> life-style appealing. They discovered that simply by joining
> the savages, they could live and enjoy themselves as only the

richest and most powerful Europeans, the royalty and rulers, were able or permitted to live—that is, with almost total personal freedom . . . [It] had a persistent unsettling and subversive influence on the frontier and, therefore, on the American imagination. Working like a chronic low-grade fever, the notion that only a feral man can be genuinely free constituted the most ironic legacy of the forest wars—the final revenge of the Shawnee, Cherokee and Iroquois.

Joe Walker was born on the Emory River in Tennessee on December 13, 1798. He was the 245th direct descendant of John and Katherine Walker, and his relatives were spread out along hundreds of miles of the frontier. The Cherokee had been subdued, but Creek war parties still ranged nearby during his childhood and adolescence, taking scalps and captives, some for the torture stake, others to be inducted into the tribe. The nearest town was Knoxville, a collection of crude huts around a wooden fort, fifty miles to the east. To the west, the forest extended for five hundred miles, to the Missouri River and the rumored plains beyond.

We don't know much about Joe Walker's childhood. He was literate and received some schooling, but presumably he spent a lot of time hunting, trapping and roaming the woods on horseback with his older brothers, learning the skills that would carry him across the continent. The family raised hogs and cattle, and Bil Gilbert surmises that Joe and his brothers spent a lot of time herding animals in the mountains and trailing them up through Virginia to market, a round-trip journey of two hundred miles or more.

At fifteen, Joe Walker rode with Andrew Jackson's militia units, and fought the Red Sticks band of Creek warriors at Horseshoe Bend. Eight hundred Creek warriors were killed that day— March 27, 1814—and that signaled the end of the forest wars. Afterwards he ranged down through Mississippi and Alabama, hunting and trapping, and might have fought with Jackson against the Spanish in Florida.

In the summer of 1819, aged twenty, Joe Walker was back on the Emory River in Tennessee, helping the family pack up and move on to Missouri. The neighbors were getting too close, the game too scarce, and besides, everyone else was doing it. There was a folk migration pouring out of Appalachia, a westering fever that swept up a million people that decade and deposited them in the Mississippi River Valley. The Great Migration, as it was called, included many different ethnic groups, but like the settlement of the Appalachian frontier, it was dominated and led by the Scotch-Irish, and the other groups tended to take on their cultural habits.

When the log cabin was built in Jackson County, Missouri, twenty miles beyond the frontier line, Joe Walker rode out west— the first of his clan to emerge from the forests and see the treeless immensity and the horse nomads of the Great Plains. He was twenty-one years old and intending to ride all the way to California, at a time when no white man had made the journey overland. He got as far as Santa Fe and was arrested by the Mexican authorities as an illegal alien. He managed to talk his way out of jail, went north to Taos, and joined up with the first group of Americans to trap beaver in the southern Rocky Mountains. Over the next few years, he became a fully fledged mountain man, one of a new breed.

His Long Hunting forebears had set the process in motion, but it was Joe Walker's generation of frontiersmen, reaching the nomadic spaces and horse cultures of the West, who severed the last ties to log dwellings and agriculture and became full-time wilderness roamers. In the figure of Joe Walker we can see the two main tributaries of the American wandering tradition come to a confluence: the nomadic Indian, from whose culture he borrowed heavily and later married into, and the restless, rootless, sunset-chasing Scotch-Irish.

Of all the European immigrant groups in America, they were undoubtedly the most footloose, and the most concerned with individual freedom and independence. And in my experience their descendants still are. We have met a few of them already. Mike Hatfield, the truck-driving nomadologist, was Scotch-Irish and Cheyenne Indian. B.J. McHenry was Scotch-Irish to the bone. Medicine Man claimed to be a hybrid of all the world's races, but his tall, gaunt frame, reddish beard and drawling speech strongly suggested that he was another one.

It's a question I always ask: where are your people from? Among railroad tramps, highway drifters, rodeo cowboys and that vaguely cohesive class of itinerant ranch hands, carpenters, construction workers and oil-field roughnecks that one meets in bars in small Western towns "Scotch-Irish" is the second most common reply. The most common reply is a shrug and a drawled, "I don't know. Myrhh-kin, I guess."

Now let's get back to rendezvous, in late July 1833, and catch up with the expedition to California. Walker rode out with forty men, perhaps a few more, and each man was outfitted with four horses, a buffalo robe and blanket, beaver traps and a year's supply of powder and lead. Captain Bonneville, the source of this largesse, did not go with them.

One of those men requires an introduction, a twenty-three-year-old from western Pennsylvania called Zenas Leonard. Sick of chores on his father's farm, he had gone west to find adventure in 1831 and joined up with a fractious, badly organized trapping brigade. His two years as a mountain man had been a catalogue of disasters: terrible ordeals with hunger and cold, lost for weeks at a time, captured briefly by the Arikaras, wounded by the Blackfeet, and robbed of all his furs, horses and equipment. Suffice to say that Zenas Leonard was glad to join such a well-equipped brigade led by such a well-respected partisan. He signed on as the expedition's clerk and kept a journal on the trip. Later he turned his journals into a book, *Adventures of a Mountain Man*, which stands as a classic memoir of the fur trade, and the most detailed and prolonged account of what it was like to travel with Joe Walker.

Here is Leonard's first description of the man he came to idolize: "Mr Walker was well hardened to the hardships of the wilderness—understood the character of the Indians very well—was kind and affable to his men, but at the same time at liberty to command without giving offense—and to explore unknown regions was his chief delight."

They rode southwest to the Bear River and its tributaries, where Walker had made his spring beaver hunt that year. He knew they were approaching the western limit of the buffalo range, so he called a halt and sent the men out to "make meat." They hunted, they butchered, they hung up thin strips of the meat to dry in the sun and the wind. Walker kept them at it for a week, until each man had sixty pounds of buffalo jerky in his saddle-bags.

It sounds like a glaringly obvious precaution—to bring some food with you when heading into a huge uncharted desert, reputed to have very little game—but normally mountain men scorned this kind of forward planning and carried no reserve food supplies. They let the landscape of the moment shape their diet, gorging when game was plenty and going hungry when it wasn't. When hunger turned to starvation they ate their horses, their dried beaver skins, their moccasins (boiled in water to soften up and make a soup) and on a few occasions the flesh of their dead companions, which was known as "man meat" in the mountains. Riding with Walker was an irascible, eccentric loner named Bill Williams, who had once been a spellbinding teenage preacher in Missouri and later acquired a notorious reputation for cannibalism.

Walker also strengthened his party on the Bear River, recruiting fifteen or twenty trappers who were camped nearby. One of them was Joe Meek, recovered from his rendezvous hangover and looking for that feather in his cap. They rode on for the Great Salt Lake in "good cheer" and "fine spirits." The weather was clear, there was little danger from Indians and they were still finding buffalo to hunt.

We can imagine them sitting cross-legged around the camp-fires, the smell of fresh-roasted meat in the air, scenes of gargan-tuan feasting. A peculiarity of buffalo meat was that you could eat enormous quantities of it without feeling full. There are reli-able accounts of mountain men and Indians eating ten pounds or more at a sitting, per person. Afterwards, cleaning their guns, forging bullets from bars of lead, smoking their pipes and leaning on their elbows, the trappers swapped their yarns: the places they had been and the scalps they had lifted, the squaws they had bedded and how much foofaraw it had cost them. They told tall tales of glass mountains and caves that led to hell, and true stories of gruesome hardships—doling out the moccasin soup in a starving winter camp—and glorious benders at rendezvous, or back in St. Louis. And the listeners would interject now and then with a grunting roar, usually rendered in the literature as "wagh!" This was the mountain men's all-purpose exclamation and noise of affirmation, copied via the Indians from a noise made by an assertive grizzly bear, and roughly translatable to the modern "yo!"

They spoke an extraordinary dialect, a subcultural slang of their own invention—rough and salty, laced with oaths, brags and racial epithets—which was largely impenetrable to outsiders. It was delivered in an exaggerated drawl, derived from southern Appalachia, and before that from the distinctive lilting speech of the Scottish borderlands and Protestant Ulster.* Bears were *bars*, here was *hyar* and the act of scalping was *takin' har*. They filled out their speech with mispronounced words of French and Spanish, phrases and metaphors drawn from various Indian languages and hand gestures from the Indian sign language, which all the Western tribes understood and which Cabeza de Vaca and Estevan had learned three centuries before.

Another curiosity: mountain men liked to refer to themselves in the third person, as *this chile, this 'coon, this hoss, this buffler, this beaver* or *this niggur*, which was a term used for whites, blacks and Indians by the mountain men, and meant "rough disreputable fellow." (J. L. Dillard, a scholar of American vernacular, says the word "nigger" was used without racial offense in America until 1928.) This was Joe Walker's accent and idiom, although he was less garrulous than most, and these were the kind of yarns to be heard around those campfires . . .

---

* "The earliest recorded examples of this 'Scotch-Irish' speech were strikingly similar to the language that is spoken today in the southern highlands [of Appalachia], and has become familiar throughout the Western world as the English of country western singers, transcontinental truck drivers, cinematic cowboys, and backcountry politicians." (David Hackett Fischer, *Albion's Seed*)

"Mind the time we took Pawnee topknots away to the Platte?"

"Wagh! Ef we didn't, an' give an ogwh-ogwh longside thar darned screechin', I'm a niggur . . . Sez I, hyar's a gone coon if they keep my gun, so I follers thar trail an' at night crawls into camp, an' socks my big knife up to the Green River, first dig. I takes tother Injun by the har and makes meat of him too . . . I got old bull-thrower, made medicine over him, an no darned niggur kin draw bead with him since."*

Lewis H. Garrard, *Wah-to-yah and the Taos Trail*

On the western shores of the Great Salt Lake they killed their last buffalo and made their first contribution to American cartography. Walker made a careful scout and found no trace of the Buenaventura River, which was thought to flow west out of the Great Salt Lake, and perhaps all the way to the Pacific. Having debunked the last mythical waterway in North America, they rode out into the moonscape salt deserts to the west, "the most extensive and barren plains" Zenas Leonard had ever seen.

They found some Indians camped by a spring, a party of Bannocks on their way east to the buffalo grounds. Walker made the signs for peace, brought out the tobacco and the trade gifts, and asked them about the country further west. This also seems an obvious thing to do—to be nice to the locals and ask them for directions—and again, it was not standard practice, and probably caused some grumblings among the men. Some of them had lost traps and horses to the Bannocks recently, and companions in the past. Others were greenhorns, eager to take their first scalp

---

* Rough translation:

"Remember the time we scalped those Pawnees on the Platte River?"

"Wagh! And if we didn't whoop as loudly as they did, then call me a liar . . . I said to myself, I'm a dead man unless I get my gun back, so I followed their trail, crawled into their camp at night, and stabbed one of them, plunging in my knife blade to the hilt. I killed and scalped the other Indian . . . I got my rifle back, performed a magical ritual over it, and now it shoots straighter than any rifle in the mountains."

and so blood themselves as mountain men, and there were a few like Bill Williams who plain enjoyed killing Indians and considered it sport. Joe Walker was an experienced and expert Indian fighter, but whenever possible he favored diplomacy—establishing trade relations and strategic alliances—as the best way to get through potentially dangerous Indian country.

Walker took the advice of the Bannocks and struck out northwest across the desert, following Indian trails between the springs but finding no game except for rabbits and a few scrawny desert antelope. A few days later, as promised, they came to the headwaters of a river that flowed west. They named it the Barren (now the Humboldt) because no trees grew along its banks, nothing bigger than a "walking stick," which meant no campfires at night unless they found driftwood. They followed the river, tiring now and "no longer so full of sport," trapping a few beaver as they went.

Indians "of the most poor and dejected kind—being entirely naked and very filthy" began to follow them, keeping hidden by day and stealing their beaver traps at night. These Indians were Paiutes, known to the mountain men as Diggers because of the sticks they carried to dig out the roots, grubs and insects they survived on. They were probably the most primitive, undernourished people in the Americas at the time, which was a reflection on the barrenness of these deserts, rather than their own cultural shortcomings. Zenas Leonard thought it miraculous that so many of them were able to survive in a country with so little game, so few edible plants, so few living things in general. From the Paiutes' point of view, Walker's party, with some 240 horses, must have looked like a banquet on legs. They had also seen the advantage of steel knives, cookpots and beaver traps compared to their own Stone Age technology and they grew bolder in their thefts.

Walker gave orders to take no reprisals against the Diggers, but a few unnamed individuals disobeyed him, killed two or three of them, and repeated the "same violation" the next day. When Walker found out about it, he was furious, because he knew what would happen next. The next day hundreds of Indians materialized from the desert armed with bows and arrows. How could so many of them survive out there and still have the energy for war?

Walker circled his men, piled up their packs and saddles into a breastwork and staked the horses inside it. Five chiefs approached, and from 150 yards away they made signs to say their people wanted to come into the white men's camp, to smoke and parley. Walker thought it was a trick and refused, signing back that he would meet them halfway. Then a group of warriors walked toward the breastwork, having decided they would enter the whites' camp with or without permission. Walker signed that if they came any closer, they would be killed.

The Paiutes laughed—how did the white men intend to kill them from such a distance without bows and arrows? Walker realized that they had never seen rifles before, or even heard stories about what they could do. So he put on a shooting exhibition. His riflemen picked off some ducks on a nearby pond and then riddled a beaverskin on the bank, which the Paiutes had left there as a target. The noise of the guns terrified the Paiutes, who fell flat on the ground and then ran. But they evidently failed to grasp the lesson Walker was trying to teach them.

The next morning Walker broke camp early and got the column moving. Indians began converging from all directions. Again Walker warned them to keep their distance or they would be killed, and again the warning had no effect. A hundred warriors cut in front of the column, apparently trying to delay the whites until the rest of the tribe could surround them.

"This greatly excited Captain Walker, who was naturally of a very cool temperament, and he gave orders for the charge, saying there was nothing equal to a good start in such a case," writes Leonard. "We closed in on them and fired, leaving thirty-nine dead on the field—which was nearly the half—the remainder were overwhelmed with dismay—running into the high grass in every direction, howling in the most lamentable manner."

The massacre of the Diggers has come down as an ugly stain on Joe Walker's reputation, but it's hard to imagine what else he could have done to avoid violence. And harder still to imagine another mountain man who would have done so much. The threat was real enough. His men were outnumbered ten to one, they had no cover and their powder-and-ball rifles took thirty to forty seconds to reload. An Indian could shoot off five or six arrows in that time. If the Diggers had surrounded them and charged, which looked to be their intention, Walker's party stood a strong probability of being wiped out. And bear in mind that Walker was also struggling to control his own men, many of whom were spoiling for a fight, and apparently went into a killing frenzy once it began. "Our object was to strike a decisive blow," writes Leonard. "This we did—even to a greater extent than we had intended." Afterwards, they were somewhat chastened by the scale of the massacre (none of Walker's party was killed or wounded) and, according to one account, they decided not to scalp the dead.

At any rate that was the last they saw of the Diggers. They were in an area of marshes and stagnant lakes in the middle of the desert, where the Humboldt River dies into the Humboldt Sink. Walker turned south, rode across the present-day Walker River Indian reservation, past a large lake now called Walker Lake, and the next night they were camped at the foot of the Sierra Nevada. It was early October and already the snowline was halfway down the mountains. The horses were tired and thin after crossing the desert. The buffalo meat was almost gone and they had no other food.

Walker sent out parties of hunters and scouts into the foothills. They found no game, nor even any recent sign of game, but one of the scouts discovered an Indian trail leading up into the mountains and this encouraged them. A few days later they were up on the central ridge of the Sierra in a high frozen country of cols, peaks and snowfields, with no navigable routes down to the west. The horses were emaciated now and barely able to walk. The men were eating insects and juniper berries.

Mutiny broke out in camp. Some of the men wanted to turn around and try to make it back to the buffalo country. Walker made "earnest appeals" to them not to go and then forced them to stay by refusing to give them horses or ammunition. That night, to revive morale, he ordered two of the horses to be killed. The men were so hungry that the withered black horseflesh tasted like "the choicest piece of beef steak." Two nights later they killed three more horses, which appeared to trouble Zenas Leonard more than the massacre of the Diggers.

> It seemed the greatest cruelty to take your rifle, when your horse sinks to the ground from starvation, but still manifests a desire and willingness to follow you, to shoot him in the head and then cut him up & take such parts of their [sic] flesh as extreme hunger alone will render it possible for a human being to eat. This we done [sic] several times, and it was the only thing that saved us from death.

They were up there for nearly a month, moving south along the spine of the mountain range, unable to find a way down. If that sounds like incompetence on Joe Walker's part, I advise a trip to that stretch of the High Sierras. Take a look at those peaks, crags, precipices, cols, crevasses, giant boulder fields, yawning chasms, snowfields a hundred feet deep . . . Now imagine trying to get two hundred and forty half-starved horses and sixty exhausted men over it. They called themselves mountain men, but they had no experience or knowledge of high-altitude mountaineering and were improvising techniques as they went. More remarkable is the fact that Walker managed to keep them alive and moving, and operating as a cohesive unit. The hunters and scouts were dispatched every day in an orderly fashion. There was no more talk of mutiny among these rugged individualists.

If you visit that country today the first thing that strikes you is its spectacular natural beauty. It was harder to appreciate such things when you were half-starved, shivering in your buckskins, twelve hundred miles from the nearest possibility of help, with no map and no idea what lay ahead. Leonard says they were too concerned with getting out alive to pay much attention to the "wonder of nature's handy-work." But there was one sight that stopped them in their tracks.

> Here we began to encounter in our path, many small streams

which would shoot out from under these high snowbanks, and after running a short distance in deep chasms which they have through ages cut in the rocks, precipitate themselves from one lofty precipice to another, until they are exhausted in rain below.—Some of these precipices appeared to us to be more than a mile high.

They were standing on the rimrock above Yosemite Valley, looking out over one of the most awe-inspiring sights in North America, and they were the first white men to see it. Leonard makes this brief, passing description, adding that it offered no way down, but for Joe Walker it seems to have been a seminal moment. Decades later he would request the inscription "Camped At Yosemite—Nov. 13, 1833" to be engraved on his tombstone.*

They picked their way along the narrow ridge that separates the Yosemite Valley from Tuoleme Canyon, which is almost as spectacular, and struggled on for another five or six days. The horses were dying of starvation now and furnished very little meat. The men were down to their last reserves of energy and will. Then a party of scouts came back with news of an Indian trail descending a steep, treacherous ridge to the west. They came down using hand and footholds, zigzagging from ledge to ledge and lowering the horses on ropes. That night they camped below the snowline and the hunters brought in a deer and two bears— "this was dressed, cooked, and eat [*sic*] in less time than a hungry wolf would devour a lamb."

With full stomachs, and the snow behind them, their spirits rose rapidly. Coming down the western slopes, they found easier trails, warmer weather, beautiful forests and ever more abundant deer, elk and bear. They began to revel in the journey. Leonard's aesthetic sensibilities were rekindled and his journal swelled with descriptions of natural wonders. At the base of the mountains they rode through groves of giant sequoias, a species of redwood

---

* There is confusion about the date. Leonard places them in Yosemite three weeks earlier, but this is unreliable.

that no white American had seen before, "incredibly large—some of which would measure from 16 to 18 fathoms [90 to 110 feet] around the trunk at the height of a man's head from the ground."

They followed the drainages down to the Merced River, which flowed west through "wonderful curiosities": foaming rapids, rock pinnacles a thousand feet high, and deep, placid pools of crystal-clear water, for those who were inclined to bathe. The Merced led them to the San Joaquin River, a ribbon of woodland winding across a wide level plain where wild horses and grizzly bears were seen in profusion. They found signs of white people: trees felled with axes, Indians with knives and blankets who were terrified of them.

> This night we encamped on the bank of the river in a very beautiful situation. Soon after the men went to rest and the camp had become quieted, we were startled by a loud, distant noise similar to that of thunder. While lying close to the ground this noise could be distinctly heard for a consider-able length of time without intermission . . . some of our men were much alarmed, as they readily supposed it was occasioned by an earthquake, and they began to fear that we would all be swallowed up in the bowels of the earth; and others judged it to be the noise of a neighboring cataract. Capt. Walker, however, suggested a more plausible cause, which allayed the fears of the most timid. He supposed that the noise originated by the Pacific rolling and dashing her boisterous waves against the rocky shore.

Actually, it probably was an earthquake or distant thunder, because they were still two days' ride from the coast.

Leonard goes on to describe another sight they would remember for the rest of their lives: thousands of meteors streaking across the sky, perhaps two hundred thousand in all, exploding in mid-air and sometimes "dashed to pieces on the ground."* The

---

* Once again there is confusion about dates. This meteor shower was the major celestial event of the nineteenth century. It could be seen all over the Northern

horses were terrified. So were the men, but again Walker talked them down—he comes across like a comforting father in Leonard's journal—and assured them there was no danger from the "falling of the stars."

The San Joaquin led them to Suisun Bay, an arm of San Francisco Bay, where naked Indians were fishing for shad and salmon. They turned south, riding over the future sites of Berkeley, Oakland, Hayward, San Jose. A day and a half later "the broad Pacific burst into view," and they rode on to "the extreme edge of the great west." Except for Joe Walker (during his time in Mississippi and Alabama, or perhaps Florida), none of them had seen an ocean before and they were mesmerized. Leonard tried to describe this extraordinary natural phenomenon: "Here was a smooth unbroken sheet of water stretched out far beyond the reach of the eye."

They camped at Año Nuevo Point and then went on down the coast. Now they saw an angry sea for the first time, heard the "deafening sound" of breakers crashing against the shore and came upon the carcass of a beached whale, which they measured at ninety feet. Far out to sea they caught sight of a ship and hoisted two white blankets to bring it to shore. As the ship came closer they saw to their amazement that the Stars and Stripes was flying from its masthead. The ship was the *Lagoda*, registered in Boston, trading in cowhides from the Californian ranches, and commanded by a "Captain Baggshaw" (actually Bradshaw), who insisted that his countrymen come aboard and broach a few flasks of cognac with him and his crew—"This was an invitation that none of us had the least desire to refuse."

The pitching and rolling of the boat and the incessant rounds of toasting were too much for Zenas Leonard, who left the party

---

Hemisphere, between midnight and dawn on November 13, 1833. According to Walker's tombstone, they were at Yosemite on that date. Leonard's book (the original journal has been lost) has them in the San Joaquin Valley three weeks after Yosemite, and on the brink of reaching the Pacific. There is suspicion among some scholars (Milo Milton Quaife, for one, another Western historian with a great name) that Leonard's editor rearranged events to create a more dramatic narrative: the heavens ablaze as the expedition reaches its historic finale.

sick and returned to shore. The rest carried on until dawn, celebrating the bridging of the continent.

Following Captain Bradshaw's advice, Walker went on with
two men to introduce himself to the Mexican authorities at
Monterey. Jedediah Smith had been thrown in jail on both trips
to California, mainly for being rude and arrogant—he lectured
the Mexicans on their slack morals and popish religion. Joe Walker
handled things more diplomatically, presenting himself to the
governor, showing the United States passport Bonneville had given
him and asking permission to stay the winter, trap and trade
beaver, and hunt enough game to keep his men fed. The governor
was impressed by Walker and granted permission, as long as they
stayed off Indian lands and didn't start any trouble.

With official blessing, Walker and his men were able to enjoy
the winter vacation of their lives. They went to the mission ranches
and found everything as advertised: hospitable padres with unlim-
ited supplies of wine and brandy, willing señoritas, docile Indians,
warm, sunny weather. They were dazzled by the horsemanship
and roping skills of the Mexican cowboys. Feasts and fiestas were
thrown in their honor. They were invited to bullfights, bear-bait-
ings and staged fights between bulls and grizzly bears. When they
felt restless they rode off to hunt and explore, and found the
valleys and oaklands teeming with game.

Six of the men decided to stay in California, and Joe Walker
thought about it seriously. The governor offered him thirty thousand acres of free land in northern California, wherever he liked,
if he would establish a colony of American "mechanics," or
craftsmen, which were sorely needed in California. Walker liked
the country and "had no doubt he could in a few years amass a
fortune, and be the head of a rich and flourishing settlement."

Despite these inducements, Walker turned the governor down.
He gathered up the remaining men, a huge herd of horses and
cattle, thirty dogs for an emergency food supply, and rode east,
finding an easier pass across the Sierra Nevada, recrossing the
Great Basin and delivering all his men safely into the 1834
rendezvous.

It is hard to think of another frontiersman who would have

refused such a golden opportunity to get rich. Leonard says Walker's decision was based on his "love for the laws and free institutions of the United States, and his hatred for those of the Spanish government." Bil Gilbert thinks this was patriotic embellishment by Leonard, or Leonard's editor, and certainly it raises an obvious question. If Walker was so enamored of American laws and institutions, why did he avoid them so assiduously and live so much of his life outside their jurisdiction?

The real problem with the governor's offer was that it meant settling down. It meant an end to his beloved explorations, an exchange of nomadic freedom for sedentary wealth and status. Over the next thirty years, as we shall see, Walker had several good opportunities to settle down and get rich, and he always chose to keep traveling.

Partly because a similar choice is fresh in my mind—I turned down a desk job with a British newspaper recently that would have quadrupled my annual income—I find Walker's refusal to be bribed away from his travels appealing and instructive.

The standard explanation of American restlessness is all about the prospect of getting rich. The horizontal, geographical mobility of Americans, I have read in half a dozen books, starting with Alexis de Tocqueville, is motivated by the hope of rising vertically in terms of wealth and social status. That was the main reason for the initial emigration from Europe and the habit stuck. And because there were fresh resources to be exploited in the West, for so much of the nation's history, enough of these migrations were successful to create a culture of optimism and a conviction that a better life lay over the next hill.

I have no quarrel with the validity of that argument, but it doesn't tell the whole story. It excludes most of the figures who catch my fancy in American history, who wandered above all for the simple pleasure and freedom of moving across the land. Faced with an opportunity to improve their economic situation in the settlements, they invariably turned it down, for the same reason they had left the settlements in the first place: it was an intolerably constrictive way to live.

De Tocqueville's argument might explain why the average modern American lives in fourteen different houses during his or her lifetime, but it doesn't explain those who eschew the whole idea of living in houses: a Mike Hatfield, a B.J. McHenry, a Medicine Man, a retired orthodontist in his three-hundred-thousand-dollar motor home. And though I hesitate to place him in the same company, it doesn't explain Joe Walker's wandering.

There is a diagnostic distinction to be made here between migrants and nomads. Migrants, to borrow a definition from the *Oxford English Dictionary*, move "from one place of residence to settle in another." Emigrants and refugees would fall under the same definition. The pioneers were migrants: farmers and small businessmen who traveled toward a destination with the intention of owning property there and making a better living. For many of them, the process of settlement didn't work out as they had hoped, and they moved on to try their luck in a new location. When migration becomes habitual, it can resemble and sometimes turn into nomadism, but until that point it remains a different form of restlessness.

Nomads reach a destination with no intention of settling there, or anywhere else. They regard fixed locations as resupply points, which allow the journey to continue, or as temporary harbors, in which to wait out bad weather. When travel becomes constant, it alters its meaning, at least in sedentary languages. It is no longer a trip away from somewhere. In a sense nomads never leave. They inhabit the same locations: trail and campfire, interstate highway and motel room. It is only when the rhythm of travel is halted that the nomad experiences a change and upheaval in circumstances. The nomad does not feel stable when stationary. To borrow Deleuze and Guattari's definition, he only feels stable when experiencing velocity.

CHAPTER 7

Almost one hundred and fifty years have passed since trapping beaver was an important industry in the West. Compared to later industries—mining, timber, agriculture, energy, defense, tourism—all the furs ever taken west of the hundredth meridian are barely a dot on the West's economic map . . . The story of the mountain men, on the other hand, has had a tremendous impact on the West's mental map, an impact out of all proportion to the historical importance of the fur trade. The story of the mountain men has affected the western mind directly, as is evidenced by the fascination with mountain men that continues to this day. The story of the mountain man has also affected the western mind indirectly through its reincarnations in the story of the cowboy, the ranger, the logger, the Hell's Angel, the monkey wrencher—or whatever tough, untamed character catches the western imagination.

Maguire, Wild and Barclay (eds.), *A Rendezvous Reader*

I was in Pinedale, Wyoming, doing some research at the Museum of the Mountain Man, visiting the Green River rendezvous site (a plaque, a small fenced-in grove of cottonwoods, a dilapidated outhouse), and running away from deep feelings of instability at home. I had just set an eight-year record, spending twenty-nine consecutive nights in the same bed, and it had turned into a prolonged and intractable bout of insomnia. I had heard about this syndrome on the road—the inability to sleep after two or three weeks in the same location—but I had never experienced it before, probably because I hadn't crossed the three-week threshold in so long.

The best defense against insomnia, according to medical opinion, is a fixed daily routine with regular hours, regular meals and regular exercise. To know in advance what the day holds in store, to live within the same set of visual references and social relationships: this is supposed to make you feel stable and "grounded," and promote orderly sleep patterns. In my case, of course, it had precisely the opposite effect, producing insomnia where none had existed before. And sure enough, after a rambling eighteen-hundred-mile road trip to Pinedale, fueled by irregular meals, random encounters and ever-changing scenery, I was cured and sleeping eight hours a night in the back of my truck. This, I suppose, was the routine I had fixed for myself over the years.

I liked Pinedale, a small, no-nonsense Wyoming town on the edge of the Green River plain, overshadowed by the high, sculpted peaks of the Wind River Mountains. I spent a day hiking up there, in the exposed valleys below the peaks, and that was it exactly: a river of wind. In the 1830s this was the heart of the Rocky Mountain fur country. Beaver was plentiful in the mountains, buffalo roamed the plain, the Shoshonis or Snakes (now on a reservation east of the mountains) were usually hospitable and eager to trade. Six rendezvous were held in the vicinity of present-day Pinedale, and more so than anywhere else the mountain men thought of this place as home. Now it ekes out a living from ranching, farming and seasonal tourism—sightseers in summer, hunters in the fall, a few die-hard snowmobilers in winter, when the temperature gets down to forty and sometimes sixty below zero.

The town greets its visitors with a carved wooden sign: "Welcome to Pinedale—All The Civilization You Need." Eight motels, three bars, three cafés, a couple of gas stations, a campground with cheap showers and laundry machines. Population: 1181 and falling. There were boarded-up storefronts on Main Street, and no Wal-Mart or Super Kmart nearby to take the blame.

When I arrived Pinedale was gearing up for its major economic and cultural event of the year: a long weekend of costumed parades, amateur theatricals, rodeos, barbecues, live music shows and other events known under the rubric of Rendezvous Days. Tourists were checking into the motels. Vendors were setting up souvenir stands on Main Street. Local volunteers were stringing up banners, ribbons and pennants, which flapped and rattled in the wind.

Outside the Museum of the Mountain Man, where I was ensconced in the archives, tracking down references to Joe Walker, a ramshackle fleet of camper vans, road-beaten RVs and live-in pickup trucks began to assemble in the parking lot. Tepees went up on a grassy flat behind the museum, and then a row of trading stalls, with their goods displayed on blankets and deerhides—Indian jewelry, animal skulls and antlers, antique knives, beads and powder horns, buckskin pouches, beaded moccasins, fake eagle feathers, scenes of the Old West painted and shellacked onto pieces of log. Serendipity of the road: this was a group of American nomads I had never encountered before.

The first trader I talked to was a lean, bearded, long-haired man in his early forties, chewing tobacco and spitting the juice into a beer bottle. He was wearing moccasins, a breechclout, a buckskin waistcoat and a braided buckskin headband—no shirt, no trousers or leggings. Behind him was a sign written on a piece of deerhide: "Howling Wolf Custom Mountain Man & Indian Articles." Lying at his feet was what looked to be a full-grown, pure-blooded wolf. Both wolf and owner regarded me with pale and exceptionally piercing blue eyes.

I introduced myself and asked him how he was doing. "Fine as frog's hair," came the jovial reply. "I'm Howling Wolf, and this here is Blue. He's got some malamute in him but he's mostly timber wolf. I'm a quarter Cherokee* just trying to keep the old ways alive." He was talking in general historical terms here: the

---

* Howling Wolf may well be telling the truth, but the claim of a "quarter Cherokee" automatically arouses suspicion, especially when applied to themselves by pale-faced, blue-eyed people. As Vine Deloria and other Indian writers have pointed out, an unsupportable percentage of whites claiming Indian heritage do so through the Cherokee tribe—considered the best-looking and most civilized tribe by nineteenth-century whites.

ways of the Rocky Mountain fur-trade era, rather than the Cherokee tribe, who never participated in it. (The Cherokee were farmers and hunters from southern Appalachia, forcibly removed to Oklahoma in the 1830s.)

Howling Wolf took me over to his tepee. It was made of canvas and had a blue wolf's head painted on the side. "You see the way I've got the poles set up?" he said. "This is a Lakota-style lodge. Some guys do a Crow lodge, some prefer a Cheyenne. Whatever suits you, I guess. Anyway, this is home."

He keeps a house in Wyoming and spends most of the winter there, making his jewelry and other "articles." For the rest of the year he travels a circuit of mountain man heritage festivals and rendezvous re-enactments, selling and bartering his goods, living in his tepee and wearing his moccasins and breechclout. "I'll go into restaurants and supermarkets dressed like this," he told me. "Hell, I'll walk into any shitkicker bar in Wyoming in my breech-clout. I always get a powerful reaction. The women love it. The men don't on the whole, but I haven't gotten my ass kicked yet."

There are maybe fifty thousand people in America who get dressed up in fur-trade regalia and attend rendezvous re-enactments, and they call themselves "buckskinners."* The great majority of them are part-time hobbyists, who work a regular job and go to re-enactment events on weekends and vacations. It is only the full-time traders, perhaps three hundred people in total, who live as nomads. And like Howling Wolf, most of them spend a portion of the winter at a fixed base, much as the orig-inal mountain men would wait out the snows in a winter camp: a rough-hewn log cabin in a sheltered mountain valley, or a tepee within an Indian encampment.

"There's not a lot of trapping beaver or horse-stealing or scalping going on these days, and I use a pickup truck instead of a horse and pack mule, but the life is not that different," said Howling Wolf. "I'm traveling through the same country, camping at a lot of the authentic sites, wearing the same kind of clothes,

---

* There is also a thriving buckskinner scene in Germany and the Czech Republic.

and trading the same kind of goods. Actually, a lot of people are buying my stuff online now. Isn't that a trip? A mountain man with a Web site."

Now the crowds were arriving: tourists, locals, visiting buckskinners. Howling Wolf and the other traders were besieged with customers and too busy to talk. I wandered over to a makeshift bar, which had been set up by the museum's front entrance, and there I fell in with a buckskinner who gave his name as Black Kettle. He was a big, corpulent, extroverted character, with a fake eyepatch and a gray beard turning white. He was wearing a high-crowned beaver-felt hat, a period hunting shirt, green riding britches with a leather seat, black leather boots and a string of antique trade beads around his neck. I asked him about his outfit. How come he wasn't wearing buckskins?

"Wagh!" he roared. "This hoss sold his plews[*] in St. Louis and outfitted himself with some fancy store-bought duds. Now he's come back upriver to the mountains and he aims to shine. A season's trapping and these clothes will be wore out. Like as not, this hoss'll be back in his buckskins." Then his accent, and his idiom, reverted to contemporary Wyoming: "Everything I've got on is totally authentic 1830s/1840s gear. See these beads? They were manufactured in Venice, Italy, in the early 1800s. These are the same beads that the mountain men would trade with the Indians."

With Black Kettle was a man calling himself Dead Cloud (a pun on the great Lakota chief Red Cloud), who was dressed as an Appalachian Long Hunter from the 1780s. He showed me his knife, which was manufactured by a company that went bankrupt in 1789. "Dressing up is a big part of it, getting the right clothes and the right guns and all the accessories, but it goes deeper than that," he said. "We model ourselves after those guys, and try to live up to the same principles, as far as it's possible in the modern world: self-reliance, honor, independence, an appreciation for being out in wild nature, whether you're hunting, fishing, camping or whatever."

---

[*] Mountain man slang for beaver pelts.

I wanted to know if any buckskinners went off to live in the wild, hunting and foraging for food, and dispensing with the twentieth century entirely. "There's a few of us who know how to survive in the mountains with a rifle and a knife, and a flint-and-steel [for starting fires], but it's a different deal nowadays," said Dead Cloud. "You don't have to worry about skylining your-self on a ridge, where the Blackfeet might see you, and there's hardly any grizzlies left. And if something does go wrong, help is only thirty miles away. Back then, it was a thousand or fifteen hundred miles away, on the other side of the Mississippi. You'll meet a lot of buckskinners who say they were born a hundred and fifty years too late, but there's not one of us in a thousand who would have made it back then."

Dead Cloud is a salaried engineer who works on rocket nozzles for the space shuttle at a plant in Wyoming and attends buck-skinner events in his spare time. Black Kettle does a little carpentry and house fixing when his money runs thin, but he travels and trades on the circuit for most of the year and "lives out of a mailbox." He must have been in his mid-fifties when I met him, with no savings, property or pension plan. In the usual nomadic style, he had invested all his money in portable forms of wealth and status. Year by year he upgrades his outfit, acquiring ever more valuable and authentic clothing, knives, pistols, blackpowder rifles, jewelry and accessories. His most prized possession, which he wasn't wearing that day, is a string of "Lewis and Clark" beads worth five thousand dollars—authenticated as the same type and vintage as the ones Lewis and Clark took up the Missouri in 1804 to trade with the Indians, and conceivably the actual beads themselves.

At sunset, the miniature rendezvous outside the museum began to drift apart, and we continued our discussions in a downtown bar. The place was packed and roaring. The waitresses, young and elderly alike, were dressed up as Old West saloon girls, in frills and corsets and lace-up, high-heel boots, and not looking happy about it. We staked out a table in the corner and swooped down when its occupants left.

Now came the rounds of whiskey shots and beer chasers, the

intense, insistent conversations, eyeball to wavering eyeball, the melting away of time to the point where all stories are told in the present tense, even if they happened 180 years ago. Black Kettle and Dead Cloud were puzzled by my enthusiasm for Joe Walker, who is an obscure figure in the buckskin literature, mainly because he had no interest in bragging about his exploits to journalists, traveling diarists, dime-store novelists or anyone else who might have publicized them. They had vaguely heard of him—a good man apparently, went to California early on—but what about Jim Bridger, or Tom Fitzpatrick, or Kit Carson, or Jed Smith, the front-line celebrities of the fur trade? What about John Colter, who went west with Lewis and Clark and stayed on to trap beaver and become the first mountain man? Dead Cloud told the story of his famous escape from the Blackfeet in 1808.

So there's Colter, naked, unarmed and barefoot, surrounded by a hundred angry Blackfeet warriors. They have just killed his only partner, hacked him into pieces and flung his organs and entrails in Colter's face. He braces himself for death by torture but the chief decides to give him a sporting chance: a hundred-yard head start in a foot-race for his life. Colter takes off sprinting, barefoot across the cactus-studded prairie, pursued by a party of howling warriors with spears.

Colter is an exceptionally fast runner (although he told the Blackfeet otherwise), and after two or three miles only one warrior is still in close pursuit. Colter wheels around, grabs his spear, and kills him. He runs on for another three miles, reaches a river (the Jefferson or the Madison), dives in and hides underneath a pile of driftwood while the Blackfeet search the banks. The next morning he sneaks away and starts east for Manuel Lisa's trading fort on the Yellowstone, three hundred miles away. Still naked and barefoot, eating roots and tree bark to stay alive, he gets there in eleven days.

That set off a round of hairsbreadth escape stories: Joe Meek killing a grizzly with his knife, Kit Carson and a few of the boys fighting off two hundred Comanches from behind a breastwork of dead horses. Hugh Glass is horribly mauled by a grizzly on the upper Missouri, left for dead by his companions and stripped of his rifle, knife and flint-and-steel. He regains consciousness and lies there for ten days, eating berries from a branch overhanging his head and drinking from a spring next to him. Then he starts crawling east, making only a few hundred yards a day at first. It takes him a couple of months, feeding on roots, berries and rotting buffalo carcasses, but he manages to drag himself across half of South Dakota and make it into Fort Kiowa.

Amazing stories, verifiably true stories (except for a few disputed details), and none of them about Joe Walker. As far as we know, crossing the Sierra Nevada in 1833 was the worst scrape he ever got into, and that left him without much kudos in this conversation. Walker's great talent was for avoiding scrapes. He was a master of not getting men killed in dangerous places. Twenty-six of Jed Smith's men died on the way to California and back, but Walker accomplished the same trip without losing a man.

As the evening progressed, a spirit of aching nostalgia came over the table, allied with a maudlin conviction that the modern world was insufferably dull, tame and regimented by comparison. Sure it was a hard life back then, a dangerous, brutal life, and granted most of the mountain men died young and never got out of debt, but think of the rewards: to roam a million square miles of wilderness in all its primordial splendor, living by your wits and skills, free of all laws, responsibilities and social constraints, moving on from one adventure to the next. There was no doubt in our minds that this was the purest and most absolute freedom ever experienced in America, or anywhere else.

Whiskey lends itself to bold statements, untroubled by exceptions, caveats, qualifications. We dismissed the trail cowboys of the open range as a bunch of lowly hired hands who spent too much time breathing dust and staring at the rear end of a cow. Most cowboys didn't even own the horse they rode and there was no exploring left to do because the mountain men had done it all. We dismissed Indians, even nomadic horse Indians: too many obligations to tribal band and extended family; too many supernatural powers to fear and appease; no exploring left to do because their ancestors had done it all.

I might flesh out that last clause, sitting here at sober remove.

Indians traveled old, established trails for the most part, without the illusion of discovery and newness that the mountain men conjured for themselves on the same trails, even when explicitly following Indian directions, or Indian guides, into "undiscovered country" and "virgin wilderness." At that point in their history the Western tribes had no linguistic concept of wilderness, no point of comparison with sedentary civilization, nowhere to escape from or into, and therefore a lesser appreciation of their freedom than the mountain men had for theirs. It wasn't until the tribes saw how life was lived in the encroaching white settlements, and realized what they had to lose, that they were stirred into their glorious flights of oratory about nomadic freedom.

The mountain men themselves certainly thought they had reached the apogee of personal freedom and adventure. It was their reflex justification under questioning by traveling diarists and writers, and by themselves in their journals and memoirs. They were not a reflective breed on the whole, but they under-stood their alternatives well enough: jail perhaps, a desk job or more likely a life on the farm. Hoeing corn, slopping hogs, split-ting wood, mending fences, trudging along behind a plough and a farting mule, with an overworked wife in the kitchen, babies squalling with the colic and dying of diphtheria—that was how they characterized it. That was the benchmark against which they measured their freedom. A year in the mountains, went the camp-fire axiom, was like a lifetime in the settlements.

None of us at that table wanted to picture himself on the farm. Hell no, we would have been at the campfire. And the danger, the hardship, the reduced life expectancy? That was an integral part of it, inseparable from the adventure and the feeling of wildness that the mountain men cherished. It was a life they chose without illusions, and celebrated in their stories, and mourned when it was gone, because nothing else made them feel so free and so intensely alive. Or so we declaimed, ignoring exceptions like Zenas Leonard, who was only too glad to get back to the security of the settlements after his adventures with Joe Walker.

And then, as if it had just happened yesterday and the outrage was fresh in his mind, Dead Cloud began thumping the table and bellowing about the Chinese. He was half-joking, half-serious and about three-quarters drunk: "The goddamn Chinese, it's all their fault! Who else would've thought to milk a goddamn caterpillar? We should nuke those Commie bastards for what they done!"

In the mid-1830s a story began circulating at rendezvous. Its details were probably apocryphal, but in broad, symbolic terms the story explained why the fur trade was going to hell. A French duke had lost his beaver-felt hat while visiting China. Unable to find a replacement, he had ordered a Chinese hatter to make a similar model out of silk. When the duke returned to France, his hat created an instant fashion sensation. Paris fops wept with envy and rushed out to scream at their hatters. "Silk! How dare you insult me with this dowdy old beaver felt?" The cry reached London, where Beau Brummell heard it. Then Milan, Montreal, New York and so on.

There is no record of the French duke in China, but it is true that a fashion craze for silk hats, starting in Paris and London, devastated the global market for beaver furs and created a corresponding boom in Chinese silk production. In 1833 a prime beaver pelt brought six dollars at rendezvous (and that was down from eight dollars a few years before). By 1840 it was down to four dollars and the mountain men were looking around for a new line of work. Some hired on as scouts and guides for the emigrant wagon trains and the army. Some, like Joe Meek, went to the settlements and attained a measure of respectability and political influence. Others drifted into crime or drank themselves to death in frontier saloons, telling tall stories in return for drinks.

Like the Gold Rush, the buffalo-hide bonanza and the cattle-baron era that followed it, the Rocky Mountain fur-trade boom lasted less than thirty years. And regardless of hat fashions, it wouldn't have lasted much longer. The animal on which the trade depended was close to extinction. The silk hat was invented just in time. For all their Indianish traits, the mountain men went after the beaver with all the raw, rapacious, ransacking energy of expanding white America, which had already consumed most of the furs east of the Mississippi. They "trapped out" a stream, or attempted to, and then moved on to the next one.*

Eight or nine hundred mountain men, with some help from the tribes, managed to decimate beaver populations from the Missouri to the Pacific, from Canada to Mexico—a million square miles—and most of the trapping was done in a twenty-year period, between 1820 and 1840. When Lewis and Clark came into the West, the beaver was diurnal and watched them with curiosity from the riverbanks. Under pressure of trapping, the animal became nocturnal and extremely wary.

During the 1840s there were still remnant beaver populations in isolated areas, but it was no longer profitable for the fur companies to send large, well-equipped trapping brigades after them. Nor was it profitable to resupply them in the field: the last rendezvous was held in 1840, fifteen years after the first. It was cheaper to let the Indians trap (and hopefully sustain) the remaining beavers and trade with them directly, or through a handful of mountain men who had established bartering relationships with the tribes.

Jim Bridger traded with the Shoshonis from his posts in Utah and Wyoming. The Bent brothers traded with the Cheyenne and Arapaho from their adobe castle on the Arkansas River in southern Colorado, and Kit Carson dealt with the same tribes in the field. Jim Beckwourth, the black mountain man, lived with the Crows and brokered their furs, and Bill Williams took up a similar station with the Utes.

Joe Walker based himself with the eastern Shoshoni, the Snakes, in the upper Green River country, but he did a great deal more traveling than any of the other middleman fur traders, ranging from the central Rockies as far west as California. He traded with Crows in Montana, Bannocks and Utes in Utah, Paiutes in Nevada,

---

* By contrast, the British fur interests in Oregon and Canada, operating through the Hudson Bay Company and using Indian trappers, tried to leave enough beaver to ensure a steady, renewable harvest in the future—a policy that collapsed when mountain men appeared in their territory.

Navajos and Apaches in Arizona and Mexican ranchers in California. He was the only mountain man who managed to increase the free-roaming independence and license to explore they had enjoyed in the boom years. Walker led the first party of whites to cross the Great Basin from Sevier Lake to the Virgin River, the first to see the canyons and waterfalls of the upper Virgin River and the first into certain parts of northern Arizona. Unfortunately, Zenas Leonard had gone back to the settlements in Missouri, so we have no extended, firsthand accounts of Walker's life for this period (or indeed, for the next thirty years).

He crops up from time to time in fur company ledgers, bills of sale at trading posts, brief entries in travelers' journals and occasional newspaper stories. He always seemed to have a herd of horses to sell, or a pack-train laden with furs or trade goods for the Indians—whatever the market would pay for, whatever it took to stay on the move. On the Pacific coast he traded furs to the Mexicans for abalone shells and then headed back across the Great Basin, trading the shells with the tribes along the way for more furs and skins—an echo of Cabeza de Vaca's years as a wandering trader in Texas in an expanded, equestrian age.

Horses were the mainstay of Walker's trading business. He bought his herds from the Mexican ranches around Los Angeles and drove them east to Santa Fe (800 miles), Bent's Fort, Colorado (1100 miles), Fort Laramie, Wyoming (1200 miles), and sometimes all the way back to Missouri (1800 miles). If you retrace Walker's trails today, especially in the Mojave and the Great Basin, it seems unfathomable that he was able to cross such barren deserts with so many horses. Even allowing for cattle overgrazing, there is so little vegetation and so few rivers, streams and springs.

Walker had mastered a set of skills known to desert nomads all over the world, whether they were driving camels, cattle, sheep, goats or horses. Knowing where in a dry streambed to dig for water. How to locate a waterhole by the flight patterns of birds, or a distant patch of grazing by the droppings of migrating wildlife. When and where to rest the herd. When to drive them to the point of exhaustion and collapse, accepting the death of twenty animals in order to reach a stream dying out in the sand fifty miles away. When to cut open a horse's neck and revive a failing man with its blood, and do it in such a way that the horse survives.

Between trading expeditions, when opportunity presented itself and the urge took him, Walker pursued other means of travel and exploration. He guided the first pioneer wagon trains into California and blazed a new wagon trail to get them there. It skirted present-day Walker Lake, connected with the Walker River, and crossed the Sierra Nevada at Walker Pass. Arguably, he left a deeper impression on American maps than American history books. Most of this trail, like so many others first "discovered" by Joe Walker (or, more accurately, pieced together from existing Indian trails), is now a state highway.

In 1844, he hired on as a scout for John Charles Frémont of the US Army topographical corps, a great publicist and popular hero of Western expansion, who declared himself "The Pathfinder" while Joe Walker led him along trails the mountain men had been using for twenty years or more. Walker soon became disgusted by Frémont's self-promoting histrionics and rank cowardice in the field—a combination he found particularly loathsome. They parted company on bad terms and thereby Walker shunned his best opportunity to become an American legend. Frémont seized on the younger, more impressionable Kit Carson for his guide and, by fraudulent prose and a government-sponsored publicity machine, succeeded in turning himself and Carson into heroic frontier explorers and nationwide celebrities.

Meanwhile, Joe Walker was off making genuine explorations, filling in the last gaps on his extraordinary mental map of the American West and fading deeper into obscurity.

Following Black Kettle's advice and directions, I drove south from Pinedale, three hundred miles across the high plains to the flyspeck town of Hamilton, Colorado, and then ten miles up a dirt road into the mountains. I parked the truck and walked up to the gatekeepers of the Rocky Mountain National Rendezvous. This was the big one, Black Kettle had reiterated, "the World Series of buckskinning, the Super Bowl, the goddamn Olympics."

I stood there at the entry booth in jeans, a denim shirt and moccasins—the best outfit I could muster on short notice—and was given a look that I remembered from the doorways of fashionable London nightclubs.

"The moccasins are okay, but there's no way you're coming in here with the rest of it." This was a hard-faced woman in her late forties, wearing some kind of homespun pioneer smock and sunbonnet. A tall, gray-bearded man in fringed buckskins, leaning on a long blackpowder rifle, gave me the once-over and grinned. "Hell, all you've got to do is ditch the jeans and the shirt, take off your drawers and borrow a breechclout from someone. You'll be a big hit with the ladies." Another woman, also in period dress, took pity on me: "Don't worry, hon. We'll find you some britches and a hunting shirt to borrow. There's some nylon in the stitching of your moccasins but we can let that slide."

In lace-up corduroy britches and a blue linen hunting shirt, kindly donated by a man who weighs a hundred pounds more than I do, I paid my twenty dollars and walked up the trail. It was maybe a quarter-mile long, with a moderately steep uphill grade, and provoked terrible complaints from the portly, wheezing buckskinners alongside me: "Jesus H . . . Steep sonofabitch . . . *Whoof*, I got to sit down and take me a breather."

The trail crested out on a small rise and there below, in a mountain meadow with a stream flowing through it, fed by a small alpine lake, was a near-perfect replica of a rendezvous from the 1830s. There were hundreds of tepees, two long traders' rows of old-fashioned, boxy canvas tents and, by the official count, eighteen hundred people milling around in buckskins and period garb, and more arriving.

Every few seconds the air would reverberate with an enormous *BOOM!* Authentic reproduction cannons were launching bowling balls into the lake, which floated for easy retrieval by the authentic replica canoes. *Ratta . . . tat . . . TAT . . . KERBLOOM!* That was the sound from the blackpowder rifle–shooting contests, as you walked toward them with a lingering hangover. *Thonk! Schwap! Schoonk!* That was the sound of tomahawks and throwing knives, embedding themselves in target stakes and luckless trees.

When a replica strives so hard to be authentic, the eye is naturally drawn toward its failures. Plastic portable toilets, "hooters," were concealed within canvas enclosures. People were pouring their beers and Cokes into antique mugs or drinking horns and then stashing the empty cans in burlap sacks. There were propane stoves in some of the tepees, and God bless America, there were copious supplies of ice. It came in plastic-wrapped ten-pound bags, hauled up the road by an enormous container truck twice a day and delivered into the rendezvous by horse-drawn wagon, whereupon it was poured into plastic coolers, hidden inside wooden boxes, or draped with blankets or deerhides.

From time to time a group of Indians would ride by on horseback, in full plains regalia, and a couple of them had Indian features under their face paint. Otherwise, it was an entirely white crowd, from a broad mix of occupations and social backgrounds: doctors, lawyers, business people, bureaucrats, engineers, mechanics, beauticians, oil-field roughnecks, construction workers, waitresses, housewives, hunting guides, a noticeable minority of Vietnam veterans. All age groups were represented, from small babies to elderly retirees, but most people were in their forties and fifties, with the men outnumbering the women about three to two.

With a few exceptions, most notably a small German contingent, they were Westerners from the inter-mountain states— Colorado, Utah, Wyoming, Montana, Nevada, New Mexico and Arizona—and the traditional attitudes of the region held sway: love of guns, hunting and fishing; suspicion of the federal government and the coastal elites; a wariness of outsiders, outweighed by a strong code of hospitality. As a lone Brit in an ill-fitting costume bearing no weapons of any kind, I must have cut a strange and jarring figure. I received a few hostile glances and cutting remarks, but on the whole, people were welcoming and extraordinarily generous. They offered me food and drink, better-fitting clothes, a place by their campfires and floor space in their tepees at night.

I was expecting a wealth of amateur historians, with an encyclopedic knowledge of the fur trade and fresh insights to borrow, but the first twenty people I talked to had never heard of Joe Walker. Reading history books, it turned out, was not a popular pastime among American buckskinners. Their information came primarily from buckskinner magazines, videotapes and how-to manuals, which went into fanatical detail about the clothing, firearms and equipment of the fur trade, and dealt with the history in potted two-hundred-word biographies, brief anecdotes and did-you-know? trivia corners. The same balance of priorities was reflected in rendezvous conversations, which revolved around shopping and gear. The biggest, hairiest, wildest-looking men, swaggering around in grimy buckskins, bristling with guns and knives, were capable of impassioned forty-minute dialogues about historically correct needlework and beading patterns.

"Basically, rendezvous these days is an excuse to get dressed up, go on a camping trip and have a big swap meet." This was the judgement of Lance Grabowski, delivered from his tent on the far fringe of traders' row. His tone was jaded and sardonic: rendezvous was dumbing down and there was nothing you could do about it. Style was replacing substance, knowledge and commitment were giving way to empty posturing. Rendezvous re-enactments were a version of something to begin with and now they were becoming a version of a version.

"What you get now is a lot of this 'Wagh! I ar a mountain man!' attitude from people who are totally out of shape, and don't know what they're talking about, because they never pick up a book. I don't get it. If they're into mountain men, you'd think they'd want to *read* about mountain men, but apparently it doesn't work that way any more."

Fifty years old, with long, graying hair pulled back into a pony-tail, a walrus mustache and wire-rimmed antique spectacles, Lance was self-educated and enormously well read about the Rocky Mountain fur trade. He used to supplement his income as a rendezvous trader by lecturing at fur-trade museums and histor-ical sites. There was a look of quiet, keen intensity about him. He moved well, with a calm, purposeful efficiency, and you could tell he was good with his hands. He was wearing ten thousand dollars' worth of beaded, fringed buckskin clothes and accessories, most of which he had made himself, and he was living out of a 1983 Chevy van with eight hundred thousand miles on the clock, running on its fifth engine.

Lance Grabowski was the first buckskinner to become a full-time, nomadic trader. This was back in the late 1960s and early 1970s, when buckskinning was in its infancy and the first rendezvous re-enactments were taking place. The mountain men had lain dormant in the American imagination for many decades, and Lance, with his long hair, breechclout and buckskins, was often mistaken in the early days for a blond Indian with a beard, or a hippie who needed his ass kicked. Except hippies weren't supposed to carry guns and knives and act belligerent when threatened.

He started out trading buffalo hides and skulls. He bought them at a buffalo ranch in Nebraska and sold them at swap meets, flea markets and the emerging circuit of rendezvous re-enactments. Through the 1970s and 1980s the circuit expanded from coast to coast, and Lance traveled it full time, with no fixed abode. He has read and thought a great deal about nomadism, in the American West and Central Asia, and he remembers those years as a kind of nomadic idyll. "My truck was my armchair, and the country was my house. The different parts of the country were like different rooms in my house. Oh, it's October, the fall colors will be coming out in upstate New York. Let's go to that room. I never got bored. When I'm on the road I'm home, I'm happy."

Lance had just returned to the rendezvous circuit after an unhappy experiment with a more sedentary lifestyle. It was partly his own idea and partly his ex-girlfriend's urging. He bought some land south of Santa Fe, New Mexico, and built them a house—a lovely place out in the hills, filled with antiques, buffalo hides and fur-trade accoutrements, and a huge library of books. Now he had split up with his girlfriend and the house had become a ten-ton albatross around his neck. "Within twenty-four hours of getting back there I'm either angry or depressed, and I can't wait to leave. I'd like to sell it, but where would I put all my stuff? I don't know what I'm going to do. Realistically, I'll probably hang on to it and spend as little time there as possible. Either that or sell the fucking thing and go to Mongolia."

For fifteen years, on and off, he has been talking about making a four-thousand-mile horse trip across the steppes from Russia to Mongolia. He figures that Mongolia—a vast, unfenced expanse of plains, deserts and mountains still inhabited by horse nomads—is as close as he's going to get to Wyoming in the 1820s, which is where he really wants to be.

Lance was one of two people I stayed in touch with from that rendezvous. The other was George Jackson,* an elk-hunting guide, former oil-field roughneck and hydro-plant caretaker from the backcountry of northeast Utah. George had ten thousand dollars saved up and a plane ticket to Mongolia when his ex-girlfriend announced that she was pregnant. He bought a house in Vernal, Utah, and knuckled down to his responsibilities. Two years later she went off with another man and left him to raise his daughter on his own.

George gets a little testy on the subject of his daughter's mother, but he retains a slightly bruised faith in women, love and long-term relationships. Lance is more jaundiced on the subject, and at that rendezvous he was feeling more jaundiced than usual. Every two days he would have to drive into town and call his lawyer. His ex-girlfriend had tried and failed to sue him for palimony (they had no children together). Then she charged him with physical abuse, which had led to three years of Kafka-esque legal maneuvers that had cost him seventy thousand dollars to date. (When the case finally made it to court, the judge threw it out for lack of evidence. Representing herself, the ex-girlfriend produced no police or medical reports, no paperwork of any kind.)

In his darker moods Lance sees the hand of feminism at work in his recurrent girlfriend troubles. "It's making women neurotic and unhappy. It's turning them into Prozac fodder. I can't figure out why a man would want to work in an office all day and climb some corporate ladder, let alone a woman. You'd think raising children would be more fulfilling."

---

* He is directly descended from the famous Scotch-Irish mountain man David Jackson, for whom Jackson Hole, Wyoming, is named.

In Lance's perfect world there would be a lot more women who liked living in vans and tents—specifically sane, intelligent, good-looking women in their thirties and forties, whom he sees in woefully short supply on the American road. In the late 1970s he got a taste of his ideal relationship: three years on the road with Susan. Both of them were making buckskin clothes and handicrafts and selling them on the rendezvous circuit. She was earning her keep, she liked being outdoors and on the road. They were happy and in love, and Lance "basically screwed it up, by never accepting the possibility that it was going to last." Since then the biggest source of friction in his relationships with women has been the road.

"Apart from Susan, all of them have had kids or steady jobs. They can't take off on the road with me and they don't want to, and I don't blame them, but sooner or later they get fed up with me coming and going all the time. They're not used to having boyfriends like that, and they think boyfriends aren't supposed to behave that way. Even though they piss and moan about the guys who stay home and watch football every Sunday, and bring home a steady pay check, that's what they're used to, that's what they're comfortable with."

Now, by journalistic convention, I should track down Lance's ex-girlfriends and get their side of the story. But instead I will hazard a guess and quote some of my own ex-girlfriends on the subject of wandering males: they make poor long-term prospects. They are unreliable and irresponsible. They have issues with emotional commitment, especially settling down and having kids. The road can be fun for a while but not forever.

There is no statistical evidence about the ratio of men to women living full time on the American road because so many of them, male and female, live beyond the reach of statistical inquiry. Their defining quality, mobility, makes them extremely hard to count. Judging from personal experience, and backed up by Lance and other informal sources, I would say the men outnumber the women by about twelve to one. And the vast majority of those women are either under the age of twenty-five, or over the age of sixty, traveling with the RV crowd.

Why so few women? As the age breakdown suggests, a major factor is the difficulty of bringing up children on the road. It is not a prospect that many women find appealing, and there is immense pressure from the education authorities to place the child in a sedentary environment. It can be circumvented legally in most Western states by homeschooling, even if your home is a vehicle. I have met traveling hippie couples with children, some homeschooled, some off the records completely. I have met migrant workers whose children go to six different schools a year. And Mike Hatfield told us about husband-and-wife trucking teams, homeschooling their children between turns at the wheel.

Can we agree that women are more oriented toward child-rearing than men, in a biological sense? I think we can, even though we have all met exceptions. And deeply ingrained in our culture is the idea that a child needs a stable home environment. We talk about settling down and having children in the same breath.

Is there a nesting instinct in women? A natural female affinity for hearth and home? Absolutely not. Looking back over human history, it is clear that these are social constructs, peculiar to sedentary cultures. Among tribal nomads and traveling gypsies, as Bruce Chatwin points out in *The Songlines*, it is usually the women who keep their men on the road, away from the temptations and corrupting influences of the settlements, and women who insist on bringing up the children in the traditional, nomadic way. "Women, above all, are the guardians of continuity," he writes, "if the hearth moves, they move with it."

To illustrate the point, he quotes a grumbling nomad sheikh, encountered in the sand dunes of Mauritania, who sounds like a reluctant girlfriend dragged off on a camping trip: "I'd like nothing better than to live in a house in town. Here in the desert you can't keep clean. You can't take a shower! It's the women who make us live in the desert. They say the desert brings health and happiness, to them and to the children."

At the rendezvous of 1837 a young artist from Baltimore called Alfred Jacob Miller was in attendance, sketching furiously, trying to capture the wild, romantic, sublime wonder of it all. One of those sketches became a painting entitled *Bourgeois W—r, & his Squaw*. Bourgeois (pronounced *booshway*) was another word for a field commander, W—r was Joe Walker (no one knows why Miller disguised his name), and the squaw was Joe Walker's wife. A young teenage girl, with a broad face and twin braids, dressed up in full Shoshoni frippery, she is riding a decorated pony behind the shaggy, imposing figure of her new husband.

We have another sketch by Adolph Wislizenus, a German traveler who encountered Walker, the veteran fur man Andrew Drips and their Indian wives in the Wind River Mountains.

> The two squaws, quite passable as to their features, appeared in highest state. Their red blankets, with the silk kerchiefs on their heads, and their gaudy embroideries, gave them quite an Oriental appearance. Like themselves, their horses were bedight with embroideries, beads, corals, ribbons, and little bells. The bells were hung about in such number that when riding in their neighborhood, one might think one's self in the midst of Turkish music. The squaws, however, behaved most properly. They took care of the horses, pitched a tent, and were alert for every word of their wedded lords.

We don't know the name of Walker's wife, and we can only speculate in the broadest terms about their marriage. From her perspective, a white chieftain trader like Joe Walker would have been a prestigious catch, and also a risky one. Whites were considered to be more generous and romantic with their wives than Indian men (who thought white notions of romantic love were amusingly silly). And their exotic physical appearance—beards, body hair, blue eyes—sometimes added a frisson of sexual excitement, just as the otherness of Indian women excited some mountain men. The risk lay in the fact that white husbands were more likely to abandon their wives and children than Indian husbands. Tribal society produced very few loners, a type that was common among the mountain men.

From the perspective of Joe Walker and his contemporaries,

the single greatest attraction of Indian women was their gender. In 1836, when he married his wife, there were no white women west of the Missouri settlements. In New Mexico and California there were Mexican women, but on the whole they lacked the endurance, skills and experience to make good trail wives. This brings us to the second great advantage of Indian wives: they were born nomads who knew no other way of living. And the third: Indian society trained its women to be incredibly obedient and hardworking, and resentful of any attempts by their husbands to help out with the camp chores. It was akin to insulting her, announcing to the rest of the camp that she was inadequate and worthless.

By tending the horses, putting up and taking down the tepee, keeping it clean, swept and repaired, fetching the water and firewood, tanning the hides, sewing the clothing and doing the cooking, Indian wives made trail life more comfortable than any white or Mexican woman of the time was willing or able to do, and this freed up more time and energy for hunting, trapping and trading—the means by which a married couple survived and accrued wealth, possessions and status.

Some mountain men regarded their Indian wives purely as sexual/domestic conveniences, and discarded them callously when they felt like being alone again or with someone new. Others had happy, lasting marriages, and Joe Walker seems to have fallen into this second category. He was with his wife for approximately ten years. He demonstrated his commitment to the marriage by taking her back to meet his family and old friends in Jackson County, Missouri, and escorting her into Six Mile Baptist Church, doubtless through a gauntlet of scandalized whispers and gossip. And he spent several winters and hunting seasons with his Shoshoni in-laws, who semi-adopted him into the tribe. There has been speculation, by Captain Crook for one, that Walker took other wives. Polygamy was certainly commonplace, among Shoshonis and mountain men alike, but we have no confirmed sightings of another wife.

At some point the Walkers had children together, which would have presented no impediment to their travels. To give an extreme illustration, there are accounts of Indian women riding twenty-five miles, stopping by the side of the trail to give birth, and getting back on their horses a few hours later.

The newborn baby was wrapped in a cloth or blanket, with the soft, absorbent inner bark of the cedar tree packed between its legs, and carried in a tanned buckskin pouch called a cradle-board. The cradleboard was strapped to the mother's back, or to the pommel of her saddle, and the horse supplied the rocking, swaying motion that instinctively calms human babies. In camp, the cradleboard was hung from a lodge-pole and the mother rocked it by hand. By the age of four or five the children would have been riding ponies of their own.

In 1846 the references to Joe Walker's wife and children dry up in the records without explanation, and at the same time his travels took on an aimless, erratic quality. He neglected his trading business and let his partners drift away. He disappeared into the mountains for six months and emerged without his usual haul of furs. In the spring of 1847, he made a hell-bent ride with three new partners from the environs of Santa Fe to the Missouri River, covering the eight hundred miles in twenty-three days. Walker was forty-nine years old at the time, and he seems to have under-taken this punishing, record-equaling ride on a sudden whim. The other three happened to be heading in that direction when he bumped into them in New Mexico.

The most likely explanation for this uncharacteristic behavior, by Bil Gilbert's deduction, is that Walker's wife and children had died of smallpox, which was sweeping through the Rocky Mountain tribes at the time (they had no immunity to the disease), and that Walker was grieving for them. Like many a wandering male, before and after him, he was dealing with his emotional pain by trying to outdistance it geographically. For the rest of his life he avoided the central Rockies and the upper Green River country, where he and his wife had met, married and spent most of their time together.

When he reached the Missouri River, Walker rode on to Independence and spent five months there with his relatives, doing very little. He was tight-lipped about his intentions and his feelings, but some of his relatives got the impression that Joe had come back for good. At a family gathering that summer, a visiting cousin, who had become a well-to-do planter in Alabama, asked him if he had finally had enough of wandering around the wilderness. Wasn't it high time he settled down and made something of himself in civilized society? The question seemed to decide or confirm something for Joe Walker. He replied sharply that he was going back to live with the Indians because "white people are too damn mean."* He left soon afterwards, riding west, and was never seen in Missouri again.

For the rest of his life we have no sightings of another wife or girlfriend, nothing except one unfulfilled crush on a white woman he met on a wagon train.

The lone wandering male, riding off womanless into the sunset. He was a common enough figure in American history, first celebrated in the early folktales and ballads, and turned into a full-blown mythic hero by James Fenimore Cooper in his Leatherstocking novels.

Unlike Odysseus, or all those medieval knights-errant, Leatherstocking did not return and reunite with his family and community after his long, questing journey. At the end of the story—an old man now, still unmarried and quite possibly a virgin—Leatherstocking rides off again, "to seek a final refuge against society in the broad and tenantless plains of the west."

By the time Lance Grabowski was growing up, on the family fruit farm in upstate New York, Fenimore Cooper had given way to Gary Cooper and John Wayne. Leatherstocking was wearing a cowboy hat and a six-shooter on his hip, riding off into Technicolor sunsets, leaving behind the woman who loved him, and maybe her children, and always the camera, at the homestead fence.

Lance was so obsessed with cowboys at such a young age, and so insistent on dressing up like them, that his mother joked he had

---

* A rare direct quote, preserved in Walker family histories, and ferreted out by Bil Gilbert.

been born wearing a hat and a gun—it had made for a difficult delivery. Then he became obsessed with Indians as well as cowboys. In his late teens his heroes were outlaw bikers, which he sees as a natural progression: "In America you grow up with that cowboy ideal, that you should be independent and self-reliant and value your freedom above all else. That's what the films, and TV, and books, and popular culture tell you America is all about. Then you find out that, in reality, society wants you to be exactly the opposite: obedient, fearful, dependent, basically a good little wage slave. My reaction was to get a motorcycle, wear a lot of black leather and chains, and develop an extremely confrontational attitude."

In 1966, at the age of eighteen, he went to Taos, New Mexico, visited the Kit Carson Museum, and left with a stack of books about the mountain men. Two years later, at art school in Kansas City, he was wearing homemade buckskins, a breechclout and moccasins, and he wore nothing else for the next ten years. "I'd always been attracted to wandering outlaw types. I'd always been interested in the idea of living with total personal freedom. When I discovered the mountain men, it was like hitting the mother lode."

If Western movies shaped his attraction to tough, untamed, nomadic role models, had they also shaped his attitudes toward love and women? Here he was, fifty years old, never married.

"That was never my intention, I don't particularly enjoy being single," he said. "Unfortunately, it just seems to go with the territory. The women of my age that I find attractive and interesting are generally not interested in living in tents for the rest of their life. That's my dilemma. If I'm going to find someone and make it work, I'm going to have to settle down more, and that makes me insufferable to be around. Of course, the mountain men didn't have this problem. If you wanted a woman to travel with you, you would just pick one out from the nearest tribe, hand over whatever plunder her father managed to gouge out of you, and ride off with her."

Despite his vow at the family gathering, Joe Walker never did go back to live with the Indians. Instead, he did something which was to become a standard American response to the blues: at the age of fifty he went to California and made a fresh start. And it seemed to work for him. He was soon exhibiting all his old vigor and efficiency.

He arrived in the fall of 1848, when the Gold Rush was just beginning. A journalist named James O'Meara spent some time with him and was struck by Walker's indifference to the fortune he could make, his casual disdain for the idea of laboring with a pick and gold pan merely to get rich: "gold . . . had no charm for Captain Jo Walker. Although he valued money in his own provident and unselfish, unavaricious way, he was neither its slave nor its worshipper."

Instead, Walker set up a nomadic trading operation to supply the mining camps with horses and beef cattle. He bought the stock from the Mexican ranches around Los Angeles, trailed the herds north to the diggings around Sacramento, and then went back for more—a modest round-trip journey, by Walker's standards, of eight hundred miles or so.

With the profits he bought some ranch property near Gilroy, which he used to rest the livestock after the journey north and fatten them up for delivery. Walker spent very little time at his ranch, leaving its management and operation to hired hands and various family members who had followed his trails into California. A few years later he sold it and used his nephew's ranch, across the bay from San Francisco, as the resupply point for his stock-driving journeys, and as a base for launching a series of explorations and expeditions into the last pockets of unmapped country in the West.

Geographical curiosity and his abiding love for wilderness travel seem to have been the main reasons for these journeys, but he usually managed to find some practical, economic rationale: a railroad survey, a party of miners that wanted to be guided to some remote mountain range, a potential livestock market that called for investigation.

In 1858 he signed on as a scout for Colonel William Hoffman, who was leading fifty men on an expedition against the Mojave Indians on the lower Colorado River. Walker had traveled down the Colorado twenty years before, but he had never been up it.

"Nevertheless," one of the soldiers told a newspaperman, "he would make an accurate map each morning of the country to be marched over during the day, showing where mountains approached the river, and where the valley widened; where sloughs or tributaries made in, marking the halting place for the night . . . Furthermore, he would say, 'There is grass and wood in those mountains off there, with water flowing to the northward'—or whichever way it went."

Walker was sixty and, considering the quantity of sun and wind he had been exposed to, he must have looked grizzled and leathery in the extreme. The soldiers were amazed by their old scout: his powers of endurance and coolness under fire, the unerring correctness of all his predictions regarding geography, weather, game movements, Indian strategies and so on. The body of knowledge and skills that Walker had mastered was already largely extinct by 1858, at least among whites (the next generation of army scouts were Indians). The soldiers looked at him as a fascinating relic from a bygone era, a man who had outlived his time.

As Dead Cloud prophesied, I met many buckskinners who said they had been born 150 years too late. The difference with Lance Grabowski is that he sounds halfway believable making this claim. For one thing, there is the sheer virulence of his contempt for modern society: with a few exceptions, he finds the people who live in it contemptible by association. He would prefer it if 90 percent of them had never been born.

The real problem is that they are in his way. By their laws and institutions, and their viral presence on the land, they are preventing him from living in the way he wants to live. It's illegal to hunt and trap full time now unless you're a licensed government man killing coyotes and mountain lions on behalf of ranchers. It's illegal to build yourself a winter cabin in the mountains. Lance despises the authorities on principle—his politics are fiercely individualistic and libertarian, in the Scotch-Irish tradition—but he doesn't blame them in this instance. They are dealing with the same problem as he is: too many people, not enough wilderness.

By various strategies—rendezvous trading, lecturing, modeling in his gear for Western painters (among them, $150,000-a-canvas men like John Clymer)—Lance has achieved a radical degree of nomadic freedom by contemporary standards, but a pale and stunted version of what he craves. What has modernity done for him? Have there been any improvements in American life since 1840? He has to think long and hard about this question before he arrives at an answer that satisfies him: "dentistry."

He can't help admiring certain contemporary firearms, but he thinks his 1830s replicas have more style. He likes traveling in his van but he prefers riding a horse. He likes the jars of Thai curry paste now available at Western supermarkets, but he knows from experience that he is perfectly happy eating horse oats and whatever birds and small game he can bring down with a gun.

Soon after the rendezvous, I met Lance at his house in New Mexico. I wanted to look at the photographs and records of a series of wilderness expeditions he made in the 1970s and 1980s. He tried to walk from Bear Lake, Utah, to St. Louis, Missouri, fifteen hundred miles across the high plains in the three coldest months of winter, to re-create the famous "winter express" journeys of Moses "Black" Harris. Lance wore fur-lined clothes he had made himself, used his coat as a sleeping bag and carried a small buckskin pack containing thirty pounds of rigorously authentic gear. His knee gave out after two hundred miles and he had to crawl through the snow into Farson, Wyoming, and call a halt.

In 1976 he made a meandering twelve-hundred-mile horse trip from Santa Fe to rendezvous at Bear Lake, Utah, again carrying nothing but authentic gear. He stayed on national forest land in the mountains most of the way, for grazing and water, and maximum distance from civilization.

The next year, with one partner, he set off on horseback from Bear Lake to California to re-create Jedediah Smith's first trip in 1826. His partner's horse gave out in St. George, Utah, and Lance rode the last eight hundred miles alone, visited from time to time by a *National Geographic* photographer. He crossed the Mojave Desert in August, traveling by night and resting up during the 115-degree days, eating birds and jackrabbits. A few times he had to dig in streambeds for water, and in the driest section of the desert he was saved by an opportune cloudburst that left standing water on the ground.

"Obviously there were boring days and frustrating days, but it was definitely the best experience of my life," he says. "I had great dreams all the way. I felt very alive, very content, very calm. I knew I was as free as I was ever going to get."

Jed Smith had ridden into Los Angeles, but Lance gave up when he came to the San Bernardino sprawl, having covered somewhere between fifteen hundred and two thousand miles. It's hard to calculate the distance exactly because he took such a winding route, determined by the need to find water and grazing, and avoid the obstacles of civilization. "On both those horse trips it wasn't anything in nature that gave me trouble. It was highways, motorists, private land and hundreds of fucking fences. I would cut the fences and repair them behind me and it was a huge pain in the ass. When I got to San Bernardino there was just a maze of freeways, and culverts, and railroad lines, and I said, 'Okay, this has gone far enough. I'm in the suburbs of California and this is 1977.'"

The last time I saw Lance, he was talking about making another long horse trip, with no particular destination in mind. Just buy a horse somewhere, saddle it, stock up with powder and ammunition and ride out for the biggest blank spaces left on the map. "America is basically going down the toilet as far as I'm concerned," he says, "but in the West, at least, you can still make a trip like that, if you carry a pair of fence-cutters and take a few chances with the game laws. Where else in the world could you do it? Most countries won't even let you carry a gun."

The ranks of ex–mountain men, along with defeated Indian tribes, furnished the first nostalgics of the American West—the first to talk about the wild, pure, unspoiled country the West used to be and the nomadic freedom it afforded. Witness Jim Bridger in his old age, sitting on a porch in Kansas City, telling his stories about the old days and staring west with failing eyesight: "I wish I was back there among the mountains again. A man can see so much further in that country."

Even when he was totally blind, Bridger was still afflicted by a terrible, yearning restlessness. His daughter Virginia was so concerned that she got him a horse and a dog named Sultan and let her aged, blind, half-crippled father ride off and get lost in the woods and prairies outside town. "Sultan would come home and let us know that father was lost. The dog would bark and whine until I would go out and look for him."

Like Jim Bridger, the only ex–mountain man who rivaled him for longevity in the field, if not for miles traveled, Joe Walker's career was brought to a close by failing eyesight. In 1867, at the age of sixty-nine, he was traveling through Arizona with one partner. The partner wandered off from camp and got himself surrounded by bandits. He told them he was with a large, well-armed party of men and fired his gun to alert Walker. Old Man Walker couldn't see what was happening, but he made a shrewd guess and fired off several rounds in quick succession. The bandits were convinced and let his partner go.

Nevertheless, his eyesight had endangered a man's life and that was unacceptable. In all his fifty years on the frontier only one man under his command had ever been killed—a phenomenal safety record that none of Walker's contemporaries came close to matching. As Lance put it, "That was the thing about Joe Walker. If you traveled with him, you could be pretty sure that you would get there alive."

Walker rode on to California, hung up his saddle at his nephew's ranch in Contra Costa County, and settled down to a calm, pleasant, dignified retirement, with no recorded bouts of nostalgia or restlessness. Living nearby were many Scotch-Irish kinfolk he had grown up with in Tennessee and Missouri. They had followed his footsteps across the continent, as their grandparents had followed the Long Hunters over the Appalachians: migrants following nomad trails. They were eager to reacquaint themselves with Walker, and he seems to have enjoyed their visits.

His eyesight wasn't up to the trail any more, but it was still good enough to read, and he spent many hours on the porch, sitting in the sunshine with a book and a view of the California hills rolling away toward the Pacific. A few journalists came and

interviewed him. Walker gave them some sharply critical opinions of Custer and the United States Army—this was shortly after
the news of Little Bighorn. They asked him about John Frémont,
the Pathfinder, and Walker described him as "the most complete
coward I have ever known."

When it came to his own career Walker confined himself to
deflating rumors, and yes–no answers about dates, locations and
other dry details. The last journalist gave up in August 1876, and
Walker died two months later. He was seventy-seven years old.
The cause of death, says Bil Gilbert, was nothing more or less
than "having lived long enough."

How to distil that life into six lines, containing as few words
as possible? How to convey its historical importance, its adventures and wonderment, without the use of a single adjective? That
was the final task Joe Walker set himself: the inscription for his
tombstone.

BORN IN ROAN COUNTY, TENN—DEC. 13, 1798
EMIGRATED TO MO—1819
TO NEW MEXICO—1820
ROCKY MOUNTAINS—1832
CALIFORNIA—1833
CAMPED AT YOSEMITE—NOV. 13, 1833

That was typical of his terse, understated style. If you didn't understand the significance of that inscription, especially the last entry,
it would take too long to explain.

CHAPTER 8

Behold, a people comes from the north . . . They lay hold
of bow and spear; they are cruel and have no mercy. The
sound of them is like the roaring of the sea; they ride upon
horses, arrayed as a man for battle against you.

Jeremiah 6:22–23

T he written word was civilization's invention, and from the
beginning written accounts of nomads have been tainted by
civilized bias and disapproval, and often by fear and hatred. Nomads
rode into the pages of history as the enemy, thundering in from
the steppes and deserts on their horses, to raid or conquer or
exact tribute. The prophet Jeremiah was probably thinking of the
Scythians, the first recorded nomadic warriors in history, and by
any civilized standard they were a fearsome and barbaric crew. If
there are any outlaw motorcyle gangs out there looking for a
name, they could do worse than "The Scythians."

Long-haired, bearded and unwashed, they drank wine from
the skulls of their enemies and skinned their right arms in one
piece, fingernails and all, to make coverings for their arrow
quivers. Herodotus, in the world's first history book, tells us that
the Scythians also scalped their enemies and hung the dried,
stretched scalps on the bridles of their horses, like many plains
Indian tribes two thousand years later. They were superb archers
who selected a thin arrowhead for birds and shot them through
the eye, and superb horsemen who disdained walking and might

have given rise to the Greek myth of the centaur: half-man and half-horse.

In the seventh century BC the Scythians rode out of Central Asia, driving their cattle herds west—a nomadic war machine with supplies on the hoof—and took control of the European steppe. They established an empire four thousand miles wide, from the Danube to Mongolia, based on raiding, tribute, an invincible blitzkrieg style of warfare, and trading in furs, hides, gold and captive slaves. The empire lasted for nearly five hundred years, and in the end the Scythians became too wealthy to sustain it.

Laden down with gold and plunder, they began to lose mobility and settle down. They started intermarrying with sedentary peoples instead of riding off with their wives and daughters. In the second century BC the Scythians were finished off by a new tribe of ruthless horsemen thundering in from the steppes: the Sarmatians. For the next seventeen centuries the history of the steppes in Europe and Asia was dominated by nomad invasions, wave after wave, one ferocious horde after another: Huns, Alans, Khazars, Tartars, the Mongols under Genghis Khan and Tamerlane. Similar patterns evolved in India, Africa and Arabia, and wherever in the world the civilized wrote about mounted nomadic warriors, they characterized them as savage, cruel and less than human.

The Roman historian Ammanius Marcellinus described the Huns as "two-legged beasts . . . stumps rough-hewn into images." A Han Chinese secretary, passing judgement on the Huns' eastern cousins, the Hsiung-nu, wrote that "in their breasts beat the hearts of beasts . . . from the most ancient times they have never been regarded as a part of humanity." An early Egyptian official, writing about the Bedouin, stated that "their name reeks more than the stink of bird droppings." The English monk Matthew Paris, writing a hysterical letter to the archbishop of Bordeaux in 1243, described the Tartars as "a fierce race of inhuman beings . . . virgins were deflowered until they died of exhaustion."

We have abundant evidence in our libraries to demonstrate what the civilized thought of nomads, but next to nothing about the nomadic point of view: what they thought of themselves and their enemies, and how they understood the world. *The Secret*

History of the Mongols, recorded by the Chinese in the fourteenth century, from the campfire stories, songs and poems of Genghis Khan's army, is a rare and fascinating exception, but as a rule, nomad tribes leave no written records of their culture. Books and libraries are an encumbrance to a people on the move. Literacy amounts to dead weight.

In the mid-nineteenth century, pioneers in Texas were surprised to see illiterate Comanche warriors taking Bibles and other books during their raids on outlying farms and settlements. In true nomadic style, the Comanches had discovered that paper made an excellent padding for their bison-hide war shields and would absorb a bullet if you packed it in thick and tight enough. The early Texas cattleman Charles Goodnight found a Comanche war shield stuffed with a complete history of ancient Rome (its rise, efflorescence and fall to nomadic barbarians from the north).

Nomad tribes carry their culture in their heads. Their histories are oral, their religions—with the exception of Islamic nomads in Arabia and Africa—are usually shamanic, focused on dreams, visions and animistic spirits in nature, rather than written texts. Each individual is a fragile repository of all the tribe's songs, stories, ceremonies, customs, knowledge and history, and if he dies without passing it on, it is the nomadic equivalent of a library burning down. If the oral tradition falters across a generation or two, during a period of conquest and disruption, the tribe is in danger of losing its history and culture completely, or seeing it reduced to the written accounts kept by their conquerors.

This is the predicament facing the Comanches today. They still retain a strong sense of tribal identity, of being Comanche, but their language is dying, they have lost their reservation, they have intermarried with Anglos, Mexicans and other Indian tribes to the point where no pure-blood Comanches are left, and the oral tradition is on its last legs. The current generation of grandparents encouraged their children to learn English and look toward a future in the white world, and with a few exceptions they passed on little of what they knew about the old ways.

Now there is a movement in the tribe, led by college-educated Comanches who came of age in the 1960s, to preserve and resuscitate the language and record the remnants of the oral tradition. In some cases, elders who spoke English to their children are now teaching Comanche to their grandchildren. And after a long reticence with their own people, and especially with white researchers, they are starting to tell more of the stories they heard from their own parents and grandparents, about the old hunting and raiding life on the plains.

I wanted to hear some of those stories, to see if they enlarged or contradicted the written histories. Most of all, I wanted to know what had become of the Comanche. Of all the Indian tribes in America, they had always struck me as the most intransigently nomadic, the least suited to a life of farming and civic virtue, the nearest American equivalent to the barbarian horsemen who thundered across the Eurasian steppes. What had they lost, and hung on to, and gained during the painful, enormous transition from nomadism to sedentary living?

The Comanche lands today are a scattered patchwork of 160-acre allotments around Lawton, Oklahoma, held in trust for them by the federal government and largely occupied by white farmers. Driving over here from Arizona, there was ample time to reflect on the former glories of the Comanche empire. I crossed the Pecos River in New Mexico, at the empire's western edge, and was still inside it 450 miles later, driving into Lawton.

At the height of their power, between 1750 and 1840, the Comanches controlled a territory of 250,000 square miles—west and central Texas, eastern New Mexico, southeast Colorado, most of Oklahoma and southern Kansas—and this was just the launching pad for their operations. They went up into the Rockies to fight the Utes. They were sometimes seen trading horses as far north as Saskatchewan and they raided deep into Mexico. One party of Comanches, riding with Kiowa allies, reached the jungles of southern Mexico and came back with stories of multicolored parrots and "little men who live in trees," which still persists as the Comanche word for "monkey." If there were any rival to Joe Walker, in terms of miles covered on horseback, he was probably an aged, long-forgotten Comanche warrior.

They were one of the few tribes on the plains who had never

planted a seed at any point in their history. Originally, they were footbound hunter-gatherers from the Wind River country in Wyoming, part of the Shoshoni people. Some time in the sixteenth or seventeenth century, they split off after a disagreement and started a long migration toward the southern Great Plains. Along the way they mastered the emerging horse–buffalo culture and became the first tribe to exploit its full military potential. As mounted archers and lancers—a nomadic war machine fuelled by buffalo meat and horseflesh—they drove the pedestrian, river-farming tribes (including the Apaches) off the southern plains, blocked the French advance from Louisiana, kicked the Spanish out of Texas and established the first full-scale nomad empire in North America.

The Comanches had no cattle, sheep or goats, but their relationship with the horse was unique among the plains tribes, and it brought them closer to the warrior-herdsman model of nomadism which rose on the Eurasian steppes. They were the only tribe on the plains who successfully bred horses, for speed, endurance, striking colors and patterns, and they amassed far larger herds than anyone else. A Sioux war chief might boast a string of fifty horses. An ordinary Comanche warrior would often have more than two hundred, and there are accounts of individual Comanche chiefs with fifteen hundred horses or more. We think of Comanche nomadism as determined by buffalo migrations, but an equally important reason was the need to find fresh grazing for their enormous horse herds. One of the Comanche bands, numbering two thousand people, including women and children, traveled with a herd of fifteen thousand horses in the nineteenth century.

The Comanches were acknowledged by whites and Indians alike to be the finest horsemen and trick-riders, the centaurs of the plains, and many whites thought they were the finest horsemen who ever lived. They were also judged to be the most awkward on foot, walking with a peculiar, jerky, bandy-legged shuffle, which was probably a result of learning to ride before they could walk properly.

They were the only tribe who preferred to fight on horseback, instead of riding to the scene of the fight and then approaching stealthily on foot, and the only tribe reported to eat, sleep and defecate without dismounting, like the Huns. The other plains tribes rode horses for transportation, and for hunting buffalo, but they did not live on horseback like the Comanches or disdain walking in the same way.

By virtue of their proximity to Mexico, the Comanches developed an economy that was more focused on raiding the settlements than the other plains tribes, and this too brought them closer to the Eurasian model of warrior nomadism, as practiced by the Scythians, Huns, Mongols and so on.

"Behold, a people comes from the north . . . They lay hold of bow and spear; they are cruel and have no mercy . . ." Long-haired and unwashed, faces painted black for war, with human scalps hanging from their horse bridles, and some of the warriors wearing horned buffalo scalps or deer antlers on their heads, the raiding parties rode south into Mexico by the September moon—the Comanche moon, as it became known—when the grass was high and the waterholes full after the summer thunderstorms.

For the peasants, ranchers, villagers and townsfolk in northern Mexico, who were poorly defended by the army and largely unarmed, the Comanches were "*los barbaros*," the savages, the barbarians at the gates, screaming their unearthly war cries, blowing on eagle-bone whistles, snatching up captives onto the backs of their horses—a source of terror and destruction that lasted for 170 years. (Mothers in Durango, a thousand miles south of the buffalo plains, are still telling errant children that the Comanches will get them.)

Thousands of Mexicans were killed and scalped, and the Comanches were in the habit of raping the women and mutilating the dead (so they wouldn't have to fight them in the afterlife), and they were no slouches with the torture stake. Sometimes the warriors brought their families along and stayed in Mexico all winter, collecting up hundreds of captive women and children, and thousands of stolen horses and mules, before turning north for the spring buffalo hunt on the high plains.

In the 1830s the Comanches must have felt on top of the world. They controlled the entire southern plains—an empty, untilled, windswept space, four hundred miles wide and six hundred miles long, containing no permanent settlements or signs of occupation. By civilized standards it was no empire at all—it was a howling wilderness—but nomad empires function on opposite principles. Fields and settlements impede the grazing and obstruct mobility, and are best visited on long-distance raids or trading expeditions. To be surrounded by hundreds of miles of empty, primordial grassland makes nomads feel secure and powerful.

Horses were the measure of wealth on the plains, the equivalent of gold, and the Comanche herds had reached obscene proportions. The captive trade was booming, polygamy was on the rise (a sure sign of good times) and many scalps hung from their lodgepoles and horse bridles. Their numbers were increasing, despite the high rate of miscarriages that comes with a life on horseback. They were up to about twenty thousand, riding in a dozen scattered bands, with maybe six thousand warriors in total. A single Comanche moccasin print, they boasted, was enough to make their enemies turn around and go in the opposite direction.

Riding through their empire with its limitless buffalo herds, they must have thought it would last forever.

The Comanche tribal complex sits like a low-budget office park on a small windswept hill, a few miles north of Lawton. When I arrived, a group of men were putting up a sturdy, six-foot fence around an area of pasture below the offices. They said it was for buffalo, which will leap over or break through a lesser fence. The tribe has bought forty head from the federal wildlife refuge in the Wichita Mountains (a low granite range on the western skyline) and they are to be penned up here as a symbol of Comanche heritage, as a Pacific Northwestern tribe might put up a totem pole or a salmon sculpture outside its administrative headquarters. Adjoining the buffalo paddock, and completing the symbol, was a corral containing fifty horses—yearling mustangs captured a few weeks ago from the wild herds in Nevada. Forty buffalo and fifty horses: it was hard not to see it as a symbol of Comanche poverty.

There was a tribal policeman parked in front of the horses, standing by his car, watching them intently. He had the classic Comanche physique, barrel-chested and short-legged, with dark copper skin and big, broad facial features. He wore a navy-blue uniform, and his demeanor was much like that of any other Oklahoma cop. He leaned back against his patrol car, with the clouds reflected in his sunglasses, and talked in a rural western drawl, which is to say a Scotch-Irish drawl. The horses, he said, were part of the tribe's new anti-drug program.

"We've got a lot of young people messed up on the crystal meth. It's a bad scene but we're gonna whup it, I guarantee. We're gonna do whatever it takes to get all these dealers locked up, and at the same time we're gonna build up pride in our young people. Soon as we get these yearlings broke, we're starting up a summer camp, where the kids will learn all about working with horses. Young people need to feel proud of who they are, and where they came from, and heck, what kinda Comanche are you if you don't know how to ride a horse?"

My truck was parked outside the offices, about 250 yards from where we stood. He offered to give me a ride over there, and looked surprised when I said I'd just walk. It was an odd European custom, I told him: we actually liked to walk. He gave me his business card (Richard Saupitty, Tribal Police Officer, "We will serve you better today than we did yesterday") and drove away.

Approaching the front entrance, I braced myself for wariness and stonewalling, and possible allegations that I was exploiting the tribe. This had been my experience with Indian officialdom in the past, with the Lakota (Sioux), Navajo, Hopi, Apache and Havasupai, and it is often repeated among white reporters that Indians are "difficult" to deal with—"obstreperous buggers," as a relocated Fleet Street hand of my acquaintance puts it.

I went up to the receptionist to plead my case, and it was all smiles, and hey come on in, and here's a twenty-page handout packed with useful information about the Comanches, past and present, and two minutes later, with no appointment, I was shown into the office of the tribal administrator. Delphine Nelson rose from behind her desk, a small vivacious woman in a business suit, with permed reddish hair, wide curvaceous spectacles, and a tone of brisk, good-humored sarcasm. "Oh, so you want the state-of-the-tribe speech," she divined, and went right into it.

There are about 9500 Comanches on the tribal rolls, and the blood quantum is a quarter, meaning that you need at least one Comanche grandparent to qualify. Nearly half the tribe lives in greater Los Angeles, and the rest are concentrated here in southwestern Oklahoma. The good news: the Comanches have more students in higher education than any other tribe, and are producing more doctors, lawyers, business executives and teachers. The tribe has a new casino, which is already generating substantial revenues—casino gambling is rapidly becoming the staff of life for American Indian tribes. They call it "the new buffalo." The bad news: there has been little other economic development. Unemployment is high, suicide is high, alcoholism and drug abuse are high, although all these indicators are lower among the Comanche than the reservation tribes, and even the poorest Comanches are well-off by reservation standards. They all have electricity and running water, for example.

I asked her if there were remnants of nomadism in modern Comanche culture. "Well, we're not good farmers," she said. "There's a few, but on the whole we still don't like farming, and we're no good at it, and we'd rather lease out our land to white farmers. We do a lot better with stock-raising. What else? Well, the warrior tradition is still going strong."

Comanches signed up in droves for the two world wars, Korea and Vietnam, and they still join the armed forces in large numbers. "It's a way for the men to 'go out on the plains' and win their war honors," she said. "When the Comanche soldiers came back from Vietnam, no one spat at them or called them names. They were welcomed back as returning warriors, with dances and feasts, and we were all real proud of them. There was very little post-traumatic stress syndrome among Comanche veterans, compared to white Vietnam vets, and that's probably why."

The most damaging legacy of their past, she says, is genetic.

Seventy-five percent of the tribe have diabetes and 25 percent have had amputations because of the disease: legs, arms, fingers, toes. As wandering hunter-gatherers, with a diet that was mostly lean meat, grilled, boiled or eaten raw, the Comanches evolved without any exposure to refined sugars, starches and fried foods— the three basic food groups of the modern American diet. All North American Indians suffer from high rates of diabetes, but it is worse among the old nomadic hunting tribes than the farming tribes.

Indian alcoholism has spawned a welter of different theories. Is it the result of crushing defeat, loss of homelands and massive cultural upheaval? Is it a continuing response to endemic poverty and unemployment? Or does it persist because of prohibitionist Indian attitudes toward alcohol, which turn it into a dark, mysterious forbidden fruit? Or has alcohol, for all the damage it has done, been a useful numbing agent that has allowed Indians to get through a period of wrenching change? Or do Indians simply like to get drunk for the same reason as everyone else, because it feels good, and then become addicted more easily?

Delphine Nelson, who has seen two uncles and four cousins drink themselves to death, is convinced the problem is genetic to Native Americans (Comanche blood might be thinning, but most of the intermarriage has been with other Indian tribes). She doesn't believe any of the cultural upheaval theories, partly because well-educated, urbanized Indians with good jobs and families (like her cousins) seem equally vulnerable to alcoholism as poor, unemployed Indians. And partly because this vulnerability was glaringly evident during the first phase of contact with alcohol, when tribal cultures were undisturbed and undefeated.

The science is inconclusive, but there has been a lot of talk lately about certain enzymes and flushing mechanisms that Europeans use to break down and process alcohol, and which American Indians (and Australian Aborigines) seem to lack. Whether it's genetic or cultural or both, there is no doubt that the longer a people has lived with alcohol, the less prone they are to alcoholism. Mediterranean Europeans, with seven thousand years of drinking behind them, have a 10 percent susceptibility to alcoholism. Northern Europeans, with fifteen hundred years, have a 20–40 percent susceptibility, with the highest rates among Russians, Poles, Irish and Scots. American Indians, with three hundred years of exposure to alcohol, have an 80–90 percent likelihood of becoming alcoholics if they start drinking. I don't know how alcoholism is defined in these surveys, whether, for example, it's a Russian definition or a Californian definition, but the general trend seems clear.

"Indians become alcoholics for the same reason they become diabetics," says Delphine. "We're not physiologically equipped to deal with booze or junk food. It doesn't seem fair, and it's a damn shame, but that's the reality we've got to address. It was the same with all those other diseases Europeans brought us. We didn't have any immunity to smallpox either, or the common cold, and we still don't. How long does it take you to get over a cold? Two weeks max, right? For us, it's thirty to sixty days, and the purer the blood, the longer it takes."

In the winning of the American West, microbes have never got the respect they deserve. Redoubtable and remorseless, clearing the way for civilization's advance, and presumably acting with the blessing of God, immigrant germs killed more Indians than the cowboys, the army and the frontiersmen combined. We can posit historical inevitability and say that the more numerous and technically advanced people would have triumphed anyway, without the aid of microbes, but that wasn't the way it happened anywhere in the Americas. The latest guesswork indicates that diseases introduced by Europeans wiped out somewhere between 60 and 90 percent of the indigenous population of the Americas, north and south, and when they reached the Great Plains a familiar pattern was repeated: sudden, terrifying, catastrophic die-offs, social and psychic disintegration among the survivors, and an irreversible shift in the balance of power.

In 1849 the Comanches were already on the defensive. A new people, pale, gaunt and lanky to Comanche eyes, had appeared on the eastern fringes of the empire and established a frontier line of farms and settlements. At first the Comanches had underestimated them. They were laughably bad horsemen, with big, plodding horses, and their crops and cabins alone marked them as a weak, inferior people, akin to Mexicans or the Indian farming tribes, and a promising new source of captives and plunder. But the Texans had proved themselves to be a formidable enemy, and a particularly vile and treacherous one. Hostilities had hardened into permanent war when they seized and killed a number of Comanche chiefs under the sacred truce of council.

The Texans (whose ranks were dominated by southern-born Scotch-Irish) were adapting quickly to the plains. Their horsemanship had improved and they rode faster, more durable horses, and they sent out the most troublesome war parties the Comanche had ever faced. These were the fabled Texas Rangers, who had figured out that the only way to fight Comanches was to become like the Comanches. They rode in small, highly mobile, predatory bands with no supply lines and the survival skills to stay in the field for months at a time. Ranger parties had followed Comanche hoofprints for hundreds of miles, way out onto the high plains, and attacked them in their base camps, killing women and children, burning down tepees, driving off the horses, and riding away with many Comanche scalps hanging from their belts and horse bridles.

Disease had taken a heavier toll. The Comanche had already met their deadliest enemy. A smallpox epidemic in 1839 wiped out some bands entirely, and syphilis, contracted during the raiding and raping sprees in Mexico, was endemic among all the bands in the 1840s. Nevertheless, as spring turned to summer in 1849 the Comanches still held about 80 percent of their empire and remained an extremely formidable people. They had avenged their losses to the Texans, killing as many in return, raping, mutilating and taking hundreds of captives, horses and mules. For Anglo-Texans, the word "Comanche" had come to mean what it meant to the Mexicans. In frontier newspapers, memoirs and church sermons, the Comanche were compared to locusts, wolves and pestilence, to Tartars, Mongols, Huns, Vandals and the vengeful horsemen in the Book of Jeremiah. Naturally, the Comanche didn't think of themselves as a horde of subhuman savages. They called themselves Numunu or Nermernuh (spelling is fluid when oral languages are first written down), which means the one true people, living in the one true way, with the special blessing of the Great Spirit. It is symbolic of civilized attitudes toward nomads that we use the term "Comanche." That was what their enemies, the Utes, called them and it means "those who are always against us."

1849 was the Gold Rush year and tens of thousands of people poured across the northern reaches of the Comanche empire, heading for the California goldfields to make their fortunes—one of the most frenzied and deluded mass migrations in human history. The gold-seekers came from all over the civilized world, including its foulest and most disease-ridden slums, and in addition to smallpox, influenza, typhus and whooping cough, they loosed a rampaging epidemic of cholera among the southern plains tribes. Contrary to popular belief, Indians attacked the argonaut caravans very rarely. They were infected at the waterholes, from discarded clothing and blankets strewn along the trails, occasionally from trading with the wagon trains, or looting the shallow graves they left behind. The Cheyennes lost about half their population that summer, and so did the Comanches.

"It is known that every important camp headman or civil chief died in 1849," writes T. R. Fehrenbach. "The southern Comanches dissolved as a coherent band, and . . . the surviving eastern and northern bands were split into confused and traumatized fragments." Only the Quahada band, the Antelopes, who rode the remote Llano Estacado to the west, survived in numbers, and it was no coincidence that the Quahadas continued the Comanche resistance longer and more effectively than any other band.

Understand that the Comanches lived in an entirely magical universe, and understood disease as the work of evil spirits. To lose so many, so suddenly, in such hideous, mysterious ways, against the best efforts of their medicine men, implied a vast, terrifying conspiracy of malevolent forces, a giant upheaval in the balance of the cosmos—much as medieval Europeans had understood the Black Death as the instrument of God's wrath or the ascendancy of the Devil.

The agrarian tribes tended to respond to disease epidemics by giving up hope and sinking into apathetic despair. The Comanches responded by going to war with an even greater ferocity than before. Why? Because they were warriors. War offered the best hope of rebuilding their shattered morale and proving that their "medicine," their power to influence the workings of the magical universe, was still strong. War was a social imperative, and in 1849 it was also a strategic necessity. Their empire was under attack. Their enemies were invading and multiplying.

The Comanches were fighting the eastern agrarian tribes who had been removed to Oklahoma, and this was a nomad–farmer conflict as bitter as any in American history. They were fighting the Texans and managing to keep the frontier at bay, taking 150 scalps in the fall of 1849, and 100 a year through the 1850s. They were fighting the US Army which was busily establishing forts in the heart of the bison ranges and developing cavalry units that were capable of trailing Comanches for hundreds of miles. And they were still raiding into Mexico and fighting the Utes, Tonkawas, Apaches and other ancestral tribal enemies.

With half their forces wiped out in 1849 and another smallpox epidemic in 1860, the scattered, shrunken Comanche bands were outnumbered and overstretched when they needed to be at their strongest. Who knows what difference another three thousand warriors would have made, or all those chiefs who died in 1849, but the Comanches were unable to prevent the second major catastrophe to befall the tribe: the arrival of professional buffalo hunters on the southern plains in the 1860s, depriving them of their main source of food and shelter.

And so to Medicine Lodge, Kansas, in October 1867, a gathering of the southern plains tribes, in all their gaudy nomadic pageantry, and a few bewhiskered, frock-coated representatives of the US government, backed up by the army. The tribes wanted to hold the government to previous treaties and get the settlers and buffalo hunters off their land. The government wanted the Indians to stop raiding, stop interfering with roads, railroads and forts, stop inter-tribal warfare, stop roaming and become farmers on reservations. It was a key moment in the history of American nomadism: a formal, rhetorical clash of cultures and a recognition on both sides that the balance of power had shifted forever. Through interpreters and government scribes, we get a clear picture of the nomadic point of view, as they faced the prospect of confinement for the first time, and realized that the bewhiskered gentlemen were not negotiating but trying to dictate terms.

The aged Comanche chief Ten Bears was the most accomplished orator, white or Indian, at Medicine Lodge and he made a famous defense and eulogy for his people's way of life. As the translation unfolded, the whites were amazed to hear such eloquence from a murderous old savage. You will find a piece of his speech in the opening quotations of this book, but I want to pass along some more of it:

> I was born upon the prairie, where the wind blew free and there was nothing to break the light of the sun. I was born where there were no enclosures and everything drew a free breath.
>
> I want to die there and not within walls. I know every stream and every wood between the Rio Grande and the Arkansas. I have hunted and lived over that country. I live like my fathers before me and like them I lived happily. When I was in Washington the Great Father told me that all the Comanche land was ours, and that no one should hinder us in living on it. So why do you ask us to leave the rivers, and the sun, and the wind, and live in houses? . . .
>
> If the Texans had kept out of my country, there might have been peace. But that which you now say we must live in is too small. The Texans have taken away the places where the grass grew the thickest and the timber was best. Had we kept that, we might have done the things you ask. But it is too late. The whites have the country which we loved, and we wish only to wander on the prairie until we die.

The reservation was established in 1868 in southwest Oklahoma, and about half of the Comanche and Kiowa bands came in. An agency was built at Fort Sill (an army base that adjoins present-day Lawton) and the first attempts were made to turn these nomadic hunters and warriors into sedentary, civilized, Christian farmers. The initial signs were not encouraging. Farm labor disgusted them, and not just because of the sweat and drudgery. The idea of digging into the flesh of Mother Earth and removing the grasses she had placed there for horses and buffalo was spiritually abhorrent. And for what? The Comanches disliked eating grains and vegetables almost as much as they disliked growing them.

They were issued with rations of cornmeal, which they tried eating and ended up feeding to their horses. They were issued with beef and here was something they could relate to: red meat from a large horned animal. They asked for their beef ration on the hoof. The lumbering, confused animals were released one at a time. The men leapt on their horses, galloped after them and shot them full of arrows. Then the women ran up, with the traditional shrieks and ululations, and set to work with butcher knives, and the children pleaded for the raw liver (a prized delicacy among most hunting peoples, because it supplies so many vitamins and minerals).

The agent had to hire a white man to do the farming. A group of hungry Comanches raided his fields and ate a quantity of under-ripe watermelons, which gave them "devil inside the belly," and convinced them further that farming was bad medicine. There was never enough food on the reservation, mainly because of bureaucratic hold-ups and thieving contractors. There was nothing to do, especially for the young men: no raiding, no warfare, no horse-stealing expeditions, no hunting, nothing by which Comanche males measured their status and self-worth. And without stolen horses, scalps and war honors, they were considered poor marriage prospects. Small groups of Comanches, led by disgruntled males, began to drift away from the reservation and join the free bands of Comanches still out on the plains.

There was a last hurrah: a series of raids and skirmishes against settlers, army units and buffalo hunters, which the whites called the Red River War, and the Comanches called the War for the Buffalo. With the loss of that war, tribal nomadism came to a close on the southern Great Plains. In 1875 the last free band of

Quahadas under Quanah Parker, a half-breed chief whose mother was a white captive, decided to ride into the reservation and submit to the yoke. They were technically undefeated in battle, but a US Cavalry division, aided by Tonkawa scouts, had trailed them to their winter camp in Palo Duro Canyon, burned their tepees and supplies and shot 1400 of their horses. They were cold, hungry and ragged. There were no buffalo to be found. It was settlement or starvation.

And that was the end of the Comanches, according to some historians, their exit from the American stage. All that remained, in the closing phrase of T. R. Fehrenbach's book, was "the completion of their destruction" as a people.

"That whole idea, that we were totally destroyed and lost everything—we just find it funny. It makes us laugh. I mean, hello, we're still here!" This was Jimmy Arterberry, in the Office of Environmental Programs (next to the transportation office, with a picture on the door of an Indian riding a war pony, and underneath it, an Indian standing next to a pickup truck). Jimmy is one-quarter Comanche and three-quarters Dutch-American. He looks about as Comanche as I do—tall, slim, fair-skinned, sharp-featured—but he was largely raised by his Comanche grandmother and her Comanche friends. He grew up speaking both languages and pestering the elders for stories about the old days.

"We look at it as a process of adaptation," he said. "A series of choices and decisions that we've made that has allowed us to preserve as much of our culture as possible. It hasn't been easy. The whole thing has been crazy and we never would have made it through without our sense of humor. People say we laugh at the wrong times, like busting up at a funeral or whatever, but we've learned that there are two ways of dealing with harsh realities. You can cry or you can laugh."

I asked him what had been preserved and he said there were a hundred things. Customs at the dinner table and ways of preparing food. A continuing fondness for boiled meat, and boiled guts, which the Comanches call "The Bible" for the way it separates into flaky white sheets. The way the elders point with their lips. The rudeness of looking directly into someone's eyes as you're talking to them. Customs of gift-giving and hospitality. A taste for bright colors (shared by tribal nomads around the world and presumably a response to the muted hues of arid landscapes). Communalism and clan loyalty: a person with a job is expected to support his unemployed relatives, nepotism is rife in tribal hiring practices, factionalism plagues tribal politics.

"We're still basically the same people," he said. "We can still be pushy, demanding, domineering, aggressive. We're still ornery, a lot of our people are mean. Don't back them into a corner, and I'm not just talking about the men. Our women can be fighters too."

Orneriness. I didn't see any evidence of it, but one hears that word a lot talking to Comanches today. It is the blanket term they use to cover all the raiding, raping, torturing and pillaging in their past. Jimmy says that whites have made too much of it. Orneriness was but one aspect of a rich and varied culture. It was the part of themselves that the Comanches showed the outside, literate world. And they lived in ornery times, with endemic tribal warfare and white enemies who were just as ornery in return. He says that violence is natural among human beings (an assertion I might amend to normal), and that Comanche violence was small-time stuff compared to the violence committed by the most civilized people on earth: the Somme, Verdun, the Holocaust, Hiroshima, Vietnam and so on.

When I asked him about nomadic holdovers, he sprang out of his chair and started pointing at a big map on the wall. "We're still nomads!" he exclaimed. "At least a lot of us are." With a long, circling finger, he showed me where the different Comanche bands used to roam. Here, on and around the Llano Estacado, was the home territory of the Quahada band, the Antelopes, who rode with bison-hide parasols and were also known as Sun Shades On Their Backs. This was his grandmother's band, and by Comanche genealogy, which ignores all non-Comanche blood, Jimmy is Quahada and his clan within the band is the Loud Talkers. And here, further east and a little north, were the home ranges of the Nokoni band, the Wanderers, Those Who Move Often.

"All Comanches were nomadic," he says, "but the Quahadas and the Nokonis were the most nomadic. They would travel more often than the other bands and go further. What you find today is that the descendants of these two bands still do a lot more traveling than the descendants of the other bands. And they're traveling to the same places and using a lot of the same routes. They used to go down to Mexico in September to raid. Now they go down there for the bullfights in Laredo, and to harvest peyote.*
My mother would go north every year to hunt pheasant in Colorado, where we used to fight the Utes. She would go up to Wyoming to hunt bears. People are still traveling to the old sacred sites, and vision quest places. Or they'll spend a summer going round all the Indian gatherings and tribal fairs on the plains."

Jimmy has thought a lot about these matters. He has settled down now, at the age of forty, but during his twenties and thirties he wandered all over America and Europe, and his mother would always tell him, "It's that Comanche blood." That was how she explained her own love of travel—her pheasant- and bear-hunting expeditions—and Jimmy's full-blood grandmother would say the same thing about the family tradition of travel. She was a lifelong subscriber to *National Geographic*, fascinated by distant places, and when Jimmy returned from Hawaii, or New York, or Spain, or wherever he had been, she would sit him down and grill him endlessly.

Talking to Comanches myself, especially the few elders I have met, I find them uncommonly interested in my recent journeys. They don't want anecdotes or sightseeing stories, just the dry navigational details: the exact routes I traveled and the sequence of towns, rivers and landmarks I passed along the way. I had to make a couple of side-trips, and when I asked them for directions they would give phenomenally detailed instructions. Turn east at the creek with such-and-such a medicinal plant growing

---

* Peyote: a hallucinogenic cactus that the Comanches started incorporating into religious ceremonies during the reservation years, along with elements of Christianity. The practice spread to many other Indian tribes and led to the formation of the peyote-based Native American Church, and laws decriminalizing peyote possession among its members.

on its bank. You're going to see a pasture with a white barn and a palomino mare. Then they would name the next fourteen or twenty towns I was going to drive through.

I asked Jimmy Arterberry about this and he had a ready explanation: "That was how we navigated in the old days. One of the elders would draw a map in the dirt, with all the landmarks and rivers you were going to cross in the first day of the journey. You would have to memorize it and repeat it all back to him in the right order. Then he would make a notch in a stick: that was the first day. Then he would draw out a map for the second day, and you would memorize all that. He would make a second notch, and so on, for as many days as the journey was going to take. And it might take twenty days to get where you were going. There were people who had a thousand miles of country committed to memory."

In the early years of the reservation, the Comanches (and the Kiowas and Kiowa-Apaches who shared the reservation) devised new forms of nomadism, on a shrunken scale. Most of them were still living in mobile encampments of tents and tepees, and they would move up into the Wichita Mountains in warmer weather, and down into the protection of the timbered bottomlands in winter, and make frequent, extended visits to other families and clan groups camped around the reservation.

When the government started building houses for them, the Comanches were delighted. They would show off their houses to each other as status symbols, but they baulked at the idea of actually living in them. Houses had strange echoes. They attracted snakes. A few Comanches tried sleeping inside them and found the best place was directly under the chimney flue, which afforded a view of the stars at night, similar to the view through the top of a tepee. Most people pitched their tents and tepees outside, built brush-arbors for the summer, and let their dogs sleep in the houses.

These were exasperating times for the white authorities, who believed, beyond any shadow of doubt, that sedentary agricultural civilization was the crowning apogee of human progress, to which all people should aspire. The whites were operating under their own concept of Numunu. Theirs was the one true way, with the special blessing of God, and the Comanches disdained its most basic tenets: fixed dwellings, farming and private property.

In 1885 Senator Henry Dawes made a tour of Indian reservations in Oklahoma and delivered his report to the Lake Mohonk Conference—an annual gathering of influential whites who called themselves "friends of the Indian," and were dedicated to advancing their red brethren toward white civilization. The senator brought dispiriting news: "There is no selfishness, which is at the bottom of civilization." The tribes were still living within communal social structures. They were still sharing all their food and possessions with their kinfolk. They were more impressed by displays of generosity than the accumulation of private wealth.

"We need to awaken in him [the Indian] wants," said another conferee. "In his dull savagery he must be touched by the wings of the divine angel of discontent . . . Discontent with the tepee and the starving rations of the Indian camp in winter is needed to get the Indian out of the blanket and into trousers—and trousers with a pocket in them, and with a pocket that aches to be filled with dollars! . . . this is the first great step in the education of the race."

The result of the conference was the Dawes Act, which authorized the breaking up of the Indian reservations in Oklahoma. Communal land was to be divided into privately held 160-acre allotments, to encourage respect for private property and the nuclear family. By happy coincidence, the Dawes Act also freed up 28,500,000 acres of "surplus" land to the clamoring white settlers, and activated the Oklahoma Land Rush.

It sounds like a cynical excuse for yet another land grab, but the conferees firmly believed they were doing the best for the Indians. It was an article of faith in the nineteenth century, held to by capitalists and Marxists alike, that all human societies progressed through inexorable, unwavering stages of history. From wandering savagery, the first stage of progress was sedentary farming, which gave rise to the division of labor, private property and social hierarchies, which in turn produced civilization, feudalism, capitalism and industrialism. And like Lenin, Stalin or Mao, American leaders felt it was their duty to speed the inevitable process along by forcibly imposing a more advanced culture on the laggards.

Of course, these processes are not inevitable, especially when it comes to nomadic tribes. Nomadism generally develops in opposition to sedentary agriculture, not as a stage toward it. Looking out over the entire span of history, one can produce a few isolated examples of nomad tribes who voluntarily settled down, or were lured into settlement against their better judgement like the Scythians. But it usually takes starvation or military defeat to get tribal nomads to settle—a choice between settlement and death. This has always puzzled the civilized, made them curious. What is the big attraction? Why would people choose hardship over comfort? The civilized betray the answer through their repressed envy of nomads and their propensity to romanticize nomads once they no longer present a threat. The Comanches, for example, found themselves in constant demand for parades in Texas and Oklahoma, and were required to ride on horseback in feathered warbonnets.

As Fehrenbach says, "They will be remembered and recalled with a certain pride and nostalgia, because they . . . represented freedoms and values denied civilized mankind: freedom from subordination and slavery—men who took no orders except by choice, lordly creatures living as they pleased across the land."

The Comanches, Kiowas and Kiowa-Apaches managed to postpone the division of their reservation until 1901. Now came an influx of white settlers, thirty thousand of them over the next twenty years, and the spread of a mathematical gridwork across the land: 160-acre allotments fenced off with barbed wire and section-line roads which intersected at right angles. As the circle is sacred to plains Indians, so the grid, with its insistent linear geometry, is the sacred symbol of American civilization. It was no longer possible to move freely across the land, or camp wherever you wanted. The smooth space was gone. Even sounds were restricted in their travels by physical obstructions like barns and farmhouses and by a general increase in noise levels. The Comanches could no longer hear their drums, calling in the different groups for social meetings or peyote ceremonies.

But they remained a social people, accustomed to gathering in camps, and they found ways to perpetuate this tradition. They made circuits of each other's allotments. The peyote enthusiasts held pre-arranged meetings every weekend in different places. And there were large-scale tented encampments every New Year and mid-summer. The converts to Christianity, known as "church people," came together for revival meetings: prayers, sermons, testimonials. The more traditional Comanches gathered for ceremonial dances, attended by prayers, gambling and "giveaways" of money, food and gifts—to honor certain families or individuals (First World War veterans, for example) and redistribute the wealth. These dance gatherings, developed as a response to allotments and as a way to resist the intentions of the Dawes Act, became known as powwows and are still going strong.

Twenty miles north of Lawton, in the small town of Apache, the sound of drumming and singing emanates from a low concrete recreation center. The big summer powwows still take place outside, with tents and tepees, but there are smaller powwows almost every weekend, and most of them are held within walls.

I should also mention that powwows have become a pan-Indian institution. All the plains tribes have them and borrow powwow dances and costume styles from each other.

Inside: metal bleachers around the walls, white lines on a polished wood floor, hoops at either end—a basketball court. People are sitting in deckchairs, arranged in rows around a central space, where dancers are shaking gourd rattles and eight men are pounding an enormous drum and singing. Thump, thump, thump: a steady, monotonous rhythm, the heartbeat of Mother Earth, with an occasional THUMP–THUMP. "Hey-a-hah! Hey-a-hah! Hey-a-hah!" and sometimes, "Hiya-hey! Hiya-hey!" The dance is a simple, low-energy shuffle-step, as it needs to be. Today, the powwow will go on for eight hours, and sometimes they last all night.

There's Melvin—Melvin Kerchee Senior—eighty years old, dancing with a walking cane in one hand and an eagle-wing fan in the other. Some of the dancers are wearing elaborate costumes of satin and buckskin, with fringes, ribbons, tassels, jingling bells, brightly colored sashes and feathered headdresses. Melvin is dancing in jeans, sensible shoes, a regular shirt and a baseball cap that announces him as a Second World War veteran. He has close-cropped white hair and is wearing a pair of sunglasses that Elvis Presley might have worn. It is the younger generations who like to dress up for powwows, and his son Melvin Junior, with his long braids and eagle-feather warbonnet, is a particularly resplendent example.

Melvin Senior beckons me over and hands me a gourd rattle. There is no way to refuse without being rude. Raised on African-American music (jazz, blues, soul, funk, rock and roll), I have to fight the impulse to shake the rattle on the off-beat, or chanka-chanka-chank it on the quarter-beats, instead of bringing it down on the thump–thump–thump of the deep bass drum: the heartbeat of Mother Earth does not allow for syncopation. It's as rudimentary as music gets in the world, but after a while the insistent monotony of the rhythm and the repetitiveness of the chanting begin to work on me. I trance out a little, shaking the gourd and shuffle-stepping without thinking about it, or how out of place I look, and when the song eventually ends I want it to continue. Spectactors drop crumpled dollar bills at our feet. "Pick it up," says Melvin Senior. "That's hamburger money."

There is a break for a buffet dinner (boiled meat, corn and macaroni cheese), and I sit down to eat with Melvin Senior, his wife Nettie and some of their relatives. True to form, Melvin behaves scandalously. There are many facets to him, but above all he is known as a rascal, a prankster, a mischief-maker. He delights in making crude jokes and outrageous remarks in polite company, especially if he can get a rise out of Nettie, who is hard to shock after fifty years of marriage. At one point, an aged, dignified Comanche gentleman comes over and announces sadly that he has been diagnosed with diabetes. "Don't worry," says Melvin Senior. "I'll give you mouth-to-mouth when you collapse. Give you a little tongue if you want it." That wins him a gasp, a scolding and a slap on the arm from Nettie, which Melvin receives with enormous satisfaction, and the elderly gentleman walks away, grinning and shaking his head at the outrageousness of Melvin.

When you catch him in the right mood, Melvin Senior is a fount of oral history about the tribe. He is a fluent Comanche speaker, directly descended from important chiefs (Ten Bears, White Wolf) on both sides of his family. His grandfather was born into the old life on the plains and then became a trail cowboy, riding with Charles Goodnight and delivering herds from Texas to Kansas—a way to continue roaming the plains on horseback. In his old age, settled in Oklahoma, he made a concerted effort to pass on what he knew about being Comanche to his grandson.

Melvin has been solving ethnographical puzzles for me all week. Reading about the Comanche diet in the old days, I wondered why there was no mention of mare's milk, a calorie-rich food that was the staple diet of Eurasian nomads, and which the Comanches possessed in abundance. "Sure we drank mare's milk," Melvin told me. "Not if we had buffalo meat, but we would drink it. We would make a medicine out of it that's good for cataracts in the eyes."

I wondered how Comanches had been able to navigate so well on the flat and almost featureless plains that made up so much of their territory. What did they use for landmarks? Melvin said there were seven different words in Comanche for different types of small hill: round hill, hill eroding on the east, "tit hill," and so on. He told me about leaning trees: they would tie down a sapling so it pointed toward a waterhole and the tree would grow leaning in that direction. (Later, I discovered that a chance remark by Melvin Senior about leaning trees, or "turning trees," to a historian in Texas had produced a flurry of historical papers and the discovery of a few of these trees.) He is acutely aware that what he knows will die with him unless someone records it. He would prefer it if Comanches were doing this work, and a few of them are, but white people are better than nothing. He keeps admonishing me: I need to stay for a few months and bring a tape-recorder.

He has warned me repeatedly against camping in the Wichita Mountains because of the ghosts. A lot of Comanches are buried up there, he says. Their bones lie in caves and crevasses, and their spirits reinforce the old taboo against visiting burial sites and places of death. I have ignored these warnings because I like it up there and the buffalo herds are calving. Of all the North American mammals, there is something particularly poignant and hopeful about watching a buffalo give birth.

Melvin shakes his head over my stubbornness. I woke up this morning with a crick in my neck: what more evidence do I need? He leads me outside to the parking lot with Melvin Juniojr, who has prepared a brazier of coals in a coffee can, and two other relatives. Melvin Senior takes a plastic bag of dried cedar sprigs from his pocket and sprinkles them on the coals. He calls us up one by one and wafts the smoke over us with his eagle-wing fan while saying a prayer of protection in Comanche. I'm not a believer in this kind of thing, but the smoke has a wonderful aromatic smell, and the brush of the eagle wing and the soft, murmured prayer are soothing and relaxing. "Maybe that'll help with the spooks," he says.

Meanwhile, not fifty yards away, groups of teenage Comanches are lounging around in their cars and trucks, inhaling a different kind of aromatic smoke. They could be teenagers anywhere in America, in their baggy brand-name clothes, baseball caps and sun-visors, passing a joint back and forth with practiced nonchalance, nodding their heads to a parental-advisory rap CD. The license plates on their cars feature the tribal logo—a horseman with a war lance—and the legend "Numunu, Lords Of The Plains." I think of the second- and third-generation Mexican-American teenagers in my neighborhood in Tucson who speak very little Spanish and paint Aztec figures and symbols on their lowriders. I think of Irish-Americans drinking green beer on St. Patrick's Day. Italian-Americans, Jewish-Americans . . .

The Comanches have been on American soil for thousands of years, but they are immigrants into American culture, dealing with immigrant concerns. The elders still speak the old language and retain many old customs and beliefs—Melvin Senior's generation were the first Comanches to grow up in houses, instead of tents and tepees. Their children grew up speaking English and developed a hybridized or hyphenated identity. Elders are perfectly happy with the term "Indian." Their children, especially if they have been near a university, are more likely to use the white term "Native American." Their grandchildren, by the looks of things, are further down the road of assimilation—too far, according to the older generations, who have responded by setting up Comanche language classes, cultural heritage programs and anti-drug programs based on camping with horses.

As Italian-Americans have retained distinctive customs through the process of assimilation—the kiss between male relatives, ways of gesticulating, culinary traditions, ideas about family, religion and social etiquette—so it is with Comanches. They have assimilated further than the reservation tribes, but they still have their powwows, peyote meetings, customs of gift-giving (it is impossible to get out of their houses without something), eating the "Bible," communalism and all the things Jimmy Arterberry listed.

And what about travel? Are Comanches more likely to hit the road than other people in the American West? Yes, absolutely, says Jimmy Arterberry. Maybe the men, says Delphine Nelson, but not the women—"We're too busy keeping it all together." As always there are no statistics. There are obvious semantic difficulties: hit the road for how long, how often and compared to whom exactly? I ask Melvin Senior if Comanches still like to travel and move around and his answer is probably the definitive one: "Some do, some don't."

Among those who do, one finds a distinctive cultural attitude toward nomadic or quasi-nomadic travel. The experience of roaming around the American West is different for a Comanche, or so they say. They understand it as their tribal heritage, their birthright, their genetic legacy—a way of being Comanche.

Down at the tribal headquarters the construction of the buffalo fence has stalled, for some reason, but progress has been made with the mustangs. They are partially broken now, no longer crashing into the fence rails, and loving the rich new diet of sweet feed (an unfortunate metaphor, I suppose, for the Comanches and diabetes). The men working with horses are using a mixture of old and new techniques: hobbling them with ropes and breathing into their nostrils in the traditional Comanche way, doctoring them with modern medicines, spreading their manure with a tractor.

They take a break and pull out Pepsis and Dr Peppers from a cooler. I get talking to Tim Saupitty (cousin of Richard Saupitty, the tribal policeman), who has spent most of his adult life on the road, selling his artwork at Indian gatherings, tribal fairs and pow-wows all over the West—the Indian equivalent of the rendezvous circuit. "We're still nomads in our hearts," he says. "Whenever I'm on the road, especially going down to Texas, I'm aware that I'm crossing the same ground as my ancestors. It used to be you'd pick your best horse for the journey. For me, it was whatever old beat-up car I could get hold of. I'm forty years old and I must have owned twenty cars."

Donnie Parker is there, one of the myriad descendants of Quanah Parker and his seven wives, and he tells a story about his grandmother. "We were having dinner one night and she started talking about one of her sons, who was living in Albuquerque, New Mexico. So after dinner we jumped in the truck and drove over there to see him, five hundred miles, like it was nothing. That's how it is in my family. We always keep food and water and camping gear in the back of the truck, so we can just take off at the drop of a hat. That's how it's always been. It's in the blood."

And I thought how nice it must be to have such a neat, tidy, culturally approved explanation for your wandering ways, to say with absolute conviction that it's in the heart, in the blood, in the genes. Try explaining to a Comanche with wanderlust that he is suffering from a disease, listed in psychiatry manuals as dromomania and apparently treatable with sedatives and a course of therapy.

CHAPTER 9

Whenever an American wants to drop out or back into
Nature, invariably he "becomes an Indian" . . . seeking to
participate in their occult power, their mythic radiance. From
the Mountain Men to the Boy Scouts, the dream of
"becoming an Indian" flows beneath strands of American
history, culture and consciousness.

Hakim Bey, *T.A.Z.: The Temporary Autonomous Zone*

Medicine Wing is slouched behind the wheel of his 1976 VW
microbus, inching along a dirt road in the Allegheny National
Forest in western Pennsylvania, stuck in a long and seemingly
endless traffic jam. He is tired, having driven the fifteen hundred
miles from Colorado in three days, and he is deeply stoned on
top-grade, red-haired, skunky-smelling, four-hundred-dollars-an-
ounce marijuana—"The Superdank." You might think that a small
pipe would be more convenient for cross-country work, but
Medicine Wing travels with a glass water bong, sealed with two
corks between uses, and housed under his seat in a padded nest
of foam and velvet.

"How did you end up living on the road?" I ask him.

"Right," he says. "The road . . ." He gazes out of the window,
trying to collect his thoughts, and becomes distracted by the
shifting patterns of sunlight in the foliage. Thirty seconds go by.
"Whoa," he says. "Dude, that is so fucking trippy."

Interviewing him has been a faltering, haphazard process but this is what I have learned so far. Medicine Wing: twenty-five years old, born and raised in various suburbs around Washington, DC, perennial source of disappointment to his parents and step-parents. They still call him Scott and cling to the hope that this is just a phase—"Dude, they're, like, so heinous. They want me to be, like, this lawyer guy or this Wall Street guy or something, you know? The whole yuppie headfuck thing. It's actually sad, dude, but that's their whole trip."

He has close-set blue eyes, a wispy blond beard, a stud through his nose and a row of silver rings along his left eyebrow. Blond dreadlocks coming in nicely after a year of no shampoo. A thin face—no, a narrow face: full-lipped and Roman-nosed, but oddly constricted for width, as if a giant had reached down into his cradle, clasped the sides of his face and gently pressed them together.

On his arm is a tattoo of a plains Indian in a feathered warbonnet. It strikes me as an odd symbol for a devout pacifist and vegetarian, but Medicine Wing says I have it all wrong when it comes to Indians: "We were warriors for the earth, dude. We only fought to protect our sacred lands from the white man." What about raiding, inter-tribal warfare, captive-taking, scalping? "Babylon lies," invented by white historians. What about hunting and meat-eating? "No, dude, we were mostly vegetarian." He claims a deep knowledge of these matters because in a past life he was a Lakota shaman, and before that a Hopi mystic, and he still feels essentially Native American, "in my heart, in my soul, the vibes I'm putting out."

He reaches under the seat, plucks the bong from its velvet nest, uncorks it and loads in another pinch of The Superdank. *Hubble-bubble-bubble.* Holding the smoke in his lungs, he raises the bong to the sky (swiftly and a mite furtively, for fear of cops) and croaks out a brief, strangulated prayer to the Great Spirit. Exhaling now, and borrowing from Rastafarianism, he describes marijuana (and only top-grade marijuana) as the "holy herb," the sacrament of his religion, to be taken first thing in the morning and at regular intervals throughout the waking hours. Imagine a Catholic priest addicted to communion wine, and you have an idea of Medicine Wing's relationship to The Superdank. Low-grade marijuana is "schwag" and does not necessitate the same ritual and prayer. Alcohol is "Babylon poison" and he never touches it.

How can I describe the smell in here? It is a rich, pungent, complex aroma, dominated by gasoline fumes from the old, leaky VW engine and the cloying scent of patchouli oil. The patchouli is intended to mask the other smells in the van but it acts more like olive oil in a sauce, as a conduit or a medium in which the other smells can express themselves: body odor and bad breath, stale smoke and bongwater, spilled coffee, rotting fruit in the food crate, old pizza boxes converted into ashtrays, a damp, sour, mildewy smell emanating from the mattresses and sleeping bags in the back, where Medicine Wing's traveling companions—Hawk Feather and Julie, who is now Willow Leaf—are crashed out in a stupor. For a newcomer to the van, the smell is a big, domineering presence, but Medicine Wing doesn't notice it any more. This is the smell of home, the smell of life.

The traffic jam moves forward thirty yards and comes to another standstill. Medicine Wing sighs and slumps back in his seat, rolls himself a Bugler cigarette, loses his lighter, wishes he had a cup of coffee. He tries to rally himself, to contact the excitement and anticipation that have been building inside him all week, all month, all summer long, but he is too tired, and too blearily stoned. Maybe a sugar rush will pull him out of it.

He turns off the engine and gets out of the microbus, a lean scarecrow figure in cut-off army surplus fatigues and an old tie-dyed Grateful Dead T-shirt, standing about five feet ten in his bare feet. He pads up to the white rental car in front and squats down on his haunches by the driver's window.

"Hey, welcome home, brother," says the driver.

"Welcome home," says Medicine Wing. "Hey, brother, d'you have any zuzus? I'm in, like, *baaahd* need of a sugar rush, dude."

The two dudes have never met each other before, but everyone is family here—the Rainbow Family of Living Light—come together in their thousands for the national gathering in the woods. Casting around for a point of reference, I find myself comparing the gathering to an outdoor music festival, but there are no scheduled bands here, no admission fees, no concession stands or portable toilets. Maybe the Gathering is better summarized as a mobile backwoods commune. It forms every summer in a different location then dissolves and re-forms at smaller, regional Rainbow gatherings through the rest of the year—a "Nomadic Utopia"* founded on the principles of peace, love, spiritual harmony and communal sharing. In Rainbow parlance "zuzus" are sweets or candies, highly prized items at the gatherings, where the staple diet (doled out free of charge by the volunteer kitchens) is a beige vegetarian sludge. Nevertheless, it would be unthinkable for a Rainbow who was holding zuzus not to share them with a brother in need.

"Here you go, dude," says the driver, handing over a cellophane packet. "Welcome home!"

"Awri-i-i-ight!" says Medicine Wing. "Gummy Bears, dude! Most excellent zuzus." He chomps down a few of them, then wanders up and down the traffic jam calling out, "Hey, who wants a zuzu? Medicine Wing has got the righteous Gummy Bears to feed the Family."

"Right on! . . . Over here, brother! . . . You're beautiful! . . ."

A line of hands appears, outstretched from the car windows, and Medicine Wing walks along it, giving out Gummy Bears until the bag is empty. Walking back, he sees smiling faces framed in every windshield, that special beatific Rainbow smile, and as he passes by the faces turn and say, "Thank you, brother," "Loving you," "Welcome home," and one sister jumps out of her car to give him a hug.

Medicine Wing is grinning and energized now, shaking his head at the wonder of it all. "There's the Rainbow magic, dude," he says, sitting back down in the driver's seat. *Hubble-bubble-bubble.* "It's like this whole incredible vibe that just *happens*, you know, when the Family gets together, and everyone gets in tune with Mother Earth, and the forest vibes, and the Great Spirit,

---

* A phrase borrowed from Michael I. Niman's book *People of the Rainbow: A Nomadic Utopia.*

and the miracles just start to happen! It's all connected, dude! Every molecule in your body, okay, *every* molecule, is like every other molecule in the universe so how can it *not* be connected? There's no way, dude! It's like wherever you are, there you are, and you've already *been* there, man! It's like next time, you might be a grain of sand and that's totally cool. Or a tree, or a bird, like the winged brothers, or, like, an alien in another galaxy, or whatever, dude. It doesn't matter. One love. Universal vibes. That's what it's all about."

I latched on to Medicine Wing by pure happenstance. In an hour of wandering up and down the traffic jam, he was the first Rainbow I found who lives on the road year-round. As an entity, the Rainbow Family is nomadic—it has no fixed location, it takes form wherever the mobile commune is set up—but most of its members make their living within sedentary society. Of the estimated twenty-two thousand people at this year's Gathering, maybe two thousand are full-time nomads. The rest, in Medicine Wing's estimation, are "weekend hippies," taking a brief vacation from Babylon, or "yuppies," a term he uses to describe anyone who has a salaried job. Even in the Rainbow Family, which prides itself on tolerance, inclusiveness and egalitarianism, one finds the old nomadic disdain for the sedentary.

And talking to the sedentary Rainbows about the nomads, one hears the usual sedentary mixture of disapproval and envy: a tendency to characterize the nomads as irresponsible escapees and imbue them with a certain untamed romance. I first got a sense of this from a twenty-nine-year-old paralegal called Chris Wagner who had driven here from Philadelphia and was sitting in a Honda Accord with his wife and baby daughter. "I've got love for all my Family," he said. "I'd love to be out on the road with those guys, but I guess we're looking for a little more comfort and security in our lives right now. She's got to go to school for one thing, but it's more than that. I don't know, Babylon is fucked up, but it's our responsibility to change it, you know? If you want to drop out altogether and spend your life on the road, that's cool, but we also need people to work within the system, organizing in their local communities, trying to change people's perceptions and make a better world for our children."

The Rainbow nomads belong to several different groups, distinguished by social backgrounds, accents and modes of transportation. The more affluent nomads, traveling in RVs and schoolbus conversions, call themselves "gypsies" and tend to come from a well-educated, middle-class background. Medicine Wing and his companions, despite the shabby condition of their microbus, might be pegged on the lower fringes of "gypsy" and this is the term they use to describe themselves. Below them are the "tramps," "hoboes" and "road dogs" who roam the country in ancient, shit-heap vans and trucks, by hopping freight trains and hitchhiking (Medicine Man in the Dragoon Mountains, for example). They tend to come from blue-collar backgrounds in the South and West, and have Scotch-Irish ancestry.

Among the tramps and road dogs there is a hardcore cadre of belligerent alcoholics, many of them Vietnam veterans, who are in and out of jail for petty crimes—driving with expired tags, begging in a town that requires a begging license, trespassing on railroad property, hitchhiking in an unauthorized location, possession of marijuana, public drunkenness, bar-brawling or urinating in public, which in many states is equivalent under the law to masturbating in public. Although most Rainbows would wince and object to the term, these drawling, alcoholic tramps represent the Rainbow underclass and they are required to camp apart from the main Gathering.

This is the dreaded A-Camp. The A stands for alcohol, and A-Camp is the only place in the Gathering where alcohol is permitted. Violence is commonplace, lewd remarks are yelled at passing women and peace-loving dudes sometimes get threatened with knives for money. A-Camp is the dark side of the Rainbow Gathering, the ultimate test of the Family's tolerance and inclusiveness, a place where all taboos are broken. Medicine Wing is horrified to learn that I was invited here by A-Campers (encountered at a flea market in Arizona) and advises me to steer well clear: "Dude, it's like *monstro* bad vibes."

We're nearing the main parking area now, a mad melee of

people and jostling vehicles in a forest meadow. Volunteer organizers are yelling and directing traffic, handing out leaflets and maps, and here comes a young, bearded, bare-chested Rainbow, wearing purple pantaloons, pink sunglasses and an enormous foam-rubber stovepipe hat. He looks in the van and says, "Hey, seat belts on, people. Don't give the man an excuse to bust you." Then he catches a whiff of The Superdank. "Damn, brother, you've been smoking that kind bud! But hey, be cool all right. The cops have totally been busting people for herb."

There is a delicate legalistic balance here, a palpable tension between the forces of control and the forces of anarchy. This is national forest land, theoretically owned by the American people, but administered and policed by the federal government, through its appointees in the National Forest Service. And here are twenty thousand people prone to nudity, drug-taking, and ecstatic dancing, assembled on the government's land without permits or permission, engaged in an experiment to show that government itself, or any kind of coercive, hierarchical power structure, is unnecessary and poisonous.

As you might expect, the authorities—state, local and federal—have repeatedly tried to ban the Rainbow Gathering, but it has taken place every summer since 1972 because of a pesky clause in the Bill of Rights. The First Amendment guarantees the right of the people to assemble peaceably, and since there is no commerce of any kind at the gatherings the Rainbow Family is legally entitled (by prevailing judicial interpretation) to assemble on national forest land—"public" land—without a permit.

Defeated in the courts by unpaid volunteer Rainbow lawyers, the authorities have come to a kind of sullen, reluctant accommodation with the Family. They allow the Gathering to take place but subject it to various kinds of petty harassment: stopping and searching vehicles on vague pretexts, videotaping license plates, patrolling with sniffer dogs, planting undercover agents dressed up like hippies, filing new lawsuits and trying to whip up a public outcry by spreading rumors and misinformation to the media. The authorities have alleged that the Gathering is a thin excuse for interstate drug trafficking, that Rainbows are dealing crack and heroin, and trading runaway children into prostitution and white slavery.[*]

I arrange to meet Medicine Wing later and hop out of the microbus to talk to the local sheriff's deputies. There are four of them, leaning against a Ford Bronco, big solid country boys with huge, beefy forearms. They have been giving out tickets for seat-belt violations, arresting a few people for flagrant marijuana smoking, but on the whole they are retaining an attitude of detached amusement toward the freak show passing through their county. "If we wanted to, we could stop this thing in a heartbeat," one of them assures me, without being asked.

"But how?" I say. "You've got twenty thousand people here, spread out through ten miles of forest, and most of them are an hour's walk from the nearest road."

"Don't you worry," he says. "If we wanted to, we could call in the National Guard, go in there and drag every one of them hippies out of the woods." He turns to his partner and says, "Shit, look at that crazy hippie over yonder."

"Which one?"

He points to a small dervish hippie in his early fifties, wearing a loincloth and a pair of black socks and hiking boots. He is whirling around in circles, flapping his arms, cackling, squawking, hooting, and he's coming this way. He stops and points his finger at the cops. "Alcohol deaths in America," he yells, "one hundred thousand a year. Marijuana deaths a year: zero! Hell, I don't drink but I don't want to stop you from drinking. Why do you want to stop people from smoking pot? Are you *nuts*? Do you believe in *lies*? Is that the problem here? Hah!"

One of the deputies—the alpha cop, a 240-pounder with a shaved head and wraparound Oakley shades—grins back and says, "All right, brother, you've persuaded me. I'm gonna grow my hair real long, quit bathin', and sit around on my nature-lovin' ass all day. Why don't you give me a joint, brother? I won't bust you. I just wanna get *stoned*."

---

[*] This last ridiculous item from a 1983 FBI memo, quoted in Niman.

Well, everyone cracks up at that one: the deputies, the bystanders, even the cavorting hippie. "That's a good one," he allows, "but hey man, I own my own business."

"What kinda business would that be, brother? A little horticulture, perhaps? I know you ain't in the soap business."

"Hey man, fuck you, man! I smell like a human being is supposed to smell after four days on the road. I drove up here from Austin, Texas, man. That's where I've got my business. Computer software, man! I made sixty-five thousand dollars last year. Hah! Smoked pot every goddamn day! Hah! How much money did you make last year, Officer! Whoooooooooh-hah!"

The alpha cop just smiles behind his Oakleys and turns to get back in his vehicle. "Well, it"s been real nice visiting with you, but we've got work to do," he says. "Watch out for them brown recluse spiders. We've already got eight spider-bit hippies in the hospital. And watch out for them timber rattlers in the rock piles."

"Aw hell man, don't give me that shit!" squawks the hippie. "Spiders and snakes don't wanna bite nobody. They're my brothers. See, when you're in tune with nature, every living thing in the woods is your brother."

"Oh that's it, huh?" says the alpha cop. "If you love up on that ol' brown recluse, he ain't gonna crawl in your tent? That ol' rattler ain't gonna bite you when you step on him? I see a timber rattler in the woods, I love on him with this." He pats the gun on his hip, to loud hooting guffaws from the other deputies.

The cavorting hippie goes off and comes back at the wheel of a pickup truck. I get in the back with four others and he ferries us to a trailhead that leads into the Gathering proper. We strap on our backpacks and start walking down a muddy trail, toward the distant sound of drums. A few people are pulling wooden carts through the mud or pushing wheelbarrows, and one couple has rigged up their dog with a harness and travois poles.

Sitting on a log by the side of the trail, a naked man is rolling cigarettes from a big bag of tobacco and offering them to passersby. He has long blond curls, a deep Southern accent and a prosthetic leg. "We're collecting wood for the bliss fire at the Yin–Yang

Kitchen tonight," he says. "If I give you a cigarette, how about picking up a piece of firewood and taking it down there?" There are many of these requests along the trail, especially to the empty-handed. "Carry this watermelon as far as you feel like carrying it and pass it on to someone else." "Help us break up this fire-wood." "Does anyone feel like taking this sack of lentils to the next kitchen?"

This is how the logistics of the Gathering work. All the labor is voluntary and shared, and everyone is expected to help out—shirkers are known as "Drainbows." I stop off and help dig one of the slit trenches that serve as the Family's latrines. With twenty thousand people and no toilets there is a very real danger of fly-borne disease, not to mention fouling the woods, and the Rainbows, through trial and error, have come up with a simple, effective solution. The trench is covered by a piece of wood with a foot-wide hole cut in it and a lid. Next to it is a coffee can full of ashes from the fire and toilet paper, both of which you throw in when you're finished, and a bucket of bleached water for washing your hands. When the trench gets too nasty, you throw in some lye and fill it up with earth. They are called "shit-ters" to remind people not to urinate in them—urine impedes the chemical breakdown.

Everyone is encouraged to bring their own camping gear, and food to donate to the kitchens, and once a day the Magic Hat goes around the Gathering, collecting monetary donations ("green energy") for food, gasoline for the ferry vehicles and other supplies. It is, however, perfectly acceptable to show up at a Rainbow Gathering with nothing—no food, no money, no camping gear, no shoes. You will be outfitted from a pile of donated clothes and gear, fed at the free kitchens, and unless you are a complete Drainbow you will gladly give some free labor in return.

From the trailhead it's about two and a half miles to the center of the Gathering: a large, open meadow filled with tented camps and kitchens, tepees, spiritual workshops, drum circles and a great milling throng of thousands of people. I pass a meditation group, a sweat lodge, a crèche, an amateur theatrical, a Tarot workshop, a dozen naked women standing under a rigged-up shower, a dozen whirling, chanting Hare Krishnas with sharp elbows and dead, humorless faces.

A group of scrawny teenage hippies are "fishing for a bowl": holding out an empty marijuana pipe in one hand and pretending to reel in a fish with the other. Sooner or later someone will fill the pipe bowl. Over by the Rainbow Crystal Kitchen a teenage gutter-punk is thrashing on the ground and screaming, in the throes of a bad acid trip, and a circle of people are standing around him, chanting, "Ommmmm." And it works. He calms down. People hug him and he starts to smile. There's plenty of weed, acid and mushrooms around, but no sign of dealing and no powdered drugs. What I'm craving is a cold beer, but A-Camp is four or five miles away. Apparently, they were throwing quarter-sticks of dynamite into their fire last night.

You might call it a diverse crowd. I come across lawyers, bankers, organic farmers, social workers, infants and octogenarians, Christians and pagans, stoners, ravers, punks, tramps, trustafarians, original hippies, nouveaux hippies, every type of hippie imaginable. Or you might call it a homogeneous crowd, because about 95 percent of the people here are white.

I'm looking for an American Indian, a real one. I want to know how this looks through Indian eyes: the white people with feathers, beaded medicine bags and ersatz pipe ceremonies, the tepees and sweat lodges, the names like Medicine Wing and Hawk Feather, the invocations to the Great Spirit, and so on. In leaflets, newsletters and conversations the claim is repeated that the Rainbows embody "the true spirit of the Native Americans," "the pure Indians of old," "the wise Indians of old," "the joyful Indians of old." What would a living, breathing Indian make of all this? Would he feel flattered that his ancestors are so revered? Or would he take it as an insult, a suggestion that living Indians are false, impure, stupid and miserable? Would he find it ridiculous? Presumably it would depend on the Indian, but I can't find one to ask.

Posted all over the Gathering is a piece of doggerel masquerading as an ancient Hopi Indian prophecy: "It is said that when the earth is weeping and the animals are dying that a tribe of people who care will come. They will be called the Warriors of the Rainbow." The Hopi prophecy is a prime example of what Michael Niman calls "fakelore," the tendency of Rainbows to invent romantic myths about themselves and appropriate other people's history as their own. The Hopi elders have no knowledge of this supposed prophecy, and they have asked the Rainbows to stop using it. Well, try telling that to Medicine Wing. You'll get trumped every time. After all, he *was* a Hopi, back when Hopis were really Hopis, so he ought to know.

Fakelore aside, the Rainbows—at least the traveling Rainbows—probably are the nearest equivalent to a nomadic Indian tribe in modern America. Why? Because they have a communal ethic, a consciousness of belonging to a tribe, a spiritual connection to nature. And a few of them, at least, travel with mothers and children.

In the bus village, the gypsy camps and tramp camps there are families and groups of families who manage to live on the road year-round, as migrant farm workers, flea-market traders, computer programers and consultants ("technomads"), craft workers, artists. There are others, like the Ohana Tribe (not to be confused with the native Hawaiian tribe of the same name), who spend the whole year in national forest campgrounds, raising their children on a circuit of smaller, regional Rainbow Gatherings and supporting themselves within the Rainbow economy.

How do the nomadic Rainbows educate their children? There are three basic strategies available: homeschooling, by mail or e-mail; moving from school to school, enrolling and withdrawing your child, like migrant fruit-picker families; or staying off the grid entirely, avoiding the education authorities and breaking the truancy laws. I can't find anyone who admits to using this third strategy, but people say it is easily done. You stay mobile and stick to remote areas. If cops or forest rangers start asking questions, you tell them that you are in the process of relocating the family to a new town, or traveling to the next crop harvest, and will enrol the children in school when you get there.

Former British prime minister John Major ran away from a circus family to join an accountancy firm, and one wonders how many of these nomadic Rainbow children will rebel against their

upbringing in the same way, and become lawyers, tax account-
ants, business executives. One imagines the crushing disappointment of their parents.

Turtle Momma sits in the back of a tarpaulin lean-to, at Chico
Sunie's Yin-Yang Kitchen, with two babies sleeping on a blanket
next to her. This is a Rainbow tramp camp, predominantly male,
which moves around the country in a loose convoy of old vehicles, with others hitchhiking and riding the rails to the next
assembly point. They have been here for two weeks already, making
trails, digging shitters, hauling in gear, setting up the kitchen and
dumpster-diving in town for their food until the Rainbow supply
trucks showed up a few days ago.

"A lot of people look down on the tramps and road dogs and
A-Campers," she says, "but we get here first, and we're the last
to leave, and we do most of the work around here."

"Damn right," says Peg Leg, who is still naked, and has hobbled
into the tent to unhitch his prosthesis. "When all these weekend
hippies have gone home, we'll be picking up every piece of trash,
filling in the shitters, sowing seeds in the muddy, tromped-out
areas to bring back the grass and replanting over the trails. A year
or two from now it'll look like we were never here."

Turtle Momma is a good name for Turtle Momma. She is wide
for her height, a broad, oval shape you might say, and she exudes
an earth-motherly warmth and kindness, a deep, calm patience.
The babies are not hers. Their mothers wanted to drop acid and
dance around the bliss fire tonight, and she told them to get to
it and have a beautiful trip. The other women would watch the
babies, and who knows? They might even get a man to help out.
Peg Leg harrumphs when he hears this slur against his gender.
"Hell, I don't mind. I'll watch these kids with you." He puts in
ten gallant minutes, then rehitches his leg and gets back to the
party at the bliss fire.

Turtle Momma started traveling in the late 1960s, attending
the love-ins, be-ins and free festivals that laid the groundwork for
the first Rainbow Gatherings. She describes herself as a "nomadic
soul" who has raised generations of Indian children in past lives,

but she has conflicted feelings about nomadic motherhood in this incarnation. In principle she supports the idea as a matter of personal liberty and a way of protecting children from the corrupting influences of Babylon. In practice she settled down to raise her own children because it was easier to keep them fed, clothed and schooled that way. Giving up the road, she says, was the hardest thing about motherhood, the biggest sacrifice.

"I put in twenty years on the home front, and I raised great kids, but it wasn't me," she says. "As soon as they were grown up and out the nest I bought an old motor home and picked up where I left off." She laughs. "Now here I am, postponing adulthood all over again."

She moves awkwardly, with obvious pain. She needs operations to remove what she calls "ticking time-bombs" in her insides, but she can't afford the medical bills. She doesn't have thirty thousand dollars lying around, and since she is already sick no health insurance company will give her coverage. That probably sounds outrageous to a European reader, but millions of poor, sick Americans are in the same predicament: unable to get health insurance because they are a bad financial proposition. Conceivably, Turtle Momma could find an employer willing to take her on and pay her medical insurance through the company, but she would rather spend what time she has on the road, going to Rainbow Gatherings. Here she finds peace, love, hope, harmony, communal sharing, an appreciation of the sacred in nature—the nearest actualization of the principles she has held all her adult life.

It's not perfect, as she readily admits. The sedentary Rainbows need to get over their snobbery toward the tramps and A-campers. There have been conflicts over resources, such as financing A-Camp's beer consumption, and she sees more Drainbows than before. But these are minor flaws, easily remedied. For Turtle Momma, the Rainbow Gatherings add up to a good working model of utopia, and infinitely superior to anything Babylon has to offer.

Medicine Wing and Hawk Feather are not affiliated with the Yin-

Yang tramps. They came over here to check out the bliss fire and the rumors of some righteous acid going around. Willow Leaf is asleep again, back in the tent. I worry about Willow Leaf. Sallow and painfully thin, she has no stamina, no energy, no trace of anything that you could reasonably describe as buttocks. It looks like an eating disorder to me, because the act of putting food in her body is so fraught with anxiety and devoid of pleasure, but she calls it organic veganism. Her traveling companions, whose staple diet is dumpster-dived pizza, with any meat picked off and discarded, worry about her too. But what are you going to do? You can't even buy organic produce in most of the country, let alone find it in a dumpster.

These concerns are far from their minds now. The rumors were true. They brought some firewood with them and gave a bud of The Superdank to a good brother by the name of Medicine Wolf, and he steered them toward the acid. Righteous? You don't even know how righteous. Listen up and watch Rainbow fakelore in the making.

At first, they were told that the acid was fresh out of the lab of a Rainbow chemist, clean and pure as it gets. Now the story has moved on and launched into orbit. "This is some shit kicked down from 1964, brother!" announces Medicine Wolf, a red-bearded, biker-looking tramp who is tripping out of his gourd on the stuff. "Sandoz Laboratories, the original shit, back when acid was still *legal*, man." Someone somewhere had kept the acid refrigerated or otherwise preserved all these years because they knew this would be the perfect moment, and the perfect setting, for the acid to release its energy. And no one doubts this story, because miracles like this happen all the time at Rainbow Gatherings.

A troupe of drummers has materialized from the woods. I have driven three hundred miles today, walked about eight miles and filled up three-quarters of a notebook. The drummers keep me there for another hour. These goateed, tattooed, thirty-something white guys put together a kind of drum travelogue. They begin in West Africa, with something loosely borrowed from the Fela Kuti back catalogue, and keep returning to it.

They make excursions to Jamaica and turn back. They head north to the Berber rhythms of Morocco and turn back. They cross the Atlantic to Cuba, and then down to Georgia for some James Brown funk.

People are shouting encouragement. The tripping tramps in the kitchen are beating on pots and pans, and everyone is up and dancing around the bliss fire. The girls make a lot of sinuous, serpentine hand and arm movements, the kind that leave cool tracer lines when you're on acid, and the boys do a lot of head-bobbing and elbow-waggling, with occasional hopping twirls and tai chi moves.

A trumpet-player appears from the woods. He looks like one of those hippie jazz musicians from the 1970s—the white guy on the back cover of an obscure Miles Davis or a Pharoah Sanders album—but he is too young to be one of them. It takes him a few minutes to get warmed up and find the rhythm (James Brown has led us back to West Africa), and then he starts blowing a wild psychedelic blues over the top of it, hitting and holding incredible high notes.

I feel a stab of jealousy for Medicine Wing and Hawk Feather. I gave up LSD many years ago, but I know how this must sound to them, and how it feels when a group of dancing, tripping people peak on the music at the same time. I can see the mind-blown, bliss-drenched expressions on their faces. Why do they live on the road? There is a short answer to that question: to get from one of these moments to the next.

The full story comes out over the next two days. How three well-bred scions of the DC suburbs became nomadic Rainbows and assumed American Indian identities. The story stretches out over many past lives, but let's begin in high school, in Arlington, Virginia, in the late 1980s. This is when they became friends, and they say it has been a friendship entirely uncomplicated by sex. (They seem curiously disinterested in sex, regarding it as more hassle than it's worth; they'd rather get high.) Scott/Medicine Wing's mother was, and is, a policy analyst for a conservative foundation. Drew/Hawk Feather's mother is a lawyer. Julie/Willow Leaf's mother is also a lawyer. I mention the mothers because, in all three cases, they were granted custody after the parental divorce.

An easy theory presents itself here. These children of broken homes ran away and joined the Rainbow Family to find the love and sense of belonging that was missing in their own families. It sounds persuasive enough, and there may be some truth in it, but as they point out, most of the children at their high school went through a parental divorce. And there was only one other kid, from the grade below, who became a full-time traveling Rainbow.

The collapse of your parents' marriage, the interrogations in lawyers' offices and courtrooms, the arrival of stepdads and step-moms in your life—none of it was easy but somehow the whole process seemed normal and inevitable, a basic rite of passage that kids had to go through, like dealing with puberty. Anyway, they never saw much of their parents, who were putting in twelve- to fourteen-hour days at the office, trying to pay the bills and save up for the college fund.

Nor was it unusual for them to start smoking pot at the age of twelve. There were eight-year-olds in the DC suburbs who got high every day, ten-year-olds who were urine-tested once a month by their parents with the new home-testing kits adver-tised on television. Twelve, if anything, was a little on the late side, but once they got started, Scott, Drew and Julie became more ardent, devoted pot-smokers than most of their classmates. By the age of fifteen they were at the nucleus of the high-school stoner clique and making a little money, enough to cover their own consumption, by supplying their fellow stoners.

At seventeen they started going to Grateful Dead concerts together, and this was a major formative influence in their lives. They took acid for the first time and met people who followed the Grateful Dead year-round, taking acid all the time and going to Rainbow Gatherings in the first week of July.

In the media the Deadhead scene was usually described as a "hangover" or a "leftover" from the sixties—something tired and stale that had outlived its time, even though most of the people at Dead shows were under twenty-five. There was no buzz for a journalist to chase. The band had been touring, almost continuously, since the late sixties. Their followers, of whatever generation, were listening to the same old songs, taking the same old drugs, wearing the same fashions, repeating the same hoary aphorisms.

Well, it didn't seem that way to Scott, Drew and Julie. They were on the loose from uptight parents and weird step-parents, the dull regimentation and petty viciousness of suburban high school, and the Deadhead scene blew their minds. LSD was a major part of it, of course, the feeling of communal psychedelic ecstasy, but something more than drugs and music was working on them. They were welcomed with smiles and hugs. They were treated as equals by Deadheads young and old, surrounded with love and assurances of love. Gently, casually, painlessly, they were initiated into the tribe.

After the shows, in concert-arena parking lots and nearby camp-grounds, sitting in the back of a van or around a campfire, smoking weed to ease out the acid come-down, they received their instruc-tion in the tribe's philosophy and belief systems. These long, stoned nights constituted their true education, shaping their under-standing of the world more than anything they learned at school or absorbed through popular culture.

I once spent a week trailing the Deadheads, making notes at those same campfires. As an environment for learning, it was both solemn and intense, and incredibly vague and forgiving. Whatever was said, no matter how ill-informed, half-baked or self-contradictory—even, as I discovered, if the remark was intended as a joke or parody—it would be greeted with an automatic "Right on" and an earnest nodding of heads. A statement might be expanded or elaborated upon, but never challenged. That would be confrontational: bad vibes, a form of violence, a threat to the fragile bliss of the tripping brain.

In addition to rejecting the materialism and competitive indi-vidualism of Western civilization, Medicine Wing and his cohorts also came to reject its rationalist underpinnings—the dictates of logic, the demands for empirical evidence and scientific proof, the whole linear, cause-and-effect, Cartesian logic trip. Look what it had produced! A culture of greed and spiritual emptiness, nuclear weapons, alienation from nature, a suicidal, matricidal war against the Earth. Babylon was a product of Babylon Mind, this cold, scientific, heartless way of thinking.

At Deadhead campfires and Rainbow Gatherings, a different criterion for truth prevails. If it rings true in your heart, if it sounds appealing, if it manages to float up into your consciousness and make it out through your lips, that is good enough. Unless it smacks of Babylon Mind, anything is permitted, everything is true. What does it matter that the information has traveled through dozens of stoned brains? Who cares that it is long divorced from any written text or verifiable fact? And since everything in the cosmos is connected and interchangeable, malleable at a molecular level and responsive to the wishes and fancies of the human mind, how can any conclusion be judged as too far-fetched?

Scott had always felt an affinity for Native Americans. Even as a kid, even if it went against the intentions of the filmmaker, he had rooted for them on TV. Gracing his bedroom wall, back in Arlington, and now in tatters on the back door of the microbus, is the famous poster of Chief Seattle, with his poignant, stirring, ecological oratory printed underneath his photograph (unbeknown to Medicine Wing, the speech was heavily rewritten by a Hollywood screenplay hack, Ted Perry, in 1971).

Having shed himself of Babylon Mind, Scott came to understand that he actually *was* an Indian, and had been in at least two of his past lives. A Rainbow elder named him Medicine Wing at his first Gathering, and divined that the eagle was his animal totem. Then came the last year of high school, the worst year of his life. Grounded from Dead shows, threatened with urine-testing, guilt-tripped with stories of how hard his parents had worked to send him to college, he toughed it through and managed to graduate. So did Drew, who was already Hawk Feather, and Julie, who was still Julie. She started working in a health-food co-op. The boys went on to college and dropped out after the first semester.

"I was hoping college would be a cooler scene, but it was like Babylon Central, dude," says Medicine Wing. "It's like, here's all these preppy dudes, spending beaucoup bucks and racking up monstro debts so they can go and work for some corporate Babylon headfuck. Me and Hawk were so outta there."

They traded two ounces of The Superdank for the keys and title to the microbus, sold off or gave away most of their belongings, and hit the road. To an outsider, perhaps, it looked like an act of escape, but to them it felt more like a conscious, positive decision to link up with a mobile community that was out there and waiting for them. There were thousands of people who followed the Grateful Dead year-round, and went to Rainbow Gatherings in the summer, and they seemed happy, free, enlightened and welcoming. No one seemed to work and yet no one went hungry. The tribe had a vague, happenstance economy of its own, and it was easy to find a niche, especially if you had good pot connections.

For instance: a dude hears that Medicine Wing is holding The Superdank. He wants a quarter-ounce but doesn't have the hundred dollars. He does have a handmade African drum worth two hundred dollars, so a trade is made to the satisfaction of both parties. A week later Medicine Wing trades the drum for a quarter-ounce of weed, five tie-dyed T-shirts and a handcarved wooden bong, which he sells outside the next Dead show. It just seems to happen that way, as if by magic, with no one trying to drive a hard bargain.

Medicine Wing and Hawk Feather followed the Grateful Dead for two years, stopping in at the summer Rainbow Gatherings. Then came the great tragedy of August 1995, the death of Jerry Garcia, singer and lead guitarist of the Grateful Dead, and the breakup of the band. They spent a couple of months recuperating in Flagstaff, Arizona. They liked the town and the country around it, but all they could get was cheap Mexican weed. Flagstaff was Schwagstaff so they moved on to northern California. The next year they hit the road full time, following Phish and the various Grateful Dead offshoot bands, dropping in on Rainbow Gatherings, national and regional, stopping off to see friends around the country, and that has been their pattern ever since. A year ago they swung back through DC and picked up Julie, who is now Willow Leaf.

Understand the sense of mission they feel. As Rainbows, they belong to a tribe—the one true people, living in the one true way—which the Great Spirit has brought into being for a task of vital importance. The task is nothing less than saving the planet from nuclear war and/or environmental apocalypse, and ending human suffering and exploitation. You might, from the perspective of scientific rationalism, doubt the effectiveness of their methods. You might say, "Wait a minute, you're going to do all this by sitting around in the woods and getting high?" But having rejected scientific rationalism and embraced a magical universe, as all religions do to some extent, they have no such doubts. They are filled with utopian fervor. By setting a positive example to the rest of the world, by beaming out love, prayers and positive energy, they confidently expect to bring about a new dawn in human history, a new age of peace, harmony and spiritual enlightenment, and the Rainbow Gathering is proof that it is already under way.

There are two signs hanging from a tree limb above A-Camp, each keeping a running numerical total. One says "KEGS." Two weeks in, the keg count is up to 89 (no one is keeping count of the empty liquor bottles). The other says "FIGHTS" and stands at 27.

It is early afternoon, a fact that means very little at A-Camp. The pattern here is to drink until you pass out, wake up and start drinking again. Some people are so saturated, so ruined by drugs and alcohol, that they can only manage two-hour shifts before passing out again. Others can drink for eighteen or twenty hours at a stretch, although this usually requires the aid of LSD. At any hour of the day or night there will be people passed out on the ground and people drinking around the fire, sitting in a circle of old lawn chairs, and people staggering around, roaring and bellowing. Perhaps the clearest delineation between night and day is the use of dynamite, which seldom occurs before sunset.

The boss of A-Camp, whose word is absolute law, is a short, sturdily built woman in her fifties. Her name is Eileen, but the A-Campers call her Mom. She sits on a lawn chair, in black shorts and a black T-shirt, with a tobacco tin full of money on her lap. She has long, gray, frizzy hair pulled back in a ponytail, and a big, tough face that has seen a lot of hard living—a face like Charles Bukowski's. Stern and watchful, smoking her cigarettes, drinking her Pepsi, sometimes adding a little whiskey after dark, I never see her drunk, I never see her smile.

The only time I see her rattled is when a drunk comes over to give her a hug and inadvertently collapses on her and showers her with beer. She shoves him off and roars like an angry bear, "Get the fuck out of here, you sonofabitch! GET OUT!" He turns tail and staggers out of the camp. If he had disobeyed an order from Mom, the other A-Campers would have ejected him forcibly and almost certainly beaten him up.

Why is she here? What's in it for Mom? I assume it's the power she wields, and the unconditional love and devotion she receives. Maybe she just figures someone's got to do it. She takes my offered ten-dollar bill. Visitors to A-Camp are expected to contribute to the keg fund, to pay for their own beer and a little extra to support the regulars. She tells me that Chad and Tiffany, the couple who invited me here, are asleep, and that's all she's got to say to me.

She has a steel-trap memory. She knows which visitors have donated how much money to the keg fund, and how many beers they have tapped. With these donations, and a share of the Magic Hat fund, she keeps A-Camp constantly supplied with beer, ice, liquor, tobacco and food without leaving her chair. "Okay, we need sixteen bags of ice. Hey Doc, go find someone who's sober enough to drive. Here's twenty bucks." She keeps track of which A-Campers have eaten lately. "Hey, Cosmo, you need to eat some-thing." There is a big pan of fried venison by the fire and we are a long way from hunting season.

The deer was donated by a local biker, who has been drinking here, on and off, for a few days. At all Rainbow Gatherings a contingent of the local bikers, jocks and hard-cases will show up to party with the hippies and throw their weight around, but they can't imagine a party without beer. So they are directed to A-Camp and the threat of violence is confined and localized, away from the main Gathering. Most of the fights at A-Camp are between regulars and visitors, and they usually begin with wild drunken misunderstandings. Fight number 28: Cosmo attacks a visitor who was gathering wood for the A-Camp fire because Cosmo thought he was a "butthole-watcher," spying on the A-Camp women at the A-Camp shitter, even though no women were anywhere near the shitter at the time.

Fight number 29 is started by a guy named Joe, a part-time tramp in his thirties with a scraggly blond mullet. He used to be an A-Camp regular but he has missed the last few Gatherings. He has been living in Tucson in a biker/tramp commune on the edge of town and he wants to know why he hasn't seen me there. Suddenly, his face is six inches away, his breath is foul and he is yelling that I'm an undercover cop. Mom intervenes (thank you, Mom). "Look, Joe," she says. "The guy is a friend of Chad and Tiffany's. He's not a cop. I know you want a fight, Joe, but I can't help you with this one."

Five minutes later Joe takes a swing at Animal, a wiry, bearded, feral-looking Vietnam vet, with scars and scabs all over his face and a nose that has been broken too many times to count. There is a flurry of fists, Joe goes down, and Animal, quite literally, kicks his ass as he stumbles out of camp, knocking him down on all fours and kicking his ass some more. Afterwards, Mom summons Animal to her chair. She wipes the blood off his face and puts on her glasses to inspect the damage. "You're okay, Animal. You caught him a good one, too. If you hadn't hit him he would have caused even more trouble. You did good."

Tiffany appears. For someone who has just woken up and crawled out of a tent, after two weeks at A-Camp, she looks remarkably fresh-faced and clear-eyed. Being twenty-four helps, of course. And while Tiffany likes to get drunk and take drugs, she is an amateur by A-Camp standards, a tender young green-horn. We sit and talk while she works on the A-Camp flag, cutting slogans out of T-shirts and sewing them onto a big piece of canvas: "100% Whoop Ass," "Beer Is Food," "Blood Alcohol Experiment In Progress," "When You Step Through The Ropes, Your Ass Is Mine," "Fuck You, I've Got Enough Friends."

She has long brown hair, a sunny, relaxed disposition and a dirty laugh that goes well with her fresh-complexioned face. You get the impression that finding boyfriends has never been a problem for her. Tiffany tried the straight life. She got an office job out of high school in Ohio and filled an apartment with possessions—"I was bored out of my fucking mind." She hit the road three years ago, driving down to New Orleans with a friend and then striking out on her own. Memo to lone female hitch-hikers in their early twenties: "There are some sick, crazy men out there, and you better have a knife or a gun."

Chad is a hardened A-Camper twenty years her senior. She met him on the road two years ago and has been with him ever since. He is not every girl's dream catch, but he has an undeniable charisma and roguish charm, and an antic, twisted sense of humor that keeps her laughing. They travel the country in an old tradesman's van, with a belligerent black chow called Derail. They sell old pieces of junk, collectable rocks and minerals, and home-made jewelry at flea markets and swap meets, making the occasional fifty- or hundred-dollar drug deal with another tramp, stopping off to see Tiffany's family and do odd jobs for her father. "They get on great with Chad," she says. "We all have a good time together."

Chad appears in the late afternoon, walking toward the fire with loose soles flapping on his cowboy boots, a big, red, droopy mustache and a battered old cowboy hat. His face is puffy and swollen and there is a ghoulish yellow tint to his skin and his eyeballs—a sure sign of a failing liver. He sits down in his lawn chair, and doesn't say hello, doesn't say a word to anyone until he's got three beers inside him.

With eight beers inside him he starts to perk up. They call him Namegiver, and he starts listing some of the A-Campers he has nicknamed over the years: Puddlescum, Twisted Gizzard, Timmy Two Tokes, Mario Machete, Puff Nuggy, Shitstained Mike. Most of them didn't make it to A-Camp this year, because they're dead or in jail, and when their names are mentioned people pour a ceremonial splash of beer on the ground.

Chad is up and strutting now, with a beer in one hand and a

tattered old book in the other. He has renamed himself Bellerin"
Idiotfeather and assumed the role of a football coach. Last year,
A-Camp played a hard-fought, no-rules game of American football with the gutter-punks, which ended with three gutter-punks
in hospital, and the rematch is planned for tomorrow. Chad is a
die-hard Oakland Raiders fan, and the book is *They Call Me the
Assassin*, by a Raiders hardman named Jack Tatum.

"All right, we're gonna read from the sacred book! We're gonna
teach those pantywaist motherfuckers what it means to bleed!
We're gonna rip some heads off and shit down some necks!
Cosmo! I know you're short on wind, but you're my defensive
end . . ."

Mid-rant, a young, muscular, goateed hipster-type walks coolly
past him, gives five bucks to Mom, draws a beer and sits down
in a lawn chair. He is wearing baggy shorts, a wifebeater's under-
shirt and a thick-furred fedora hat. Chad stomps up to him and
gets in his face. "I don't like your hat. I don't like you. What do
you think about that, motherfucker?"

"Hey, it's all good. You don't like my hat. So what, man? I'm
cool with that."

"Hey, you're all right kid," says Chad, backing off and grinning. "Welcome home, brother."

The kid relaxes a little deeper into the chair, thinking he has
won a small victory, then Chad lunges forward and grabs him by
the shoulders. "Now get your pansy ass out of my chair! Put on
some tie-dye and go on up to the Buddhist camp, motherfucker!
I said it, I meant it, and I'm here to represent it." The kid gets
up and leaves.

"Man, how do I get away with it?" Chad guffaws, watching
him go. "Did you see the muscles on that guy? He could have
whupped me like an uppity stepchild."

The Rainbow Gathering reaches its grand culmination on the
Fourth of July. The morning is spent in silence (except at A-
Camp), and processions of people from all over the Gathering
(except A-Camp) make their way to a high meadow to pray for
world peace. Marijuana pipes are passed around in solemn silence,

people sit cross-legged and meditate. Others stand with their arms in the air and their palms raised. A man in a long white robe, belted with a chain of marijuana leaves, and a marijuana-leaf head-band waves a hawk's wing and executes a curious hopping dance step. Then he sets up a camcorder and tripod, and repeats the ritual in front of the lens. At twelve noon a soft "Ommmmm" begins and grows in volume. Didgeridoos join in, women ululate, beatific smiles everywhere.

I want world peace. I'm against nuclear war, environmental destruction and human misery, but there is a self-congratulatory quality to the Fourth of July prayer that puts my back up, like this is all we need to do. The truth is that I'm losing patience with hippies. I'm tired of being welcomed home a hundred times a day, tired of uninvited aura readings, tired of fakelore and the idea that vibes alone can change the world, and love is all you need. In my Babylon mind I'm more impressed by the practical workings of the Rainbow Gathering. It's not my scene but I've got to hand it to them. They have succeeded in creating a functioning anarchist utopia.

Being nomadic is its greatest strength. Stationary utopias—communes, for example—have to pay property taxes. They are far more visible and vulnerable to the authorities, and they are notoriously prone to develop internal leadership and faction struggles, and to move away from their original principles. The Rainbow Family, which only takes form at Gatherings, in remote forested areas, is a lot harder for the authorities to deal with. Each Gathering is an example of what Hakim Bey calls "the temporary autonomous zone," a place where people can do exactly as they please without interference by the state. When the authorities get wind of a TAZ and find a way to suppress it, you dissolve it and set it up again in a different location. Hakim Bey, the nom de plume of the subversive New York intellectual Peter Lamborn Wilson, believes this is the only workable form of anarchy that exists, given the power of the modern state and the fact that it's not going to be overthrown any time soon. This is a way to experience anarchy, rather than preach about it.

If you stay in one place, refuse to pay taxes and flout the law (drug laws, gun laws, nudity laws, school truancy laws, sexual age of consent laws), sooner or later the state will bring you to heel. If you keep moving, dissolving and re-forming the TAZ, it is harder for the authorities to keep an eye on you. He doesn't cite the nomadic Rainbows in the book, but they are the clearest living proof of his theory. As one Gathering ends, another begins. It's not pure anarchy—highway cops, forest rangers and other forms of state authority have to be dealt with or dodged around—but it's as close as you're going to get.

The other thing that impresses me about the Rainbow Family is their tolerance of A-Camp. They have made room in their utopia for behavior that breaks their taboos and horrifies them. This is unprecedented, from what I know of other utopian experiments. On my way out of the Gathering, I stopped off at A-Camp to say my goodbyes and got sucked into another long afternoon of beer-drinking and mayhem. Let me tell you about fight numbers 34 and 35, and the way the Rainbow Family responded.

Flat Nose Kelly was bombed out of his mind on beer, whiskey, weed and LSD, and half-crazy to begin with. He made a lunging grab for one of the A-Camp women, and Mom told him to get out. He protested his innocence, thereby disobeying a direct order from Mom. So Animal and Lori Lori, a tough and ferocious woman in steel-toed logging boots, rushed over and flattened him, and Lori Lori gave him a vicious kicking. Exit Flat Nose Kelly, covered with blood.

An hour later he came tottering back with a knife, looking even more wasted than before. "What do you think about this, motherfuckers!" he yelled, and then he stabbed himself in the chest.

This was a clear sign of disrespect and Animal was enraged: "You don't stab yourself in our camp, motherfucker!" He charged Flat Nose Kelly, the knife went flying, and then Animal bit off the top half of Flat Nose Kelly's ear. Then Lori Lori gave him another kicking. (Lori Lori is also known as The Keg Ogre: when beer supplies are low she stands over the keg to frighten away visitors.)

Later, an earnest young Rainbow organizer came up to A-

Camp to find out what had happened. He had just got back from
the hospital. Lori Lori stomped up to him and in her hoarse,
croaking voice she tried to explain: "Fucking asshole stabbed
himself. It was his own fucking knife."

"Okay, I'm not saying I don't believe you. He seemed crazy
enough to actually do something like that. But how does he bite
his own ear off? The doctor said . . ."

"No, man, Animal bit his fucking ear off," she said, "and I
kicked the shit out of the motherfucker. You don't fucking stab
yourself in our camp."

He was still trying to digest that piece of logic when Animal
showed up and accused him of stealing the ear. Animal wanted
it for a trophy; necklaces of human ears were sometimes worn
by American GIs in Vietnam—"Where's that fucking ear, you
faggot motherfucker? That fucking ear is *mine*!"

"The dogs got your fucking ear, man," said Lori Lori. "I think
it was Derail." And then she caught the expression on the young
Rainbow's face, a freaked-out look of fear and total bewilder-
ment, like a rabbit in the headlights, and she cracked up laughing.
"Hey, you're beautiful, man. Now go on and get your ass outta
here before Animal does something crazy."

Half an hour later, three young Rainbow hippies came up to
A-Camp, looking very serious and slightly nervous. I assumed
they wanted to talk to Animal and Lori Lori about the legal
repercussions of the Flat Nose Kelly incident, or ask them to
leave the Gathering. But no. The Rainbow way is to counter
bad vibes with love and acts of kindness. They were carrying
backpacks full of food for A-Camp: potatoes, onions, green
peppers, rice. They were greeted with ugly drunken threats and
taunts.

They didn't say a word. They unloaded the food and started
scrubbing out some pots and pans. They collected wood and got
a cookfire burning. Squatting on their haunches, they sliced up
the vegetables and threw them into a big skillet. The threats and
abuse subsided, and an odd woozy calm settled over A-Camp.
The staggerers sat down, the bellowers fell quiet. One of the A-
Campers pulled a bloody hunk of venison from a cooler. "Here.

Th'ow this in. Veggies can't hold a drinkin' man." The young Rainbows looked at each other, looked at the meat. They were obviously vegetarians. They cut up the meat, cooked it with the vegetables and boiled the rice. When the food was cooked they got up and left without saying a word, or hearing a word of thanks in return.

CHAPTER 10

Morally, as a class, they are foulmouthed, blasphemous, drunken, lecherous, utterly corrupt. Usually harmless on the plains when sober, they are dreaded in towns, for then the liquor has ascendancy over them . . . their earnings are soon squandered in dissoluteness.

"The Cowboys of the Western Plains and Their Horses," reprint from the *Providence Journal* in the *Cheyenne Daily Leader*, October 1882

Spike wakes up on the backseat of the car, with an aching head, a tongue like sandpaper and a cramp in the calf muscle of his right leg. He curses and pulls on the toe of his cowboy boot until it passes. He gets out of the car, rolls his shoulders, scratches his belly, unzips his Wranglers and darkens the dirt with a long stream of last night's beer. Last night . . . last night? I give him a cup of coffee and the details swim back in focus.

They drove five hundred miles across the desert, from El Paso to Yuma, and partied all the way; snorting hits of speed off Jimmy's bowie knife, drinking their way through three cases of beer, smoking up the last of the weed. Billy had his .38 and a box of bullets, and they took turns leaning out of the window and blasting holes in the highway signs. The radio was broken so they chanted obscene cowboy poetry to while away the miles.

We're rough and tough and all that stuff
We piss through leather britches
We drag our cocks on ragged rocks
We're hearty sonsabitches.

Periodically they exposed themselves to passing female motorists, who saw three grinning cowboys lined up across the bench seat of a faded green Chevy Impala, with matching black hats and their jeans around their knees, cans of beer in one hand and stretching out their peckers with the other, like some kind of perverted Western cartoon.

Jimmy's got warrants out against him for drink-driving and assault, Billy owes the state of Arizona $350 in speeding fines, so Spike did all the driving. Spike was the getaway man. In Las Cruces, New Mexico, he screeched out of a gas station without paying, fishtailing across the lot on four bald tires and almost sideswiping a dumpster. In Deming they ran out of a restaurant without paying— "eating at the Dine 'n' Dash." Across the state line somewhere— Was it Willcox? Was it Benson?—Jimmy came bolting out of a Circle K with two cases of Budweiser, bandy-legged and wild-eyed: "Open that motherfuckin' door!" He leaped into the passenger seat, yelling, "Woooo-hah! Haul ass and drive like Jesus!"

It was five in the morning when Spike pulled into the Yuma rodeo grounds. When he closed his eyes, he could still see the white line of the road, running through his mind's eye, and it stayed there as he slept. Strange creatures flashed across his dream highway and streaked off into the desert, leaving vapor trails of light—a coyote with a devil's head, a deer that shapeshifted into a giant jackrabbit and flew past the windshield. He wanted to turn the wheel and follow them, to get a closer look, but he knew he must keep his eyes fixed on the white line. Eventually, the temptation proved too much and a giant spectral jackrabbit lured him off the highway into the desert. He crashed into a tree and woke up on the backseat. The cramp in his calf muscle was from keeping the gas pedal pressed down in his sleep.

It's eight o'clock now, a piercing blue desert morning. Jimmy and Billy are still asleep in the front seat. A molting hound named

Bubba snores in the foot well, on a carpet of empty beer cans, and will soon wake to a hangover like the rest of them. Spike hooks out a razor and soap from the trunk and shaves in the side-view mirror.

He stands just over six feet tall, with a powerful, slightly stooped frame and a habitual grin. His face is big, solid and rawboned, the chin and forehead like ramparts, the nose broken five times in various rodeo accidents. Crooked teeth, stained brown by Red Man chewing tobacco. A long white scar across his neck from a bull's horn. He is thirty-one years old, a professional rodeo cowboy from central California and a full-time citizen of the road.

Spike and Billy ride bulls. Jimmy rides the broncs. In the last ten days they have driven five thousand miles, competing in rodeos from California to Florida and back, and do not consider this hard traveling. I've been in faltering pursuit of them for the last month or so, sometimes intersecting, sometimes missing them because of changes in their schedule, wrought by vehicle break-downs, run-ins with the law and side-trips to hospital emergency rooms.

Spike averages eighty thousand miles a year, and sometimes tops a hundred thousand. Billy hasn't spent more than a week in the same town for eighteen months. They think nothing of driving a thousand miles to some dusty corral in the middle of nowhere, to risk their necks for an eight-second adrenaline rush on the back of an enraged animal, and the hope of a pay check to keep going. It is a life of motion—short bursts of high velocity followed by long, smooth stretches of highway, soaring and crashing on various combinations of drugs and booze—and it never stops.

"The road burns out a lot of rodeo cowboys," says Spike. "You learn to sleep fast, a night's sleep in an hour sometimes, but shit, I can't imagine a better life. I've tried settling down: working construction, renting an apartment, living with a woman. I wouldn't say it's all bad, but after a few weeks of it, my feet start to itchin' and I got to hit the road. My dad was a rodeo cowboy and he always said they were the best years of his life."

He stuffs a breakfast wad of Red Man under his lip and pulls on a black 20X beaver-felt Resistol cowboy hat with a silver buckle on the band. Like most nomads, rodeo cowboys wear their wealth. Spike's belt buckle is the size of a small dinner plate, worked with real gold and fake gems. His boots cost $215. He reaches down into the left one, pulls out his wallet and surveys its contents. "I need me a gut-stompin' bull today," he says. "A rank, wild, buckin', money-makin' sonofabitch." He has eleven dollars to his name.

"I been ridin' bulls for fifteen years," he says. "I seen my pardner Neil git his ear ripped off. I seen another good buddy git stomped in the head so bad his brains popped out his ears. I seen Lane Frost, the purtiest bullrider of 'em all, git gored to death in Cheyenne. After a while, it don't affect you too bad. When you put on your chaps and spurs and git on that bull, you got to put all them negative thoughts out your mind, and just ride like Jesus."

"*Carpe diem*, that's my motto," says one rodeo cowboy to another. "Seize the day. Grab it by the nuts and squeeze until it hollers. Stomp a mudhole in its ass and . . ."

"Kar-pay dee-M? What the hell kinda Anglish is that?"

"Oh, I guess it's Eye-talian or Meskin or some shit."

Spike stands behind the bucking chutes, feet planted a yard apart, thumbs hooked in the front pockets of his Wranglers, spitting thick brown ropes of tobacco juice into the dust. He has borrowed seventy-five dollars to pay his entry fees and drawn a big red Brahma bull, which snorts and thrashes in the bucking chute, clanging its horns against the steel bars. When I say big, I mean close to a ton, with eyeballs the size of grapefruits and a look of brute fury in them. Spike fidgets with his fringed leather chaps, adjusts his spurs, stretches out his leg muscles, paces up and down. The rising adrenaline has wiped out all traces of hangover and exhaustion. He looks tense and alert.

The bullriders all have their different rituals. Some prepare for the moment with savage karate kicks. Others gaze quietly into the middle distance, emptying their mind of all distractions, in a quest for a pure, Zen-like state. Cody Custer, the former world champion, resplendent in a custom-made pair of Glory to God chaps, closes his eyes and lays his hands over the bull, to exorcise any demonic spirits that might be lurking under its hide. Then he kneels and prays, shielding his thin, scarred face with a black cowboy hat.

Bullriding is rodeo stripped down to its gladiatorial essence, a contest between man and beast in which the beast holds the advantage. The cowboy, with one hand clutching a rope, the other held aloft, attempts to stay on the back of the bull for eight seconds, with as much flair and poise as he can muster. The bull, using an unpredictable, rapid-fire sequence of bucks, leaps, plunges, kicks and spins, tries to throw him off. If the cowboy is successful, he stands to win a check for a few thousand dollars and a large, ostentatious belt-buckle. If the bull is successful, he gets the opportunity to trample and gore the cowboy, although not all bulls will try. Both partners in this frenzied, high-velocity dance contribute equally to the score. The cowboy is marked out of fifty for the assurance of his ride, the bull for its "rankness": the ferocity of its efforts to buck off the cowboy.

First up is Charlie Sampson, a lone black bullrider from South Central Los Angeles in a world of white country boys. He stretches out his groin muscles and climbs cautiously on the broad, brindled back of his bull. He ties a gloved hand into the rigging and punches the knot. The cowboys sitting on the fence rail call out encouragement, "Ride tough, Charlie," "Git up over him."

Charlie nods to the chute man, the gate flies open and the bull leaps out into the arena, six feet in the air, bucking and spinning, trailing long strings of mucus from its nostrils. A roar builds in the crowd as Charlie works the bull, "doing the windshield wiper" with his flailing free arm, jackknifing his body in perfect synchronicity with the thrashing bull, perfectly balanced, even through the final whirling spins. He is tapped off, on the jazz, in the zone, where time is bent out of shape and the soul seems to rise out of the body—"Like you're sitting in a chair looking down at yourself, making the perfect moves in slow motion." He dismounts at the eight-second buzzer, the rodeo clowns rush in to distract the bull, and Charlie scrambles up the fence, trembling and wild-eyed from the adrenaline. He takes the lead with eighty-two points.

Spike is up a couple of bulls later. He ties his left hand into the rigging and crams his hat down low. The gate opens and the bull jumps out into the arena. It gives a few halfhearted bucks and a tired-looking spin, and after five seconds or so, Spike is so disgusted that he wants to take off his hat and fan the lazy, worthless beast across the head—the ultimate gesture of contempt. He's drawn another dud. He scores sixty-five points and is out of the money again.

Billy fares no better. He stays on his bull for eight seconds but it doesn't buck for him. Jimmy puts together a good saddle bronc ride, but he's out of the money too. "Maybe we'll have better luck in Indio tomorrow, if we can figure out a way to get there," says Spike. "Right now, we've got a quarter-tank of gas and about eight bucks between us."

Jimmy roots around in the trunk of the car and pulls out five copies of a homemade pornographic video in which he stars. He walks over to the beer stand and tries to sell the videos to a trio of Marines, off-duty from a nearby military base. "Man, it's some wild-ass shit," he tells them. "She's wearin' red leather gloves and she's all tied up. I got my chaps and spurs on and I'm slappin' her around with my hat . . . Thirty bucks, man . . . How about twenty-five?"

Jimmy is a methamphetamine fiend: wiry and rodent-faced with a manic cackling laugh and glittering eyes, half-concealed by hooded lids. He does not tell the Marines that his co-star and girlfriend charged him with rape after the making of the video. He served a year in prison for it and married her the day he got out.

The marriage has not prospered. Jimmy is on the road all the time, drinking and snorting meth, screwing whores and rodeo groupies, never wearing a condom and calling up once in a blue moon. Last time he went home Jimmy found another man drinking beer on his couch and beat the shit out of him. He slapped his wife across the face, kicked her in the ass and slammed the door. She called the cops and filed an assault charge, but Jimmy was gone, cursing his way down the highway with a case of beer at his side.

There are no takers for the video, but Jimmy manages to sell his jacket to one of the Marines for forty bucks. First things first: he buys a bag of weed from another rodeo cowboy and takes Spike and Billy off behind the horse stables to "skip rope." (In the Old West rope was made out of hemp, the cannabis plant, and cowboys would light up pieces of rope and smoke them to get high. Hemp has long been outlawed in America, but the terms "smoking rope" and "skipping rope" still prevail in rodeo circles.)

Jimmy grinds out the roach with his boot-heel and says, "Awright boys, let the party commence! Let's see if we cain't hunt us up some buckle bunnies." You see them at every rodeo in America, girls in their twenties and early thirties, with big hair, skin-tight jeans and some kind of breast-enhancing top—rodeo groupies by another name, mainstay of a cowboy's sex life. They call them buckle bunnies because the first thing they look for on a man is a big, gold trophy belt-buckle, which indicates a rodeo champion.

In Yuma this afternoon the pickings are slim. There is only a handful of buckle bunnies and they are already paired off with the winners. The rest of the women here are either over sixty or young, prim, churchy types, the daughters of local ranchers and businessmen. The cowboys stay at the rodeo grounds for three beers then drive over to the organizer's dance, sneaking in without tickets and disappearing into a dark corner at the far end of the hall. Jimmy pulls out the speed, and his huge bowie knife, and they each take a snort under the cover of their hatbrims. A country and western band is playing on the stage, and when people get up from their tables to dance, the three cowboys saunter by and steal their drinks. It's a dull scene, elderly couples doing the two-step. No girls, no action.

The next stop is a bar in Yuma known informally as the Black Eye Factory, the haunt of bikers, truckers, off-duty soldiers and tough-looking women with tattoos. There is a group of rodeo cowboys at the bar spending their winnings, and Spike, Billy and Jimmy join in the celebrations. The whiskey flows, the singing and storytelling begin: tales of whorehouse sprees and narrow escapes from the law, practical jokes and epic drinking binges, famous bulls and the cowboys they've killed and crippled. At one point a steer wrestler, a big, strong country boy with a head like a boulder, stands up and issues a challenge to the bar: "I got fifty bucks says I can beat the shit out of any four of you."

Four soldiers stand up from their table, and half the bar empties out into the parking lot to watch the fight. The steer wrestler knocks out two of them early on and then it reaches a bloody stalemate. The soldiers keep catching him with punches to the head, but the cowboy won't go down and he keeps punching back. They keep swinging at each other until someone steps in and calls a draw.

At one o'clock, Arizona time, the Black Eye Factory closes and we drive over the Colorado River for another two hours' drinking on the California side. Jimmy finds an old cowboy there who keeps the whiskeys coming, glad to find an audience for his own rodeo stories. "Best days of my life," he says. "For twenty years I lived like a free man, loose-footed as a tumbleweed in a windstorm. Ridin' bulls, drinkin' my whiskey, grabbin' any piece of pussy I could get my hands on. Then I bust up my back real bad, spent six months in the hospital. The doctors said if I went back to ridin' bulls, I'd likely cripple myself. So I quit rodeoin' and tried to settle down. Let me tell you boys, it don't come natural to a cowboy."

At closing time we climb back in the Chevy and Jimmy drives the backroads to Yuma. The next thing I know it's four in the morning. I wake up on the backseat, the Chevy is parked outside a Motel 6. Two Mexicans are trying to break in, rattling the handles, and then Jimmy appears and points the .38 at them. The Mexicans leave and I pass out again.

At seven in the morning I wake up to find Jimmy rooting through my possessions. He finds a bottle of hair conditioner and holds it aloft with a manic grin. I ask him what he needs it for. "Lubrication," he says. "We couldn't afford no whores so I stole me a Pocket Pussy from the sex shop. Damn near got caught too."

I point out the brand name on the conditioner bottle: Suave. "Purty got*damn* suave, you ask me!" He cackles. To the horror of the elderly couples checking out of the motel on their way to Sunday morning breakfast and church services, he takes the Pocket Pussy out of its box, holds it to his chest and waltzes around the parking lot on his tiptoes, singing love songs to a pink plastic sheath: "You are the sunshine of my life/You are the apple of my eye . . ." Then he takes the contraption up to a motel room and five cowboys all take their turn—a scene I did not witness, but heard about later.

Later that morning they pile into the car and point it toward Indio, California. None of them has slept. A bronc rider named Jeff is at the wheel, drinking a breakfast beer and preaching cowboy philosophy: "Sometimes you've got plenty of money and you spend it like there ain't no tomorrow. Drinks for everybody, steak dinners, girls, gambling, maybe git yourself a fancy new pair of boots or a couple of whores. And sometimes you're broke and you do what you have to do to carry on down the road. Either way, you have a blast. Shit, them old-time cowboys was a bunch of rowdy outlaw bastards. I like to think we're just keepin' the spirit of the Ol' West alive."

Teddy Abbott was ten years old—a pale, sickly child with huge, mournful eyes—when his father moved the family from Cranwich Hall, in England, to a cabin on the Nebraska frontier. In England his father had been a well-to-do gentleman farmer, cultured and well educated, with forty cap-doffing villagers at his beck and call. Needless to say, he was appalled by American society, such as it was in Lincoln, Nebraska, in 1871: the ignorance and brutishness, the barbaric mangling of the English language, the ear-biting and eye-gouging contests in the taverns. There were other English settlers in the area, but he refused to associate with them and referred to them as "cart-horse-bred buggers." He took refuge in English newspapers, months out of date, and squandered his inherited wealth on various lake-building and tree-planting schemes—ill-advised attempts to make the bleak, arid prairie look more like England.

Young Teddy, meanwhile, was adjusting fine. Teddy was going native. By the age of twelve, he was out riding the open range for weeks and months at a time, herding the family's cattle, cooking and sometimes hunting his own food, sleeping under the stars. His mother said there must be gypsy blood in him, because at every opportunity he would ride off with the Loup River Pawnees, and his most fervent desire was to become an Indian and follow the last of the buffalo herds. When the Pawnees were shunted off to Indian Territory in Oklahoma, Teddy decided to become a cattle drover instead, figuring that was close enough. As his friend Charlie Russell, the cowboy artist, used to say in later years, "We were just white Indians anyway."

In the early 1870s Lincoln lay at the northern end of one of the Texas cattle trails, and the country around it was full of Texan cowboys. They were a new, emerging type on the western plains, not yet a romantic archetype. Most of them were young, discharged Confederate soldiers, inured to death and violence by the war, bitter over its outcome, accustomed to hardship, danger and constant travel, a roving, reckless, hedonistic breed.

Returning home to Texas after the war (in the spring of 1866) they found the crops failing and the economy devastated, with little or no Northern money in circulation. Beef, however, was plentiful. While the men were away fighting, feral cattle had multiplied exponentially in Texas, until half a million or more roamed the thorny brush country between the Nueces River and the Rio Grande. They were descendants of the black Spanish cattle that had escaped from the early missions and later bred with runaways from the American settlers' herds. They were spooky as deer, wilder and more dangerous than buffalo. Texans called them outlaw cattle or Longhorns, because on a full-grown bull or steer the horns might measure eight or nine feet from tip to tip. Using techniques borrowed from Mexican vaqueros, the Texans began to capture and brand them, supplementing their herds by stealing from each other and raiding the Mexican ranches across the Rio Grande.

There was no market for beef in Texas, but the North was crying out for it, so the Texas cattlemen began to drive their herds to the railheads in Missouri, Kansas and Nebraska, across hundreds of miles of open prairie. An animal worth five dollars in Texas

could be sold for fifty up north, assuming it wasn't lost in a stampede or run off by Indians or by the murderous gangs of white
rustlers who roamed the plains and the Missouri borders (and
sometimes dressed up in moccasins and feathers to shift the blame
on to Indians). A few men made fortunes on the early drives, but
many more were bankrupted, and dozens were killed, mostly by
drowning in rivers and being struck by lightning. The Texas
cattlemen were undeterred, however, and during the late 1860s
a great seasonal migration of livestock and men was established,
a new form of American nomadism.

> The drovers now were all kinds . . . hound-gutted
> Confederates, experienced stockmen who had been fighting
> Indians and Mexican raiders for years, army mule skinners,
> and professional Indian fighters, to the riffraff of the Southern
> river towns, gamblers, con men and hide-outs from the law
> and just plain murderers.
>
> Mari Sandoz, *The Cattlemen*

They wore wide-brimmed beaver-felt hats, black or brown with
a low crown, fancy shirts, leather chaps and often a ratty old
Confederate coat that served as a blanket and a slicker to keep
off the rain. As a rule, they were small, wiry men, a heavy man
being too hard on the horses. They prided themselves on their
toughness, the Texans in particular, and boasted that they could
go any place a cow could go, and stand anything a horse could
stand. Bragging, cursing and storytelling were their art forms.
Whiskey and violence were their vices. It was said that they were
only afraid of two things: a decent woman and being set afoot.

While the other Lincoln boys were in the schoolhouse, Teddy
Abbott was out on the range with the cowpunchers, learning
their techniques of riding, roping and trail-driving, sitting at their
campfires, soaking up the stories of stampedes and swollen rivers,
killings, gunfights and hangings, the wild, drunken sprees in Dodge
City or Abilene. By the age of fifteen Teddy was making money
tending his neighbors' cattle, and spending most of it on whiskey
and whores. He carried a revolver and, like any teenager with a

gun, he was itching to use it. In the company he was keeping, killing was a rite of passage into manhood, as it was for the plains Indian tribes.

In 1876 Teddy stood before a photographer, "tough, drunk and sixteen," with a cigar in his mouth and a bottle of whiskey in his hand, held out of the frame. Later that year, as had become his custom, he was galloping his horse through the streets of Lincoln, roaring drunk, whooping and howling, and shooting out the streetlights. The town marshal called out, "Halt! Halt! Throw 'em up." Teddy galloped straight toward him. He shot him through the shoulder but he was aiming for the heart.

When his older brother Jimmy died, Teddy lost what little religion he had left. At the funeral the wind blew his hat into the grave and he asked his mother if God could have prevented Jimmy's death. "Yes," she replied, "God is all powerful. He could have prevented it if he wished to."

"Then I'll never go in one of your damn churches again," said Teddy, and he never did, for the rest of his life.

Ninety percent of those early cowboys, in Teddy's experience, were "infidels." They lived in nature and slept under the stars, and, like Indians, they found it hard to relate to a God who lived in a building with a roof and showed up on Sunday mornings. Unlike Indians, they had no faith in the power of prayer.

> After you come in contact with nature, you soon get all that stuff knocked out of you—praying to God for aid, divine Providence, and so on—because it don't work. You could pray all you damn pleased, but it wouldn't get you water where there wasn't water. Talk about trusting Providence, hell, if I'd trusted in Providence, I'd have starved to death.
>
> E. C. Abbott ("Teddy Blue") and
> Helena Huntington Smith,
> *We Pointed Them North: Recollections of a Cowpuncher*

Christianity on the frontier was very much a religion of the settlers, the farmers from the Midwest and New England who started to appear in Kansas and Nebraska in the late 1870s and who closed off the range to cattle. The cowboys hated them, with the usual contempt of the horse nomad for the sedentary farmer, and called them "grangers," "hoe men," "pumpkin-pilers" and most of all "nesters"—"psalm-singin,' sodbustin', goatfaced, prayer-bayin' nesters."

To Teddy's disgust, his father gave up on cattle, ploughed under the range, and joined the enemy's ranks. All his brothers became farmers too. In the autumn of 1878, aged eighteen, Teddy left home for good, following the cattle herds north. He drifted up the Platte River Valley, visiting the ranches along the way, and hired on to an outfit contracted to deliver a herd to the Pine Ridge Indian Agency in South Dakota, where the Oglala Sioux had recently been confined. Winter found him down in Austin, Texas, fifteen hundred miles to the south. He was leaning up against a bar and a trail boss asked him, "Want to go up the trail?"

"What outfit?"

"Olive outfit. Thirty dollars a month and found."

The Olive brothers—Ira, Marion and I. P. "Print"—were some of the most violent and feared cattlemen in the West, which made the outfit all the more appealing to young Teddy Abbott. Print had already murdered nine blacks in Texas (which was not a matter for the law at the time) and several whites (which was a matter for bribing the judge and intimidating the witnesses). In Nebraska, Print Olive was known as "The Manburner." In 1878 he had hanged two nesters near Plum Creek, doused their bodies in coal oil and struck a match. Teddy got on fine with Print and Marion, but he never did like Ira.

Coming up the trail in 1879, Ira started in on a black gunman named Kelly who worked for the outfit. Ira found some provocation and pistol-whipped him in the mouth, knocking out two teeth, then waited for Kelly to draw so he could kill him. Teddy told Ira that if he hit Kelly again, he would shoot his eyes out. Ira put away his gun, got on his horse and left the herd, never to return, which tells us something about the look in Teddy Abbott's eyes at that time.

That was the only trouble I ever had in the outfit. The

Olives was mostly hard on Mexicans and niggers, because being from Texas they was born and raised with that intense hatred of a Mexican, and being Southerners, free niggers was poison to them. But they hired them because they worked cheaper than white men.

Kelly was known as "Olive's bad nigger." His job was to scare off the settlers, who had begun fencing off the waterholes and trying to charge the cattlemen a fee to water their herds. Kelly would walk toward them with his gun drawn, rolling his eyes crazily and gnashing his teeth. Most of the settlers were Northerners, unused to blacks but afraid of them anyway, and they soon dropped the price for watering for the herd.

They drove the cattle from Austin to Loup River, Nebraska, that summer, a distance of eight hundred miles or so, averaging ten or fifteen miles a day. They swam swollen rivers, endured forty-mile drives between water. They were pounded by giant hailstones. In Indian Territory, the herd was run off by a gang of Mexican, white and half-breed Indian rustlers, but the cowboys managed to recover it without bloodshed.

During the prairie lightning storms the air would fill with static electricity, and suddenly a bluish phosphorescent light would appear on the horns of the cattle—St. Elmo's fire. The electricity would flash from horn to horn, and balls of it would appear on the horses' ears, and in a man's mustache, little balls of light about the size of a pea. Then, with the first clap of thunder, the herd would stampede. The cowboys would try to gallop out ahead of them and get them running in a circular direction so they expended their energy going round and round—a full-tilt ride in the dark across broken ground, littered with cut-banks and prairie dog holes, knowing that if your horse slipped or stumbled, the stampeding herd behind would trample and literally flatten you. Teddy had seen it happen.

For the most part, the work was exhausting drudgery, in the saddle eating dust from sunup to sundown, and then two hours apiece of night-guard duty. The worst of it was the lack of sleep. On a good night, with the weather calm and the cowboys singing lullabies to settle the herd, you might get five hours. On a bad night you were lucky to get an hour, and cowboys regularly went two or three days with no sleep at all, rubbing tobacco juice into their eyes to keep them open. And if they complained, the trail boss would say, "What the hell are you kickin' about? You can sleep all winter when we get up North."

After two months on the trail, two months of sobriety, bacon and beans, hard work and danger, they delivered the herd in Loup River, got their wages in North Platte, and made for the nearest saloons, gambling dens and sporting houses, "to cut the wolf loose." Teddy wasn't a gambler, which left him all the more money to spend on whiskey and whores. Given their nomadic life, and low social standing, prostitutes were the only women available to the trail cowboys, often the only women they knew, and on the whole they treated them well. Teddy liked to "marry a girl for a week," take her to breakfast, lunch and supper every day, and hear her life story, and he was ready to pull his gun on any man who insulted her honor.

He went up the trail again in 1881 and 1883. He was knocked off his horse twice by lightning and saw three cowboys killed in stampedes. Between drives he drifted around the cowtowns, drinking and whoring, picking up work at ranches, trying his hand at trapping for a winter. He became a friend of Calamity Jane, offering a shoulder to cry on when she was drunk and mooning after Wild Bill Hickok.

"Teddy Blue" got his nickname at a theater in Miles City, Montana. A girl came up to him in a short skirt and "tights that looked like she'd been melted and run into them." She invited him to share a bottle of wine in a private, curtained box on the balcony. Teddy had seven hundred dollars in his gun-belt, and on the way to the box he had second thoughts and decided the girl was leading him into a trap. He spun around, caught his spur on the carpet and crashed through a partition onto the stage. He figured the audience needed entertaining so he grabbed a chair, straddled it backwards and bucked it over the stage yelling, "Whoa, Blue! Whoa, Blue!" The nickname stuck to him for life.

★   ★   ★

During the mid- and late 1880s the long trail drives came to an end. The range was overgrazed, there were terrible die-offs in the Northern winters and with the invention of barbed wire, private ranchers and settlers were able to fence off the open range, making the free movement of men and cattle impossible. The nomadic heyday of the plains cowboy lasted twenty years at most. The total number of men on the drives is estimated at thirty-two thousand. So why did they furnish so much American mythology? How did the word "cowboy" manage to change its meaning so dramatically?

It began as a typical sedentary insult, denoting a lawless, rootless, threatening, disreputable nomad, with no place in a decent society. Once the preconditions for his life—unfenced, unregulated space—had been removed, and his nomadism curtailed, he turned into a romantic, nostalgic, enviable figure, imbued with nobility and simple, primitive virtue. Like the plains Indian and the mountain man before him, he came to symbolize a time of freedom and adventure that had passed.

As Buffalo Bill Cody's Wild West Show was touring the world, with defeated Indians (including Sitting Bull) and out-of-work trail hands playing theatrical versions of themselves, the rest of the cowboys were drifting into ranch-work, prospecting, odd jobs and outlawry. Teddy Abbott made the transition better than most. He stayed up in Montana, quit drinking and married a woman he loved, the half-Indian daughter of a famous Montana cattleman named Granville Stuart. He bought his own ranch and started sleeping in a bunkhouse, riding a fence-line and gathering cattle in a fenced pasture. He found it a poor substitute for his wild days on the open range, but it was better than farming, an occupation to which he remained virulently opposed for the rest of his life.

Many cowboys found it impossible to break the old patterns of mobility. They seldom stayed at the same ranch for more than a season or two, and in the winter they would "ride the grubline." Every ranch in the cattle country was obliged, by the codes of hospitality, to give a traveling cowboy a free meal and a place to stay. In return, the grub-line riders spread news between the isolated ranches and gave them something to gossip about over the winter.

In the days of the open range, cowboys used to make a sport of their work skills. When different outfits met on the trail they would often hold impromptu riding, roping and horseracing contests, gambling heavily on the outcome, and this tradition was kept up by the ranch cowboys. In 1883, in Pecos City, Texas, cowboys from all the ranches in the area rode into town on the Fourth of July, and started drinking in the Bar 7 Saloon, knocking back Hill and Hill whiskey at $1.50 a quart. As cowboys will, they got to bragging, and, examining the annals of 1880s folklore, we can imagine the tenor of the exchanges . . .

"I'm half horse, half alligator, with a little touch of snapping turtle. I clumb a streak of lightning, and slid down a locust tree a hundred feet high, with a wild cat under each arm and never got a scratch. Whoopee-yip-ho!"

"Raised in the backwoods, suckled by a polar bear, nine rows of jaw teeth, a double coat of hair, steel ribs, wire intestine and a barbed-wire tail, and I don't give a dang where I drag it. Whoopee-whee-a-ha!"

It was decided to settle these claims by means of a roping and bronc-riding contest. A group of cowboys galloped off to round up some steers and drove them down Main Street to an alkali flat adjoining the courthouse, enclosed by a line of wagons and a plank fence. A. T. "Trav" Whitman won the steer roping, with a time of twenty-two seconds, and proceeded to get roaring drunk on the prize money at the Bar 7 Saloon—an event that is generally hailed as the birth of rodeo.

During the 1890s, as the last trail cowboys faded into history, similar contests sprung up all over the West, memorializing the skills of the range, and, as cowboys started traveling from rodeo to rodeo, restoring an approximation of the old seasonal migration patterns. Organized bullriding, which went on to become the most popular event in rodeo, emerged later, in the 1920s. It's an activity with no practical application for a working cowboy, a pure test of skill and daredevil courage. To ride a bucking bronc or wrestle a steer was dangerous, but to climb on the back of an angry, one-ton, bucking bull was like "looking down the barrel of a gun," according to one early bullrider. At Fort Worth, Texas, in 1937, a Brahma bull jumped a nine-foot fence, charged through the crowd and left the arena by the front entrance. The police fired forty rounds into it and then had to cut its throat.

The opening strains of the national anthem come blaring out of the PA system. In the stands fifteen thousand people rise to their feet and place their cowboy hats over their hearts. There is a moment of silence after the finale and then all the hats rise as one and a great roaring and yelping fills the stadium. This is the final Sunday of Cheyenne Frontier Days in Wyoming, the world's largest outdoor rodeo. As the announcer keeps repeating, "This, friends, is the daddy of 'em all!"

There are an estimated three hundred thousand visitors in Cheyenne this week, a town of fifty thousand, and everyone is wearing a cowboy hat, from the three-year-olds to the television weathermen. Wherever you turn there is an Old West shoot-out, a period melodrama or a chuckwagon race, and the store windows are all daubed with images of cowboys, bucking bulls and slogans such as "Howdy Pardner!" and "Yippi Ki Yi Yea!"

Modern rodeo describes itself as a sport, but the governing body, the Professional Rodeo Cowboys Association, sells it in the manner of Wild West circus show, a light-hearted day out for all the family, a celebration of American pride with plenty of corporate merchandising, references to Jesus and patriotic razzmatazz. At the center of all this merry pageantry is the emblematic figure of the cowboy, unpopular with the animal rights crowd perhaps, but otherwise understood as the living embodiment of American pride and virtue. There are many rodeo cowboys who fit the bill perfectly: polite, conservative, Christian athletes, wholesome as can be. And there are others who more closely resemble a roustabout trail hand from the 1870s: foul-mouthed, irreverent and hard-drinking.

Behind the bucking chutes, a French camera crew is interviewing Jimmy Morris, a chubby twenty-one-year-old bullrider from Duncan, Oklahoma, wearing ostrich-skin boots. Spike stands next to him, grinning stoned at the camera in a pair of cheap sunglasses.

"Ow do you feel about riding zees bull?" asks the Frenchman.

"Well, I've drawn a purty good one here this afternoon," says Jimmy Morris. "I'm just gonna try as hard as I can, and hopefully I can put together a good ride."

The camera moves away, zooming in for a close-up of a cowboy praying into his hat. Jimmy Morris turns to Spike, stuffs a golf ball of chewing tobacco into his cheek and switches back into cowboy vernacular: "I tell you what, bub, ahmoan tear a motherfuckin' rib off this bull, stomp the livin' shit out of the bastard. They better bring a gotdamn prybar to get that bull's ribs off my spurs. I got to ride this sumbitch. Got to. Spent too much damn money at the bar last night. I just went in there to get me some food and one drink with my meal, you know. I come out of there seven hours later, drunker 'n shit, and I still couldn't sleep for thinkin' about this bull. I feel like shit warmed over."

Spike couldn't afford the entrance fees, but he was only four hundred miles away so he drove to Cheyenne for the party. Billy is holed up somewhere, recuperating from a wrenched back. Jimmy is back in prison for assaulting his wife. Another one of Spike's old buddies, Ricky Lindsay, who gave up bullriding to become a pimp in Las Vegas, is in prison for "big-time federal shit." Spike has been living as normal, winning a little money here and there and blowing it as fast as he can. A rich woman in Dallas has been sending him plane tickets, and once in a while he flies off and spends the weekend with her. She makes him wear his chaps and hat and sends him on his way with fifty or a hundred for services rendered.

In the stands the fans drain their beer from souvenir cups and whoop obediently as each sponsor's flag is paraded around the arena by a cowgirl on horseback. "And presenting the flag of Ford is Codi Ann Bybee! Let's raise a cheer for this purty little lady!" Behind the bucking chutes the bullriders are taping up sprained joints, torn muscles, broken fingers and ribs. They eat ibuprofen— "cowboy aspirin"—by the handful.

Buddy Gulden, an old friend of Spike's from California, is

swathed from neck to hip in heavy strapping. Two weeks ago in Salinas, a fifteen-hundred-pound bull stomped on his left shoulder, separating the joint and tearing up the cartilage. It's a nuisance, but not the kind of injury to stop him riding bulls. He also has a broken finger, which seems to bother him about as much as a shaving cut. Buddy is thirty-seven now, probably the oldest bull-rider on the trail with all his own teeth. He is starting to tire of the rodeo circuit—the endless miles, the constant injuries and hangovers, the irregular pay—and he wants to settle down. He's married a former rodeo queen named Sheri, and they have bought twenty-eight dry and treeless acres in central California. Buddy calls it home, but as yet there is no well on the property, and no house. He still lives in his truck, a 1974 Ford with 344,000 miles on the clock.

A good bullride today would win him a well and a place in the National Finals Rodeo in Las Vegas, the only event of the year where a rodeo cowboy stands to win big money. A good score in Vegas and then, maybe, it's time to quit. Go back to California, build a house and try to find some other way to make a living. Exactly how, he hasn't figured out yet.

The corporate pageantry draws to a close. The bullriders pick up their rigging—a braided rope with a bell on the end of it—and walk over to the chutes with a melancholy clanging. They tie the ropes around the bulls, climb the chute fence and lower themselves onto the bulls' backs. Bubba Monkres, from Everman, Texas, is first up. He is bucked off immediately but his hand gets caught in the rigging and the bull wheels him around and around like a helicopter blade, snapping its horns back into his face. The rodeo clowns rush in and try to distract the bull, but to no avail. Eventually Bubba's hand works free and he staggers to the fence, bleeding from the eye and cheekbone.

Buddy Gulden ties into the rigging and jams down his hat. He nods at the chute man and bull and rider shoot out into the arena. "High, wide and wicked! That is a rank bull, friends!" calls out Spike, sitting on the top fence rail. The bull drops into a series of tight, bucking spins, generating maximum velocity, but Buddy stays with him, counterbalancing every move, whirling around in circles with one arm arched high over his head. Scrambling over the fence, he says, "If I felt any better, I'd call it a sin. I think I won my well." He scores eighty-four points and wins second place.

After the bullriding come the celebrations. There are drunk cowboys everywhere and buckle bunnies fifteen deep at the bar. The cowboys pour beer into one another's hats, so that it funnels around the curved sides and shoots down your gullet in a foaming stream. They lick the nearest cleavage and sprinkle salt into it as a prelude to a tequila shot. "He just bit my left tit!" A girl with bovine eyes smiles vacantly as a cowboy clamps his mouth on to her breast. Another cowboy has his head buried in a pair of skimpy cut-offs and receives a gentle reprimand—"A little less teeth honey." Then he jumps to his feet and looses a blood-curdling howl, which sets the whole crowd off whooping and yelping, like a pack of coyotes.

Buddy is half-drunk and fully exhausted, having driven fifteen hundred miles in the last two days and ridden four bulls. He has his arm around his wife and he stands apart from the main melee. "The only thing that gets most cowboys to quit rodeoin' is a real bad injury of some kind," he says. "I'd like to think I could quit before that point, but it ain't easy. You get accustomed to the freedom and independence of the life. Most cowboys would go crazy working the nine-to-five. I figure I'll make a go of ranching, maybe start up a bullridin' school or something. I guess the first thing we're gonna do is get that well dug, and then build a house. Ain't that right, honey?"

The winner of the Cheyenne trophy belt-buckle, a 20X beaver-felt hat, a fancy pair of boots and a check for $8,015.37 is hungover, twenty-one-year-old Jimmy Morris, now drinking again with Spike and a couple of other cowboys. "Eight thousand dollars!" he says. "Can you believe I don't know how to spend it? I done got me ten acres already, as a gift from my girlfriend's dad. Maybe I should buy some lumber and build me a home."

He ponders that for a moment and then he's struck by a grander inspiration. "Shitfire! I could put down six grand on a motor home. That's what I'm gonna do, boys. This here cowboy's gonna travel in style."

"That's a damn smart deal right there." Spike nods. "What the hell do you need with a house?"

I returned home after the rodeo circuit in a state of collapse. I mean that quite literally. Five minutes after walking in the door I dropped a cigarette, bent over to pick it up, blacked out and crumpled in a heap on the floor. Do you recall the woman who kicked the glass out of my front door with a motorcycle boot? Gale was back from France. We were trying to make it work again. She helped me up and I went into the bathroom and urinated something that looked and smelled like last night's whiskey.

I hurt everywhere and I hadn't ridden a single bull. I had made a valiant effort to keep up with the drinking and the traveling, but I was way out of my league, lacking a basic toughness and stamina. I never mastered the technique of "sleeping quick"— drinking all night, passing out for a couple of hours somewhere and then driving four, or five, or seven hundred miles to begin the process all over again. I wanted to sip spring water for a month and eat leafy vegetables. I wanted all things soft and tender. I wanted to crawl into Gale's arms and not come out. That was the first night we slept together, instead of having incredible soul-trembling sex and then sleeping together.

The sex was like a gift we had been given, something rare and priceless that we didn't know what to do with. It had brought trouble and confusion into our lives. We had tried many times to give it back, leaving each other, sometimes for a year or more, finding other people, and then deciding we had made a terrible mistake.

She knew the gift was love, but I didn't want to be tied down by love, so I looked for other explanations. It was a prolonged infatuation of some kind, a strange and uncommon form of lust. That summer, I realized how tolerant she had been of this stupidity. Things got better between us when the phrase "I love you" entered my vocabulary. And then they got worse again.

She thought that I was grudgingly in love with her, and would rather not be in love with her, which was true some days and not others. She listened to many ringing denunciations against the institution of marriage and wondered if she was wasting her time. And it wasn't easy being in love with a man who was always leaving.

I told her not to take my absences personally. It was how I made my living, and how I was meant to live, and in several different ways this made her feel jealous. There was something else, or perhaps someone else, or perhaps a whole circuit of someone elses, that kept calling me away from her. She was also jealous because she was a free spirit, with a streak of wildness and wanderlust of her own, and I was off having more adventures than she was. At the end of that rodeo summer she left me and went to Alaska for a year.

CHAPTER 11

They feared drys, cops, jailers, bosses, moralists, crazies,
truthtellers, and one another. They loved storytellers, liars,
whores, fighters, singers, dogs that wagged their tails, and
generous bandits.

William Kennedy, *Ironweed*

I sit at my desk with a box of notebooks, accumulated over the
last ten years. In a few hours the dawn will creep across the
sky and it will not feel like a fresh new day. It occurs to me that
the contents of this box would make better ammunition for a
sedentary propagandist than a defender of nomadic living. It
would be all too easy to hold up these notebooks, in the manner
of a prosecutor or a preacher, and declare that the American road
is tawdry and depraved, the last refuge of scoundrels, wastrels,
mountebanks and lunatics, and that the American rails are even
worse.

Here are the FTRA notebooks, travels and interviews with the
Freight Train Riders of America, the so-called "hobo mafia,"
suspected of orchestrating dozens of murders and using freight
trains to transport large shipments of drugs around the republic.
Listen to the song of the contemporary American hobo, the heir
of Jack London and Woody Guthrie:

I'm drunk off my ass and I don't give a fuck
Batshit in the daytime and batshit at night
I'll ride this old rail and I don't give a fuck
Batshit in the evening and I'm kicking your ass
Crazy motherfucker and I'll fuck you all up.

Here is a notebook entitled "Lot Lizards," a slang term used for truckstop whores by their clients. Here is a notebook entitled "El Pistolero," about an assassin for a Mexican drug cartel who moved from one contract to the next and thought it prudent to keep no fixed address. He was an amiable psychopath and a reluctant nomad who had the misfortune to get killed before he could give me his full life story. I was introduced to him at a backyard barbecue in south Tucson by a friend of mine who moves in that world. The assassin wanted me to write his biography and sell the screen rights to Hollywood, so he could retire from the killing business and settle down on a ranch in northern Mexico with a big herd of cattle and many children.

That was another long, drunken night. There has been so much drinking, justified in the name of immersion reporting, and it shows up in my handwriting from time to time. Where were the happy, clean, well-adjusted nomads, the Joe Walkers of our age? Where were the role models? Where were the love stories?

Chuck and Linda got married in Reno. The wedding cost twenty-five bucks and that left them with ten dollars to their name. On their wedding night Linda blew a truck driver for twenty dollars so they could get a motel room. She had done this a few times before in her life, but only in emergencies. "Honey, this is a special night and I want us to have a nice bed and a room," she said to Chuck.

"All right then," he sighed, and she was pleased he didn't kick up a fuss.

They set out on their honeymoon in a 1973 Buick, pale blue with a sun-blistered vinyl roof, and drove the interstates back and forth across the country, never stopping anywhere for more than a few days. Sometimes they got a motel room. Mostly they slept in the car. Truck drivers kept them in gas money and fast food.

A year after the wedding I met Chuck and Linda outside the TTT truckstop in Tucson. "We've talked about settling down, renting an apartment, getting jobs, raising a family, all that stuff," she said. "Maybe one day, but for right now we're happy to keep living on the road." She laughed. "It's like our honeymoon never ended."

We sat and talked in the Buick for a few hours. Every now and then Linda would excuse herself and be gone for ten minutes or so. When she returned Chuck was there for her with a big reassuring hug and a pint of Old Crow to take away the taste. She would swill out her mouth with the whiskey and spit it on the ground. Then Chuck would give her a tender kiss on the lips.

Love story number two: Jason Rogers and Scrap Iron met at the annual biker gathering in Sturgis, South Dakota. Jason was forty-two years old, an ex-serviceman who "went bad upstairs," as he puts it, and retired on mental disability payments. He had been a road tramp for thirteen years, a small, wizened, bearded man with the letters LETS FUCK tattooed across his fingers. Scrap Iron was an eight-week-old pitbull puppy. Jason traded a quart of beer for him because he wanted a dog for protection, something that would grow up vicious. He was tired of being beaten up and robbed by other tramps.

I picked them up under a bridge in Mississippi, driving west on Interstate 20. A wet snow had been falling for two days. I saw the little white puppy, looking mournful and piteous, and its hopeful, imploring owner. At the sound of my brakes the puppy bounded up the highway and was there at the door of my truck, thirty yards ahead of its master, squeaking and wagging its tail.

"Best move I ever made, getting that pup," said Jason, sitting down and arranging his gear. "People couldn't give two shits about a homeless guy, they figure it's his fault, but they feel sorry for a dog. Especially a cute little guy like ol' Scrap Iron here."

He fished around in his pack for dog biscuits, to give Scrap Iron his treat for getting the ride. This was a canny piece of dog

training. Scrap Iron had learned to associate tragic roadside
performances with praise and dog biscuits. He had learned to beg
for a ride, hence the wagging of his tail at the sound of brakes.
For the next four hundred miles Scrap Iron lolled contentedly
on Jason's lap, taking naps, getting his belly scratched and his ears
massaged and hearing a lot of "There's a good ol' boy" and
"Wooza-wooza-wooza, you ol' canine."

A curiosity about Jason: he doesn't drink water. He hates water,
and will only drink it in the direst emergencies. He restricts his
intake of liquids to coffee, Mountain Dew, beer and whiskey,
which might account for his strikingly wizened appearance at the
age of forty-two. All these drinks contain caffeine or alcohol, both
of which are dehydrating agents. (He won't drink wine because
he doesn't want to look like a wino.)

Another curiosity, more common than you might think among
road tramps: he never leaves the interstates. He travels constantly
but his environment stays the same, generic and interchangeable.
Everything he needs from society is laid out in a convenient,
predictable strip—a restaurant to beg outside, a convenience store
for tobacco and beverages, a motel or a bridge to sleep under,
depending on his funds, and a highway ramp from which to catch
a ride to the next strip of franchises. He avoids scenic byways
and rustic backwaters like the plague. The begging is no good,
and the traffic flow is too light for efficient hitchhiking.

Jason wanted a vicious guard dog. He wasn't expecting the
love and companionship that has blossomed between them. Jason
is part of a team now, and the team is blazing a hot streak across
the country. The rides come effortlessly. Hitchhiking with Scrap
Iron is like hailing a taxi compared to the old days. Money flows
into their hands like magic, more money than Jason knows what
to do with, dangerous amounts of money.

Christmas found them in Nashville. They stood outside franchise restaurants and exit-loop churches, Scrap Iron doing his
tragic puppy routine and Jason holding up a sign that read,
"Homeless. Need Help and DOG FOOD."

"It was wild, man. People would come up and give us twenties and tens. Big ol' bags of dog food. The waitress in the

Cracker Barrel bought Scrap Iron a dog sweater, which was real sweet of her. Course we couldn't use it, because it was bad for business. Man, we were making two, three hundred dollars a day without hardly trying! Christmas Eve, we made four hundred and twenty-five dollars, and Christmas Day we made another three hundred!"

They had to leave Nashville because they were making too much money. Without poverty, there were no brakes on Jason's drinking and drug-snorting. He knew he was killing himself, and where would his death leave Scrap Iron? It was time to move on, in search of leaner times. He blew five hundred dollars in a final frenzy in the downtown bars, buying drinks all around, tipping the bartender an extra fifty to let Scrap Iron sit under his chair. Then he caught a taxi to the city limits with his last twenty-five dollars and passed out in a culvert. The next morning he was up early with his thumb out, and Scrap Iron beside him. They got a ride down to Jackson, Mississippi from a drug dealer in a Ford Mustang, who gave Jason a bag of weed, a gram of coke and fifty dollars—"I'm telling you, man, we're on a roll." They worked the Cracker Barrel in Jackson for a while and then decided to go to California.

I dropped them off on the outskirts of Dallas, a franchise strip on the second exit. I offered Jason ten dollars and he turned it down. He already had eighty-five dollars and that was enough for a motel room, a bottle of whiskey, a case of beer and a three-course dinner for Scrap Iron, to be laid out on the bed while they watched wrestling on TV. "I figure Scrap Iron earns the money in this outfit, so he gets whatever he wants: cheeseburgers, fries, burritos, hot dogs, ice cream, you name it. He's real partial to chicken-fried steak with mashed potatoes and gravy. That's probably his favorite."

Where are the golf professionals who spend their lives on tour and move from one manicured grassland to another? Where are the traveling salesmen and the swelling legions of "road warrior" business executives who live in airports, aeroplanes, rental cars and extended-stay hotel suites? Where are the roving computer wizards, camped in their motor homes on corporate office parks? Where are the idle rich, the peripatetic playboys of Aspen, Martha's Vineyard, the Hamptons and other ports of call? Where, for that matter, is Keanu Reeves? He keeps no fixed address and lives year-round in hotels and movie-set trailers, or so I read a few years ago.

There is a bias reflected in these notebooks: "The pure nomad is the poor nomad." During my forays into the scholarship of nomadism, I found this axiom quoted time and again, affirmed, refuted, reiterated with qualifications in the usual academic fashion. It was penned in the 1930s by Owen Lattimore, the great authority on pastoral herdsmen in the Middle East, and to my mind the axiom holds true in contemporary America. Take Jason Rogers as an oblique example. He was on a hot streak, but as a good nomad he understood that wealth was a dangerous temptation and that he needed the lean rigours of the trail. He had proved it to himself with a near-death drug binge in a Nashville hotel room.

Another curiosity about Jason: once a year he gives away everything he owns—his backpack and its contents, his bedroll, every cent in his pockets, everything except the clothes on his back. He does it to test his skills. He needs to know he can survive with nothing, because sooner or later someone is going to steal all his gear. His last give-away was in Tucumcari, New Mexico, in the pre–Scrap Iron days. He hitched a ride to an interstate rest area, spent the day washing windshields and made enough to re-outfit himself at an Amarillo thrift shop the next day.

I spent most of my time with the wandering poor, the nomadic underclass, "the nomadic homeless," to borrow a misleading tautology that seems to be in vogue among sociologists and social workers. When we hear the word "homeless" we think of someone who feels the lack of a home and yearns to live in one again. I don't know about the urban homeless, but in my experience this is not the case on the roads and rails, at least not with the full-timers. They use the word "homeless" to elicit sympathy and funds because they know what it means to the sedentary, but they call each other tramps, hoboes, road dogs. They have rejected the idea of living in a home for one of two reasons: they either don't want or can't handle what it entails. They find it easier to get through the day without a home and a steady job to pay for it.

Since so many of them are damaged in one way or another— most commonly by alcohol, drugs and mental problems—purity might seem like an odd word to use about their nomadism. So let me explain. They experience more of the physical hardships that have traditionally accompanied nomadic living (and helped define its purity for scholars). They are intimately acquainted with sandstorms, cloudbursts, blizzards, hunger and thirst.

More importantly, they have a quintessentially nomadic attitude toward sedentary society: they take what they need from it and then retreat, looking for temporary autonomous zones. They don't pay taxes, they don't vote, they don't consider themselves bound by the social contract. And thanks to vagrancy laws, begging laws, laws against sleeping in parks, laws against hitchhiking and riding freight trains—laws, in short, that make it illegal to be poor and nomadic—they are locked into conflict with the sedentary state and its coercive power.

This was another reason why so many of them were in the hinterlands of the West, which still contained the possibility of disengaging from the social contract, and using space and mobility to avoid the coercive power of the state, at least for a while. I tended to look for the nomads who had disengaged the furthest.

God's Love Shelter lies at the railroad end of Last Chance Gulch in Helena, Montana, among pawn shops, gun shops and rough-looking bars. A group of train tramps were standing outside God's Love, passing a can of Top's tobacco, coughing their spectacular coughs, drinking coffee from big plastic mugs with convenience-store logos on the side. Some of them were FTRA, others were friends and associates, and they were storytelling their way through a cold gray morning.

"Bullshit! I was *there*, motherfucker, and it was me, K-Y and ol' Mojave Bill what burned that motherfucker down."

"Man, I love the devil out of Mississippi, but that nigger corn whiskey like to drive you crazy."

"The judge asked me how come I couldn't hold down no decent job, so I told him society is just a bunch of other people's opinions and that's all it is, boys."

"They call her Vampirella. She's got her teeth filed down into fangs and drops of blood tattooed over her jug'lar vein. She's beautiful people, man."

"Me and Rambo took that AK up into the hills yesterday and I tell you what, boys, we ploughed up a stretch of them woods good enough to start planting."

Wild Bill was there, with a beard and a hairstyle and a fringed buckskin jacket modeled after Wild Bill Hickok's. His sidekick Rambo Junior was there, dressed in full combat fatigues, with two semi-automatic pistols and an assortment of knives on his belt, all perfectly legal in Montana. Daniel Boone was there, notorious in the media as the founder and president of the FTRA, ruggedly handsome, movie-star handsome except for the brown teeth, with plenty of sardonic outlaw cool. He looked like he had some Indian blood and he wore his long, brown hair parted in the center, held in place by a leather headband. The FTRA began as a drunken joke, he was saying, but the joke had got way out of hand, and he didn't want to be associated with it anymore. He had got himself an old van and was intending to become a traveling preacher. I thought he was kidding at the time, but apparently that's what he's doing now.

Desert Rat and Tucson Stacy were there, having pledged to be old man and old lady to each other at an informal FTRA wedding. Mississippi Bones was there, now doing twenty-five years for murder, and so were about ten other people. Living without television, radio, movies, books, magazines, newspapers, the Internet or a job, they had plenty of spare time on their hands and storytelling filled it best. I noticed that their stories kept returning to the same theme: the hobo trickster who gets the last laugh at the expense of the citizens and the authorities or his rivals.

The way they spoke—drawling, rollicking, boastful, overblown, heavily salted with oaths—reminded me of mountain men, mule-skinners and Mark Twain's rivermen, although we have no accurate records of their vernacular. Like everyone else, Mark Twain would refer to prodigious feats of cursing and leave it at that. I always felt cheated. I wanted to know what their speech really sounded like. So I will attempt an unbowdlerized rendition of its modern form, reconstructed from a notebook entry and memory. In essence it is the story of a nomad raid, and while I have my doubts about its veracity, I'm not going to give you the teller's nickname. With all the police attention on the FTRA, it might get someone arrested. (I feel safe giving half of Red's name, because there are so many Reds on the rails.)

"Me and Red come into Amarillo one time, and boys I tell you what, it was a cold, nut-freezin' sonofabitch or call me a nigger. Hell, you been up in that Panhandle country. You know them winds. She come blowin' down from the No'th Pole and there ain't nothin' but bobwar fences to slow her down.

"Me and Red hadn't eaten in three days. I was so goddamn hungry I could have ate a frozen dawg and chomped her down like biscuits and gravy. We was out of tobacco too and didn't have a dime between us. So we snuck out the yards and walked on into town, lookin' for a dumpster to dive, and we come up on this liquor store. We hadn't had a drop in three days neither. I was so goddamn dry I couldn't hardly spit, and Red, well shit, he just went fuckin' nuts.

"He carries that big ol' .45, government-issue, hard-shootin' sonofabitch, and he hauls it out of his jeans, and he stomps right on in there, and he's like, 'All right motherfuckers! Everybody down on the ground. I'll kill every one of you motherfuckers,' and I'm like, oh shit man, here we go.

"So we've got three Meskins layin' down on the floor, shittin' their pants and prayin' to the Virgin of goddamn Lupe [technically Guadalupe], and a fuckin' *A*-rab freakin' out behind the cash register. Red's got the .45 in his face and he's bellerin', 'Give me the money, motherfucker! NOW motherfucker!'

"So what does this crazy fuckin' sand nigger do? He reaches down and hits the fuckin' *alarm*, motherfuckers. Red would have killed him right then and there, 'cept he didn't have no bullets in the gun, so we grab up some smokes and a bunch of bottles like schnapps and gin and fucked-up shit, and we hear them sirens comin' and we haul ass for the tracks. There was a grainer comin' through, and we caught out on the fly. And boys let me tell you what, we got ALL fucked up that night."

Twilight in the railyards of Helena, Montana. We walked along the floor of a deep metal canyon, with freight trains towering up on either side of us and automatic searchlights swinging through the gloom and unearthly clangings and screechings as a distant brakeman slammed together a train. Bones went on ahead. He was less stoved-up physically than Desert Rat and Tucson Stacy, and more adept at reading a railyard than Windwalker—figuring out which trains are going where by their cargo, position in the yard, the time of day, the signal lights.

Bones came back from his scout and led us to an empty boxcar on a train heading west. We passed up backpacks, and two reluctant puppies, and hauled Rat and Stacy up into the boxcar. Rat got badly smashed up in a derailment a few years ago, lost a kidney, and like so many tramps he lives with severe, chronic pain and hardly ever complains about it. Stacy's left leg is "mostly Tupperware," and she has a raft of other health problems. Desert Rat, also known as Hobo Rat, started riding the rails when he got back from Vietnam in 1969. Stacy hopped her first freight train when she ran away from home at the age of thirteen.

I was greatly relieved that we were climbing aboard a stationary train. There are so many amputation and decapitation stories about people trying to "catch out on the fly," or swing themselves up into moving boxcars; so many tramps with names like One Wing, Lefty and Stumpy.

Bones jammed a spike under the door to stop it slamming shut and trapping us inside—another of the myriad forms of accidental death that await the unwary or unlucky freight-train rider. Every year, three or four hundred people are found dead on railroad property (450 in 1997), from falling off trains, being hit by trains, crushed by shifting freight loads or derailments, from natural causes such as liver failure and heart attacks, and increasingly from being shot, stabbed, beaten to death or shoved out of moving trains. Because it is so hard to tell who was pushed and who fell, there is no accurate count of the killings, but through the 1990s it averaged out to about five confirmed murders a year, plus sundry beatings and rapes (of men and women). The authorities and the media said the FTRA, and its offshoot gangs, were responsible for most of the violence.

The tramps pulled out their marker pens and signed in on the wall of the boxcar. Bones was the only one to include the letters FTRA in his graffiti, with SS-style lightning bolts, and the only one to put on his colors—a greasy old bandanna, fastened at the neck with a metal concho, a disc-shaped silver ornament, commonly used to decorate belts and saddles. The others were looking to dissociate themselves from the FTRA. It used to be such a beautiful thing, they said, all about love, pride and brotherhood, but now it had been hijacked by a younger crowd and turned into something else—a major source of heat, for one thing.

The media had gone into a frenzy ("Killer Psychos Ride the Rails With Terror" was the *Houston Chronicle*'s headline), and the cops and railroad bulls were making the yards "hotter than a pistol," as Desert Rat explained it. And all because a few FTRA members, and a few more FTRA wannabes, had got drunk and a little crazy and killed a few people. "Hell, anybody can get wild when they've had a few drinks," he said.

With a tumultuous groaning and clanging and a low, mournful whistle, the train rumbled out of the yards into a bitterly cold night. What was the purpose of the journey? They wanted to get to Washington State so they could sign on and get emergency food stamps, then move on to another state and get some more—a common practice known as "double-clutching." But the foremost reason was that they loved riding freight trains and felt wrong when they spent too much time in one place. "I got hair on the bottom of my feet to wear off," said Rat.

We were supposed to leave Helena three days ago, but Bones had trouble getting dogs for the journey. He had trouble keeping a quarter in his pocket and remembering to make the telephone call and getting over to the house, less than a mile from God's Love, where the puppies were being given away. Now he looks like a different man: alert, competent, purposeful. Riding freight trains, rolling nowhere, was what they did best and they took pride in their abilities, skill and endurance.

It soon became apparent as the train got up to speed that the boxcar was a "shake, rattle and roller." It was like riding a trotting horse if you don't know how to ride, except the floor was hard, cold steel. I bounced and rattled and shivered uncontrollably, and the puppies whimpered, and Tucson Stacy looked like she had arrived in seventh heaven. "I don't ride in nobody's airplane, or nobody's car," she prattled away happily. "This ol' boxcar is my Cadillac, my momma, my poppa, my brother, my home."

As the train climbed up into mountains, you could see thick snow on the ground by the moonlight and the temperature was well below freezing. We were going over the Rockies, "over the hump," and had I known this in advance I would have brought a real sleeping bag, instead of the $29.95 Kmart special I had with me.

About these puppies. There is, or was at the time, a hobo gang called the Wrecking Crew that wore FTRA-style bandannas and conchos and used their dogs as a reserve food supply. In the summer of 1989 a deputy sheriff in Havre, Montana, caught two of them (Matthew and Mary Boudreau) in the act of skinning a puppy next to a campfire. Bones wanted puppies for a different reason. "One of these ol' boys will put fifteen degrees on your bedroll," he said, shoving one down inside his sleeping bag. Rat and Stacy stuffed the other one down between them.

They put axe-handles, knives and railroad flares within easy reach, and arranged themselves so that their feet rather than their heads were nearest the open door of the boxcar. "I woke up one morning and some dude was whalin' on my head with an axe-handle," said Bones. "Ever since then I sleep this way round."

We passed around a bottle of something and smoked weed out of a homemade soapstone pipe, and there was some entertaining storytelling of dubious veracity that decreased into ever-descending spirals and finally reached mumbling incoherence. That was pretty much how it went for the next two days. We rode at night and hid out in railyards during the day, and as I listened to them talk I wondered if it was even possible to distinguish truth from rumor about the FTRA.

Let me tell you how the FTRA has been portrayed in the newspapers and television news reports. Let me tell you what Special Agent Jack McManigal of the Union Pacific Railroad Police and Officer Robert Grandinetti of the Spokane Police Department believe the FTRA to be, since they have been the primary sources of information for the media.

I have some of their reports and presentation packages here in front of me, hooked out of the filing cabinet, and very impressive they are too, complete with flow charts and diagrams, detailing the FTRA's command structures, seniority rankings, its various chapters and subsets, such as the enforcement unit (Goon Squad) and the assassination unit (Death Squad). I appreciate all the years of hard work that McManigal and especially Grandinetti have put into their investigations, but from what I saw and heard on the rails about the FTRA these reports constitute a monumental act of flattery.

It might be, as Rat and Bones believe, that law enforcement has built up the menace of organized hobo crime to justify more funds and resources to fight it, and put a stop to all freight-train riding. But I think these diagrams and ranking systems reveal more about the mind-set of the men who made them, because they describe something that operates like a police department— organized, disciplined, hierarchical, rigid in structure, with specialist units that carry out orders and report back to a central command.

I was more in agreement with Officer Ed Standahl, from the Omaha office of the Union Pacific, who told me that his investigators had found no organized pattern to the upsurge of crime; that the hallmark of the killings and violence was their random, disorganized quality, and that FTRA members were just as likely to attack other FTRA members as anyone else on the rails. It looked to me like violent crime on the A-Camp model—another group of alcoholic Vietnam veterans who had their own flags, tattoos and codes of loyalty.

I could see the FTRA sticking up a liquor store with an empty gun, or beating someone to death in a drunken rage, or pulling off a two-hundred-dollar drug deal, but I baulked at Grandinetti's theory that they were picking up large shipments of heroin at the Mexican border and using the freight trains to distribute them to biker gangs (I certainly wouldn't trust the FTRA with a valuable drug shipment; it would be far safer on the roads). By introducing a profit motive the drug-trafficking theory helped establish the notion of a "hobo mafia," but where were the profits? All the FTRA members I met were flat broke and running food-stamp scams to keep from starving. There was another line from *Ironweed* that kept running through my mind: "The only brotherhood they belonged to was the one which asked the enduring question: how do I get through the next twenty minutes?"

The central difficulty faced by anyone investigating the FTRA is the source of information. Like everyone else, Officer Grandinetti has relied almost exclusively on hobo informants, and they get their information from the hobo grapevine, which transmits truth, rumors and tall stories without distinction. Not only do train tramps habitually lie to the police, the press and welfare agencies, they tell a lot of stretchers to each other. Factor in the drunkenness, the drug consumption, the mental illness, the habitual myth-making and conspiracy-seeking and it becomes hard to believe anything you hear on the rails. Take the question of the FTRA's origins.

It was founded by Daniel Boone under a bridge in Libby, Montana, or maybe Whitefish, Montana, in 1981, or 1983, or 1985. Daniel Boone can't remember because he was drunk and high at the time, and has done his best to stay drunk and high ever since. Fixing the precise date and location in his mind has not been a priority. But let's say Libby in 1985. A group of Vietnam veteran train tramps were drinking under a bridge when a freight train came rolling by with the letters X-TRA on the side. "We should call ourselves FTRA," quipped Daniel Boone, "Fuck The Reagan Administration." Later they altered the acronym's meaning to Freight Train Riders of America or Free to Tramp and Ride Alone.

Mississippi Bones swore up and down that the FTRA, meaning Freight Train Riders of America, was founded in the 1940s by a black hobo called Coal Train. Bones had heard the whole story from Coal Train himself as he lay drinking wine on his deathbed in a "hoochie," or lean-to, in the Mojave Desert.

At God's Love Shelter some of the older hoboes dated the origins of the FTRA back to the 1930s. It was an offshoot of the Hole in the Wall gang, based in Minneapolis, which pioneered the fashion for bandannas and conchos and established the original Goon Squad to enforce the code of the rails and punish wrongdoers. The Goon Squad meted out beatings for such infractions as failure to share food with another hobo, or help an injured hobo, or leave a clean camp behind you, or for breaking the code of silence and snitching to the authorities.

Daniel Boone's FTRA was the product of a different era on the American rails, the post-Vietnam era. A new class of people appeared on the rails, haunted by war, vilified by society, seeking escape and oblivion. Traditionally, hoboes had ridden the freight trains to find seasonal work—harvesting crops, fencing prairie, building roads, dams, bridges and railroads. It had always been a rough, tough, dangerous, drunken life, but with the arrival of Vietnam veterans, and other sixties and seventies casualties, the culture of the rails became more debauched and nihilistic, and more violent.

According to Desert Rat, the FTRA began as a brotherhood of Vietnam veterans. It gave them a feeling of belonging. "Man when you're out there hungry and alone, freezing your ass off, there ain't no more lonesome feeling in the world," he said. "But I can walk into any brother's camp and get treated like I'm somebody." Belonging to the FTRA was also a source of protection. If someone attacked or stole from one member of the FTRA, he risked a retaliatory beating from the other members of the gang—or, as it turned out, if he verbally insulted an FTRA member, or was rumored to have insulted a member, or for A-Camp-style misunderstandings and paranoid hallucinations. The people who were most active in these retaliatory beatings became known as the FTRA Goon Squad.

During the late 1980s and 1990s things changed again. A newer, younger breed of tramp appeared on the rails, even more violent and nihilistic, and some of them appropriated the FTRA name and colors while others formed different gangs. Desert Rat and the original Daniel Boone crew talk about the new FTRA, the Baby Goon Squad, the New Wrecking Crew and a particularly violent new gang known as the Resistance Crew. I heard the same thing from the hoboes playing cards at God's Love. "There's a whole bunch of these new crews riding around, causing trouble and beating people up," said Irish. "It's mostly young kids trying to make a name for themselves and be big bad gangsters. All the publicity has gone to their heads, and the FTRA gets blamed for all the shit they pull down."

Robert Silveria ("Sidetrack") was the most notorious hobo killer of the 1990s, convicted of five murders, suspected of a lot more by the authorities, and claiming to have killed forty-seven himself, out of a "deep anger." He created most of the media hoopla about the FTRA, but he was not a member, according to the police, other hoboes and Silveria himself, who claimed to be the leader of the tramp nation—"I could have tortured others of your world, but I chose to torture my world, because I preyed on the weak." In other words his killings were psychosis-related, not gang-related.

Jeremy "Jeremiah" Abshire, convicted of slashing the throat of Barbara Boggs Richardson ("Cheyenne") in 1992, was a member of the new FTRA, thirty years old at the time. The murder was a random act of drunken rage, an impulse killing, but once again it was linked by the media to the shadowy machinations of the hobo mafia.

Mississippi Bones, so called because he is a scrawny bag of bones from Mississippi, was convicted of killing a fellow FTRA member called F-Trooper. I have an article here from *Spin* magazine by Lucius Shephard, who reached roughly the same conclusion about the FTRA as me, and talked to Bones in prison. Bones claimed it was self-defense. F-Trooper had already stabbed him in the ribs with a skinning knife in an argument over Bones' rail wife, Misty Jane. It took Bones a year to recover from his injuries and then he ran into F-Trooper again, in the railyards of Missoula, Montana. F-Trooper said he was coming to Portland with Bones and Misty Jane, and Bones, who was drunk and now admits he misunderstood the situation, shot him in the head with a pistol.

Where Officer Grandinetti perceives a criminal organization, masterminded by Daniel Boone and administered by his lieutenants, I saw a general breakdown in hobo society, the kind of anarchy that gives anarchy a bad name. I also thought Grandinetti had overplayed the white supremacist menace of the FTRA. The members I met were certainly racists who talked disparagingly of "niggers" and "shawappas," a tramp word meaning the same, while making exceptions for individual black tramps they knew and certain black soldiers they had fought with in Vietnam. Grandinetti's informants have been telling him that neo-Nazi groups are organizing the FTRA into a white supremacist army that will begin by purging the rails and then move on to greater things.

I suppose it all comes down to which informants you find most credible. I got my breakdown-of-hobo-society theory from William Blank, or "Pappy," a retired seventy-four-year-old hobo who spent his days drinking coffee at God's Love. Americans tell me it's a European tendency to look for the broad historical perspective behind a contemporary phenomenon, and Pappy was a living history of the American rails. He was a small, sprightly, bantamweight figure who wore overalls and a brakeman's cap. After a lifetime of heavy boozing, kept in check by poverty, he had switched to coffee, and he drank sixty or seventy cups a day. I never saw him without a cup of coffee and he was never more than ten minutes away from rolling himself a cigarette.

He started riding in the 1930s as a teenager looking for work in the Great Depression, and was taught the ways of the rails by some of the original hoboes, who had been riding freight trains since the 1890s. Since hobo labor had laid most of the railroad tracks across the West, and harvested most of its crops, they felt entitled to ride without paying. The origins of the word "hobo" are uncertain, but it is thought to be a contraction of "hoe-boy," meaning a migrant agricultural worker.

Young William Blank fell into the same rhythm as the old-timers, moving from harvest to harvest, to tunnel-blasting jobs with road and rail crews, knocking on farmhouse doors for food in between jobs, and doing a little stealing—clothes from a laundry line, chickens and pigs, copper wire from railyards and industrial plants. "Back then there was no welfare, no missions, no food stamps," he said. "If you didn't work, you didn't eat and there wasn't always work to be found."

He started wearing a bandanna and silver concho in 1938. The Hole in the Wall gang wore them, but so did a lot of other committed, full-time hoboes. It was a way for them to recognize each other, an outside sign that someone was pledged to the code of the rails. "If you were hurt, another tramp would take care of you, and he didn't want no thank-you. 'Just pass it on,' they would say. When you came into a hobo jungle [a trackside camp] there would be clean pots and pans, and a stack of firewood, and a piece of mirror hanging in a tree to shave by. If you had one slice of bread, you'd tear it in half to share, and if you didn't, someone would hear about it and you'd be in trouble."

The big change in hobo society, by Pappy's estimation, began in the 1960s and it was all the government's fault. With the advent of welfare, social security and food stamps, hoboes no longer had to work or steal to stay alive—"All the pride and self-respect went out the window." It became possible to get blind drunk or drugged insensible on a daily basis, rather than on payday and its aftermath. The old code of the rails, the system of mutual reliance, started to break down, because it was no longer necessary for survival.

There was a steady increase in violence, as more "crazies and troublemakers" appeared on the rails, and during the 1980s a proliferation of gangs, in the sense of roving groups of thugs. "Now it's just got stupid," he said. "People are getting beat up and killed for no reason, and everyone's scared. If they see you hurt, they figure it's gang-related, and some gang is going to come after them if they help you."

Pappy has never had any trouble with the FTRA or the Goon

Squad. He considers them "pretty decent people" compared to the younger gangs. In 1986, in the hobo jungle in Pasco, Washington, he was beaten half to death by a group of "young kids" who broke his neck and left him for dead. After that incident, which hospitalized him for six months, Pappy started riding with a sawn-off shotgun in his pack.

Another factor in the violence has been the diversification of the American rails. The unified hobo society that Pappy knew has balkanized into mutually suspicious groups: anarchist punks, skinheads, crackheads, biker types, smugglers of illegal Mexican immigrants, Mexican migrant workers, eco-saboteurs, college kids and, strangest of all, yuppie hoboes. There had always been a few well-to-do vacationeers on the rails, lured by the romance and adventure (including John Dos Passos, Clark Gable, Frank Capra and the US Supreme Court justice William O. Douglas), but during the late 1980s and 1990s, as the FTRA was gaining nationwide notoriety, it turned into a hot new craze—riding the rails with cell phones, GPS finders, down parkas, three-hundred-dollar tents, four-hundred-dollar sleeping bags, and uploading your adventures to the yuppie hobo Web sites from laptop computers.

I took it as an expression of sedentary envy for the free nomadic life, a way of capturing the romance without the hunger and freezing. Most of the full-time tramps I talked to loathed the yuppie hoboes, but Pappy had no objection to them. He understood the urge. After a lifetime on the rails, after thirty-seven derailments, four heart attacks and that terrible beating in Pasco, Pappy still thought that riding the freight trains was the greatest thing in the world. "Out there you've got total freedom and no responsibilities. Wherever you're at, that's home. It can be a beautiful life, and you see a lot of beautiful country, places where man's hand ain't fucked it up yet. Man, if my body could stand it, I'd be out there today."

At the age of seventy he retired from the rails and got married for the first time in his life. He lives with his wife in a small trailer by the railyards. Old habits die hard: he still dumpster-dives for all their food and makes a little extra scavenging junk and copper wire. He took me to visit his trailer, the first permanent dwelling of his life, and showed me freezers packed full of food, mounds of junk he was planning to fix or sell, and his pack and bedroll under the bed. "I still ride for the hell of it now and then," he said. "Next time, I'm taking my wife along. It's going to be her first ride. She figures it'll help her understand a tramp husband."

His wife was off on some errand. We sat at the kitchen table drinking coffee. We talked for hours and what I remember most clearly is the expression on Pappy's face when he heard the low, mournful honk of a freight train pulling through the yards. I had heard about the effects of this sound in a hundred old country and western ballads and blues songs, and I had always taken it as a metaphor or cliché. When Pappy heard the lonesome whistle blowing he would turn his head toward it and a look of deep, soulful, profound sadness would occupy his features—like Scrap Iron begging for a ride but entirely genuine.

Where would you choose to die if you had the choice between a hospital bed or the middle of nowhere? A few years ago I was driving along I-50, a two-lane blacktop that crosses the deserts of central Utah and Nevada and calls itself "The Loneliest Highway in America." There is a ninety-mile stretch between towns or gas stations, and somewhere in the middle of that stretch I pulled over to take a photograph of a weathered and improbable sign: "ALFALFA For Sale." Curiosity led me down a dirt road to a few abandoned buildings and an alfalfa field returned to desert.

Lying in the shade of one of the buildings was an old highway drifter with his head resting on a small backpack. His eyes were closed, his lips were cracked, he lay very still and I thought he was dead. As I bent over him to see if he was breathing his eyelids moved and opened, and he made a weak sound in his throat. I rushed back to the truck to get water.

I offered him a drink and he took a sip. Did he want food? Did he want a ride? Did he want an ambulance? In a cracked whisper he told me to go away and leave him alone. What would you have done? I left the plastic jug of water beside him and drove away, and I did not alert the authorities when I got to the next town.

Fifty miles down a dirt road in southern Utah, fifty-five miles from the nearest town, we huddle in our blankets around an aromatic fire of juniper wood. Gale has come back from Alaska. We are trying to make it work again. We are talking about death as a means of talking about love.

There is a small and exquisite canyon in the darkness to the east of us with a stream running through it, and cottonwood trees, and a series of ponds where the stream has been dammed by beavers, and a beguiling historical mystery. It is one of our favorite places and Gale decides that she wants her ashes scattered there. She gives me a look that suggests that I had better volunteer my services for this duty. The reply forms in my brain that I am five years older, and male, and unlikely to be available, but this is not the time for a lecture on mortality statistics.

So I make my pledge and ask her where exactly, and request a favor in return: "If you can fix it, let me die somewhere in the desert. I hate the idea of dying in a hospital, and I don't want to end up in a cemetery. Terrible waste of calories. Just leave me out in the desert to get recycled."

"That's illegal," she says, which I hadn't realized. "But okay."

The coyotes break the silence from time to time, yammering and howling in the distance, somewhere down in the canyons. I might feel differently when the moment is at hand, but it doesn't sound like a bad fate right now—to fuel the wanderings of these splendid animals, and the flight of vultures, and get picked clean by ants, and then to enter the bodies of ant-eating lizards and lizard-eating birds and coyotes, while my bones crumble into the soil and nourish a cactus or a juniper tree. It's enough reincarnation for me.

The night is clear, windless and very cold. Words fail me when it comes to the stars. All I can say is that there are a lot of them, and they are very bright, and the planets are even brighter. Gale points up at Mars, which is flashing red, a traffic signal red. At first I think it must be a distant airplane but it doesn't move. Her grandparents were astronomers in Tucson and she knows the desert sky at night. Behind the rock battlements to the east there is a glow of light, climbing and brightening as it reaches the rim. We are sure the moon is about to appear but it turns out to be Jupiter. How tragic it is that so many people in the world will never see a night sky like this, will go to their graves without seeing the Milky Way. And how pleasant that none of them are around tonight.

The fire has burned down to coals. I make the drinks, Scotch and water, half and half, and start roasting green chillies and grilling steaks. When the food is cooked I stoke up the fire and return to my drink to find that it has frozen solid. You don't expect a desert to be this cold, but we are five thousand feet above sea level in early November, camped above a complex of canyons that drain into the Escalante River. It is our intention to poke about and explore in those canyons for a few days, laze around a good deal and give a little more thought to the mysterious disappearance of Everett Ruess.

He rode into the Escalante country in November 1934 astride a donkey, and leading a second donkey packed with his supplies: pens, paper, watercolor paints, fine sable paintbrushes, carving tools for his woodblock prints, pots, pans, blankets and food for two months. His body was lean and honed by thousands of miles of rough wilderness trails. His face was on the chubby side, with a suggestion of puppy fat and a wide, toothy grin. For the last three years, with a few intervals, he had been wandering the deserts and mountains of northern Arizona and southern Utah, keeping a journal, writing poetry and long, rhapsodic letters to his friends and relatives, resupplying himself by selling his artwork to Indian traders and Mormon ranch families.

He traveled in a state of exalted, soul-gushing ecstasy, overwhelmed by the beauty of the landscape and the romance of his adventures. He had learned to speak Navajo, slept many nights in their hogans and sheep-herding camps, and joined in their dances and ceremonies. In August, after a two-hundred-mile solo trek across the desert, he had visited the high, windswept mesas of the

Hopi reservation and seen medicine men dance with live rattlesnakes writhing in their mouths. The Hopis liked him (everyone seemed to like this strange, impassioned young man) and he was invited to participate in the Antelope Dance—one of very few whites to be accorded this honor.

He was a romantic who avoided romantic love, a hedonist who eschewed sex, alcohol, drugs and the pleasures of the palate, a nomadic aesthete who knew exactly why he felt compelled to wander the deserts: nothing else moved his soul with the same intensity, and this was all he craved from life. Before passing any judgement on his writing, or his art, or his creed, or his reckless-ness toward danger, we must keep one fact at the forefront of our minds: at the time of his disappearance, Everett Ruess was twenty years old.

Sitting by a campfire on the rim of the Escalante canyons, on November 11, 1934, he wrote a letter to his older brother Waldo in California.

As to when I shall visit civilization, it will not be soon, I think. I have not tired of the wilderness; rather I enjoy its beauty and the vagrant life I lead more keenly all the time. I prefer the saddle to a streetcar and the star-sprinkled sky to a roof, the obscure and difficult trail, leading into the unknown, to any paved highway, and the deep peace of the wild to the discontent bred by cities. Do you blame me then for staying, where I feel that I belong and am one with the world around me? It is true that I miss intelligent companionship, but there are so few with whom I can share the things that mean so much to me that I have learned to contain myself. It is enough that I am surrounded by beauty . . .

Even from your scant description, I know that I could not bear the routine and humdrum of the life you are forced to lead. I don't think I could ever settle down. I have known too much of the depths of life already, and I would prefer anything to an anticlimax. That is one reason why I do not wish to return to the cities. I have been in them before and returned to them before, and I know what they contain. There would have to be some stronger incentive than any I know now to make me want to return to the old ways.

This was the last letter that anyone received from him. A few days later he rode down into the canyons and vanished without a trace. There have been theories that he staged his own disappearance, to shack up with a Navajo sweetheart perhaps, but there is no evidence to support this idea beyond a wisp of hearsay. Nor is there any evidence to support the more likely explanations, that he was murdered by outlaws, or drowned in the Colorado River, or was bitten by a rattlesnake, or killed in a climbing accident. From his letters, and horrified eye-witnesses, we know that he liked to scamper up and down sheer, crumbling rockfaces, without ropes, and dangle from high places.

In the decades since his disappearance Everett Ruess has become a legendary figure in the canyonlands, the immortal "artist in residence" of the region, as Wallace Stegner called him, and we must address the question of why. His poetry was heartfelt and wincingly awful, in the usual adolescent fashion. His prose, and his artwork, showed signs of talent and might have turned into something significant. All of which is beside the point.

Anyone who has fallen under the spell of this country, or any big wild place, knows the temptation. We have all wondered, if only in passing, what it would be like to go further out there, deeper into the wilderness; to cut the ties to civilization and turn trips and expeditions into a permanent state of being. I first heard about Everett Ruess from the peripatetic river runners, rock climbers and outdoor adventure guides of the Southwest, who work odd jobs to fund the next trip into the wilderness or put up with the company of tourists in order to stay out there more permanently. They had a wide range of opinions about Everett Ruess, ranging from hero-worship to laconic disdain, but there was one point of convergence. They respected him for living out his dream with such full-blooded determination and commitment, and they liked the fact that it had fulfilled his wildest expectations.

★   ★   ★

Shivering in the gray light before dawn, I heap up juniper twigs on last night's coals and blow them into flames. I unfreeze a gallon of water, make coffee and eggs. After breakfast we load up the backpacks and walk out across a plateau of naked sandstone, hummocked and domed, rising into crests and pinnacles, fissured with gullies and swales, as if a storm-lashed sea had been frozen into rock. An hour of walking brings us to the rim of Davis Gulch, the site of Everett Ruess' last known camp, the final resting-place for Gale's ashes. Looking down into the lush, verdant cleft, with its smooth, undulating pink walls . . . Let's just say that Davis Gulch has a distinctly feminine quality.

Another hour and we find the one trail by which Davis Gulch is accessible from the rim, a bench of rock that zigzags down the west wall, with steps carved into the final descent by Mormon ranchers. Everett Ruess led his donkeys down this trail and built a corral for them on the canyon's grassy floor. They were still grazing there when the first search party came looking for him in March 1935. They found his size-nine boot tracks leading into the canyon but there were no tracks leading out, and no sign that anyone else had been in the canyon. There was an inscription carved into a rock—"Nemo, 1934"—and this puzzled them too.

The searchers wrote to Everett's family about the inscription and discovered that he was an avid fan of the Jules Verne novel *Twenty Thousand Leagues under the Sea*, and fancied himself as a latter-day Captain Nemo—one who has forsaken civilization to wander wild and distant regions. This was not much help. They spent ten days combing the area, with expert Navajo trackers, exploring every canyon and side gulch for miles in all directions. Further search parties followed but found no more tracks or clues, and no sign of his camping gear and art supplies.

It is possible to climb out of Davis Gulch by a hair-raising route at its head, but not if you're carrying a heavy and cumbersome pack outfit. If he left behind his gear, and it was later stolen, where were the tracks of the thieves? If he was murdered for his outfit by outlaws or cattle rustlers, where were their tracks? In the sheltered cleft of Davis Gulch footprints last a year or more, and they had no trouble tracing his movements around the canyon floor. We know that he took at least some of his supplies down into Davis Gulch, because the marks left by his bedroll were still visible at his campsite, and empty condensed-milk cans and candy bar wrappings were strewn around.

The Nemo inscription is underwater now, submerged under the 180-mile-long reservoir and boating lake backed up behind Glen Canyon Dam on the Colorado River. It drowned the lower half of Davis Gulch and a hundred other canyons, including Glen Canyon itself, just upstream from the Grand Canyon and equally spectacular. Everett Ruess' old campsite is still above water, sheltered by a rock overhang, and that's where we spread our sleeping bags and base ourselves for the next few days.

What remains of Davis Gulch is only four miles long. In a region of mammoth rock formations and hundred-mile vistas its beauty is compact and delicate: natural stone arches, fern-fringed pools and springs, cactus gardens, echoing caves and rock amphitheaters. Clambering around in its nooks and crannies we find nine-hundred-year-old Anasazi Indian potsherds and rock art, ruined cliff dwellings and granaries, and the tiny corncobs they grew here. In the warm afternoon sun we strip naked and frolic in the water, with predictable consequences. At dusk we sit by the beaver ponds, silent and motionless. There are freshly gnawed willows and felled cottonwood trees all around, fresh tracks and drag marks in the mud, but beavers have retained the wariness bred into them by Joe Walker and his ilk. We hear one warning slap of a tail on the water but see not a single glimpse. Nights around the fire sipping whiskey. The canyon walls frame a river of stars overhead.

I feel very content, very alive, very much in love. Next spring, she says, we should buy a couple of mules or donkeys, load them up with food and take off into the canyons for a couple of months. On the way up here we heard about a way to get from Zion National Park to Arches National Park, three hundred miles as the crow flies, which crosses only two paved roads. "Then, if we feel like it, we can stock up and come back again," she says. I find myself raising objections to the idea—neither of us has dealt with pack animals, we are too inexperienced in wilderness survival, it would be so easy to get lost in the maze of canyons, I have this book to finish—and I love the fact that she is suggesting it.

Years ago, long before I had heard of Everett Ruess, I spent two weeks hiking and camping in the canyons in northern Arizona, and I seriously considered going back out there for a couple of months. Lust more than anything dissuaded me, the prospect of extended celibacy. Like T. E. Lawrence, Wilfred Thesiger and a number of other wandering desert aesthetes, Everett Ruess had no apparent difficulties with the sexlessness of the life, and no yearnings for romantic love. He was attracted to women, and had come close to falling in love a couple of times, and struck out for the deserts again before anything developed. His sworn creed was to experience life as deeply and intensely as possible, and, like my younger self, he thought falling in love would be a hindrance to this goal.

So what became of him? There are dozens of different theories, all of them pure conjecture, all of them contraindicated by some-thing we know, or think we know. I lean with the herd and favor the accidental death theories, but some key piece of evidence to the puzzle eludes us: a set of footprints obscured by a flurry of wind and sand perhaps, or deliberately erased; a satchel of letters and watercolors lying in an obscure cave, now underwater; a set of bones crumbling on a remote rock ledge. Everett Ruess' death, if that's what happened, was untimely but it was not a tragedy. It was the death he had imagined for himself. "I've been thinking more and more that I shall always be a lone wanderer of the wilderness," he wrote to his brother in the summer of 1932. "God, how the trail lures me. You cannot comprehend its resistless fasci-nation for me . . . And when the time comes to die, I'll find the wildest, loneliest, most desolate spot there is."

CHAPTER 12

Leaving the snakeskin of place after place
going on—after the trees
the grass, a bird flying after a song.
            William Stafford, "For the Grave of
                                    Daniel Boone"

So it has come to this. The largest gathering of nomads in
America forms every January in Quartzsite, Arizona, a dusty,
sunbaked strip of gas stations, convenience stores, trailer parks and
RV campgrounds, strung out along a mile of interstate frontage
road; a place with no grass, no river or stream, and very few trees.
Their numbers are estimated at three hundred thousand—local
boosters are claiming half a million—and their encampments
spread out for miles into the surrounding desert.

B.J. McHenry is here, the snake-eating hitchhiker I dumped
on the side of the highway in Texas. I saw him begging outside
the Texaco this morning and gave him a wide berth. Chad and
Tiffany are here, with a small crew of A-Camp Rainbows. Lance
Grabowski from the buckskinner rendezvous has been here and
gone. There are traveling preachers, barking out the gospel from
roadside tents, nomadic traders and vendors of every description,
a small army of tramps and drifters and petty hustlers, and all of
them are feeding on the peripheries of the main horde.

Quartzsite is the big annual rendezvous for the nomadic retirees,
the most numerous and powerful of the contemporary nomadic

tribes in America. As always, it is difficult to say how numerous. They present a familiar problem to researchers and statisticians: a moving target, dissolving and re-forming, traveling in scattered bands and hard to distinguish from their semi-nomadic counterparts, who are also at Quartzsite in abundance. We know there are 8.5 million RVs on the American roads, but how many people are living in them permanently, as their sole habitations? The guesswork ranges between 300,000 and 3.5 million, with somewhere between 60 and 90 percent of them over the age of fifty-five. The Good Sam Club, America's largest RVing organization, estimates that three million people are living in their RVs year-round, of whom 80 percent are retirees.

They call themselves "full-timers," "gypsies" or, with a smile, "Geritol gypsies." They use mailing addresses (a friend, a relative, a post office box, a mail-forwarding service) to renew their drivers' licenses and keep their vehicles registered, licensed and insured. I was interested to discover that many of them stop voting and paying taxes when they turn nomadic, but those who persist in these habits do so through their fictional addresses. As their ethnographer point out, the nomadic elderly are an invisible population to the authorities, and many of them prefer it that way. "They fear that if 'the government' finds out about them it will tax them or otherwise destroy their lifestyle and their freedom."*

At first glance they strike you as unlikely inheritors and guardians of the American nomadic tradition. In some ways Quartzsite looks more like a mobile suburbia than a nomad encampment. Witness the profusion of Astroturf lawns, rolled out next to the RVs and ornamented with plastic flowers, miniature windmills, pink flamingos and plaster coyotes. The carved wooden signs bolted on the back of the RVs: "The Hendersons—Bill and Marge," "The Marshalls—Orville and Wilma." The array of gadgets inside the RVs: dishwashers, icemakers, microwaves, washing machines and dryers, TVs and VCRs, roof-mounted air conditioners, satellite dishes and solar panels. Out in the desert they circle their RVs

---

* Counts and Counts, *Over the Next Hill: An Ethnography of RVing Seniors in North America*.

like pioneer wagons and sit on deckchairs around a bonfire, drinking cocktails, making small talk and telling jokes.* When the bonfire dies down, they head back inside their RVs and the circle is lit by the flickering blue lights of their televisions.

Americans have been traveling in vehicular dwellings since the 1920s. The early models were called "house trailers" and adapted from British motor caravans, which were two-wheeled copies of the traditional gypsy wagon. The first RVs—larger, more comfortable trailers and motorized, coach-style dwellings—appeared in the 1960s, but it wasn't until the late 1970s and early 1980s, when manufacturers developed the modern, amenity-crammed, climate-controlled RV, that nomadic retirement took off as a mass movement. Two elemental American yearnings, for comfort and mobility, were combined into one package at the same time as the healthiest, wealthiest generation of grandparents in human history reached the age of retirement.

Traditionally, grandparents have been a rooted, stabilizing force in our societies, orienting their lives around their homes, communities, children and grandchildren. The images and clichés we hold of retirement are sedentary in nature: the armchair and slippers, Grandma baking cookies in her kitchen, a well-tended garden. We think of old age as a time of slowing down and solidifying, of moving about less and less until you stop moving altogether.

The Eisenhower generation has staged a mass rebellion against this model of retirement. Some thirty million retirees have left behind their homes, families and communities and struck out for new sociological frontiers. The bulk of this movement has come to rest in the new corporate-managed, age-segregated retirement communities in the Sunbelt (where no under-fifty-fives are allowed to live), but a significant minority has chosen to abandon sedentary living altogether. After a working life spent paying off mortgages, raising families and accumulating possessions, they were called by the other American dream—"burn down the house and

---

* Here's one I heard last night: "So this ninety-year-old guy goes into a whorehouse. The madam tells him, 'I'm sorry, buddy, you've had it,' and he says, 'Oh, I did? Who do I pay?'"

saddle up the horse," as Mike Hatfield described it. Or more precisely, sell the house and buy an RV with the proceeds.

Marie Williamson is marching along Quartzsite's main drag, swinging her arms purposefully, taking long, vigorous strides that leave me struggling to keep up. She is a grandmother in her late sixties, soon to be a great-grandmother, a forceful, capable woman who spent her working life on a ranch and doesn't stand for any nonsense. Marie is my neighbor at Quartzsite. My truck is parked in a dirt lot behind Silly Al's bar, and her RV—she calls it her "tepee" or "gypsy wagon"—is parked opposite, in a small encampment of RVing singles.

The air smells of dust and exhaust fumes, fried grease and corn syrup. The traffic jam, which appears in the early morning and disperses at sunset, rolls through an avenue of roadside food stands, selling waffle cones, cinnamon rolls, corn dogs, foot-long chilli dogs, jumbo pretzels, curly fries, macho nachos, single, double and triple bacon cheeseburgers. Under the circumstances, with so many ageing hearts and clogged arteries in the vicinity, these bright, cheery, all-American menus take on a morbid, sinister quality. I have been talking to the local ambulance crews and hearing about the forty or fifty heart attacks they have to deal with every January.

Swap meets and tented flea markets extend away on both sides of the road, where thousands of retirees are milling around on foot, buying up Indian jewelry, rocks and gemstones, antique bric-a-brac, Astroturf lawn ornaments, wind chimes with magnetic attachments, magic slice-and-dice kitchen implements, miraculous anti-ageing creams and arthritis cures, ceramic frogs with Velcro feet for carpeted dashboards, sun visors, cowboy hats, baseball caps, bumper stickers ("Home Is Where You Park It," "One Bad Golfer And One 'Good' Shopper Live Here," "We're Spending Our Kids' Inheritance"). The annual gathering at Quartzsite was started by gem and mineral traders in the 1960s, but in recent years they have become outnumbered by traveling flea-market vendors.

Nowhere in the world have I seen so many miniature dogs: teacup poodles, foot-long dachshunds, trembling Chihuahuas, palpitating Pomeranians. Partly it is a matter of restricted living space, and partly the pet regulations imposed by many RV parks (no animal taller than fifteen inches or weighing more than twenty pounds), but one also senses cultural conformity at work, the miniature dog as lifestyle accessory. Nowhere have I seen so many dogs wearing cute little sweaters, and/or miniature sun visors made of colored foam or crocheted wool—the hot canine fashion item of the season. Marie does not approve. She has a limited tolerance for cutesiness.

Moving through the crowd, at a gentler pace now, as Marie inspects the gems and minerals for sale, the faces are placid or smiling. There is an amiable, light-hearted, playful mood in the air. People gather in clusters and have animated, enthusiastic conversations, which break out into peals of laughter. Look up and there are retirees whizzing overhead in rented microlight aeroplanes.

Walking toward us, with a portly swagger and a lascivious smile for Marie, is a man who looks like Ernest Hemingway. He has a white beard and a baseball cap emblazoned with Quartzsite's new nickname: "Viagra Falls." Marie looks straight past him until he passes behind us, and then she rolls her eyes and tuts. As a good-looking single woman, with the body of a fifty-year-old, she knows the type all too well.

"Tepee-creepers is what I call them," she says. "Some man you hardly know will come knocking on your door at night, shaking a jar of those pills, and expect you to jump right into bed with him. I send them packing and they get mad. 'But Marie,' they say. 'Everyone's doing it.' Well not me. I don't want that kind of reputation, and it's against my religious beliefs. If you want to try living with me, I *might* be interested, but you've got to marry me first. And if you don't want to marry me, then good riddance."

She sifts through boxes of gemstones, looking for a chunk of pietersite or lapis lazuli to polish up in her afternoon lapidary class, and make into a ring or necklace pendant. She supplements her social security checks by selling handicrafts to other retirees she meets on the road. There is an internal, untaxed, unmeasured economy on the RV circuit, and this is probably its largest sector.

Marie has done well with her fringed buckskin handbags, which sell as fast as she can make them, but she finds jewelry-making more of a challenge, and more of a reward. She is still new to it, full of curiosity and enthusiasm, learning new things every day, and this accords with her general philosophy of retirement.

Her husband was content with familiar things and familiar sights. He was actively hostile toward the idea of learning or experiencing anything new. His idea of retirement, as she saw it, was to sink deeper into the same rut and wait for death. He wondered what was wrong with her. Why would she want to tear up a perfectly good life and go chasing around the country like a gypsy? They argued back and forth, with increasing bitterness, until she divorced him. That was twelve years ago, and she has been on the road ever since.

A picture of Jesus hangs above her bed, enforcing her moral codes in the bedroom. The living-room walls are decorated with cowboys and Indians, frozen in motion on their horses. She has ripped out part of her kitchen and installed a work table, where she sits with a cup of coffee, turning a freshly polished oval of pietersite in her fingers. "Even as a little girl I was always outdoors. I loved to ramble around in the woods. They'd find me out there in twenty below zero, tramping around in the snow, just as happy as I could be."

Like so many people in this book, Marie explains her wanderlust as something she was born with, something in the blood, or the soul, but she was able to contain it for most of her life. She grew up in western New York State, married a local boy when she was nineteen, moved onto a nearby ranch, and had three daughters. "All the time I was on the ranch I was itching to just get up and go, but you can't when you've got kids." When her daughters were grown up and out of the house she saw no reason to contain it any longer. There was a thirty-two-year marriage to consider, of course, vows sworn in the presence of God, and she tried hard to persuade her husband to come along. Right up to the end he didn't think she would go through with it, because the idea made no sense to him.

She started out as a "working gypsy," living in a pickup truck with a camper shell and taking odd jobs along the way. It goes without saying that the road led west. She worked as a house-keeper at a motel in Wyoming, she provided home help for old men living alone in the mountains of Montana. She went up to Valdez, Alaska, and worked in a fishery alongside one of her daughters, then bartended for a few months in Coldfoot, a rough mining town inside the Arctic Circle.

Seven years ago, with her ex-husband dead and the ranch sold, she bought her RV. We are sitting in a Kit Sunchaser, twenty-seven feet long, modestly appointed and freshly vacuumed, which cost her twenty thousand dollars used at a dealership in Logan, Utah. It is a fifth-wheel trailer, meaning that you hitch it to the back of a pickup truck and tow it around the country. The salesmen had never sold a fifth-wheel to a woman before and didn't believe a woman was capable of driving one.

"I told them I'd spent my life hauling trailers around a ranch, but they insisted on giving me a driving test before they'd sell it to me. They had me drive around the block a few times, and back up into a narrow parking space, and show them I was strong enough to hitch and un-hitch it. I get a lot of that kind of thing: 'What's a little lady like you doing all alone in that big, old motor home?' Well, because I prefer it that way. I get a lot of offers from men, but you'd have to be really in love, or in lust, or probably both, to share a twenty-seven-foot living space and make it work."

She belongs to an RV singles club called the WINS, the Wandering Individual Network, which has eighteen hundred members and caters to "active seniors" only—no over-seventies allowed. Married or single, most RVers belong to a club of some kind (there are hundreds to choose from), which arranges a year-round schedule of rallies and events, with group activities planned out for every day: pot-luck dinners, lapidary classes, sightseeing trips, dances, casino visits, and so on. Friendships blossom quickly and easily within this structure. A spirit of mutual cooperation develops. RVers drop out of sedentary communities and into tightly knit nomadic communities, comparable to tribes, or bands within a tribe.

"When you say 'singles club', people automatically assume it's about sex," says Marie, "but it's more about the companionship, and the sense that we're all in this together." That may be true, at least in Marie's case, but when her neighbors drop in for coffee or wine, conversation has a way of turning to sex and relationships and staying there for hours. There are eighteen WINS camped here, four men and fourteen women—a typical ratio on the RV singles scene, wrought solely by the difference in life expectancy—and in the view of the women it is having an unhealthy effect on the men.

Players, tom-cats, skirt-chasers, tepee-creepers: drinking coffee and wine with the WINS women, one hears these terms bandied about constantly, with varying degrees of bitterness. Joy Lane has a kinder explanation than most: "A lot of the men have been hurt, I guess. They're grieving, or they've come out of bad marriages and been taken for a ride, and they don't want to put themselves in a position where they could be hurt again. They're looking for a woman for one gathering, maybe two, but they're terrified of commitment. There are a few women the same way, who just want something casual, but most of the women I talk to are looking for a permanent relationship. They're looking for marriage."

"You got that right," Marie says firmly. "I don't want to be girlfriend to no man. I want to be a wife or nothing." She has been seeing a man named Grant (no relation), in the sense of going dancing together, eating together, spending a lot of time in each other's company, doing a little kissing. Two nights ago he came around drunk and tepee-creeping and she gave him his marching orders.

Last night she saw him dancing with another woman in Silly Al's, and she got the distinct impression they were going to spend the night together. She pitied the woman and disliked her at the same time. She didn't blame Grant unduly, because everyone knows what men are like. And the combination of Viagra and the mortality statistics has made them even worse.

My days have settled into a strange and jarring routine, a circuit that seldom takes me more than two hundred yards from Silly

Al's bar. I move from gossipy coffee mornings to petty drug deals, from shuffleboard competitions to lice-picking contests. From Jane and Jerry Bohanan, who prayed to the Lord for a thirty-foot RV with twin air conditioners within their price range and knelt down and wept when their prayers were answered, to guys with names like Timmy Two Tokes, Puddlescum, Mario Machete and Shitstained Mike.

Across the frontage road from Silly Al's is the Hi-Ali swap meet, where Chad and Tiffany and the A-Camp crew are hunkered down in their ratty tents, tarpaulin lean-tos and filthy old vans. There was a moment in the bathroom at the Texaco station, adjoining the Hi-Ali swap meet, which brought the culture clash at Quartzsite down to a snapshot. A big, wild-looking tramp was dying his beard green in the sink while a nervous retiree stood off to the side, holding a razor and a can of shaving foam, waiting to shave in the same sink. They were both nomads, but they regarded each other with deep suspicion and a sense of otherness. They belonged to hostile tribes and saw a stereotype and little more.

Chad is drinking his fourth beer of the morning, rubbing grease into a new tattoo on his arm. The yellowness has faded from his complexion, and considering that he and Tiffany have eight dollars to their name, and Lori Lori was jailed last night for public drunkenness, and the camp is running out of drugs, he is in an amiable mood. The tattoo reads "Trav'lin Man" and commemorates twenty years on the road. I ask him what changes he has seen.

He says it's harder to live on the road these days. The cops have computerized databases now, they are stricter about vehicle licenses, registration documents and broken tail-lights. Insurance has become mandatory in all states. Drunk-driving laws are harsher and there are fewer places to camp for free. He says there used to be a wider variety of nomads on the American road. Traveling bar tricksters, for example, are virtually extinct now. They would go from bar to bar, issuing improbable claims and gambling propositions—bragging that they could snap a penny in half with their fingers or do fifty one-armed push-ups and chug a beer within a minute—and, of course, they *could* do these things, and so won the bets every time. There was one who carried a live rattlesnake in a bell jar. He would get the snake all riled up and then bet that nobody could keep his hand on the glass when the snake struck at it. Apparently, it is almost impossible to control this reflex action, but it can be done with years of practice. And so the man collected on another round of bets. Who else?

"Well, you don't see the Avocado Brothers for Christ any more. That's what I called them. They were a religious cult of traveling avocado salesmen who kept their women totally subservient. They didn't allow their women to talk in public, and made them do all the cooking and cleaning up, and packing and unpacking, and everything else. Their old ladies would nod sometimes, maybe give you a little smile, but that was it. The men would drink beer and play horseshoes and sell a shitload of avocados.

"There was another outfit called the Christ Family. I called them Sheetheads. They wore a big white sheet wrapped around their heads, and they were real strict vegetarians. They'd give you all kinds of shit if you were wearing leather: 'You're wearing death. How would you like it if an animal wore your skin?' One of them was probably the most beautiful woman with a beard I've ever seen. Man, if she shaved that beard off, she was *fine*, by God. Hey Mario! Whatever happened to the Christ Family?"

Mario Machete, Guatemalan-born food vendor and A-Camp regular, at his *churro* stand a few yards away: "They're still around. But they're all wearing black leather and driving Harleys now. Bikers for Jesus and shit."

Chad is sitting on a lawn chair behind two fold-out tables strewn with Indian and animal-themed jewelry (made by Tiffany), pieces of semi-precious rock, soapstone pipes, antique beer bottles, a bear skull, an old gasoline can and other items. Littered all around him are piles and boxes of lesser junk—a broken generator, a tangled nest of electrical cables, a rusted exhaust pipe, old bits of chain, a broken bicycle, an old toilet with rust stains. "I don't even know what half this shit is, but people sure ain't buying it," he says.

Periodically, an RVer will wander by. Here comes a woman in lime-green golfing slacks and a white sun visor, carrying a dog under her arm. The dog is also wearing a white sun visor. Chad rises from his lawn chair and puts down his beer. He picks up a piece of polished rock from the table, licks it with his long yellow tongue, and launches into his sales spiel: "Here, look at the shine on that! It'll make a beautiful neck piece and today it's half price. I want ten bucks for it and that's the deal of the day." She purses up her lips, and wrinkles up her nose, and walks off without saying a word. So it goes.

Chad shrugs and sits back down. He is dependent on RVers for his livelihood, but with a few exceptions he doesn't like them. He thinks they lack a basic human decency. "Let me put it this way. If me and Tiffany are broke down on the road, they're not going to help us. And if they're broke down and we try to help them, they're going to roll up the windows and lock down the doors and call the cops. That's how paranoid they are. They watch too much TV in those goddamn RVs."

As morning turns to afternoon he becomes more strident in his opinions. "A few years ago you could tramp up in the desert around here and just go crazy. Kegs of beer, acid, speed, you name it. We had more guns than the cops, so they left us alone, and everything was cool. Then the RVers started bitching about "unde-sirable elements" and all this bullshit, and Quartzsite hired a bunch of new cops and passed a bunch of chickenshit laws and started charging you money for setting up in the swap meet. They'll bust you for drinking a beer in public! The goddamn Texaco won't even *sell* us beer. We don't need this bullshit, and a whole bunch of vendors are saying the same thing, 'Fuck Quartzsite! We ain't coming back next year.' Quartzsite is fucking itself up the ass like a double-dicked donkey, and it's all the RVers' doing."

Harsh words, a stern denunciation. Chad is deep into his second six-pack of Milwaukee's Best Ice now ("Milwaukee's Beast, the beer that made me famous"), and there are harsher words to come: "tight-fisted, butt-clenchin', lily-livered, faggoty-dog moth-erfuckers."

The bone of his contention, the clearest proof of the RVers' moral turpitude, is their selfishness with money. Chad, Tiffany or any right-minded Rainbow tramp would automatically give their last dollar for a communal beer run, in the certain knowledge that they would get a can or two in return. If an individual manages to hustle up some money, by selling something or begging, he buys beer, tobacco and food for the group, because it will probably be someone else who scores tomorrow. Sharing is a survival mechanism, but it is also a moral code, and those who fail to observe it are socially ostracized.

So you can imagine how they feel about someone driving a half-million-dollar motor home (top-of-the-line models run to a million, if you get the built-in Jacuzzi and all the trimmings) who refuses to give a dollar to a thirsty tramp. Chad has written a song on the subject, "The Wagon Burners." There was a famous occasion a few years ago (confirmed by Tiffany and numerous A-Camp sources) when Chad and his friend Jesse Manycolors, "The Croonin' Choctaw," sang it to an audience of horrified RVers. The Croonin' Choctaw had a singing engagement on a tented stage at Quartzsite. To the tune of "Folsom Prison Blues" by Johnny Cash, the song goes like this:

> Well, we went out on a beer run
> The wagons circled up
> They gave us no donations
> So we scalped their little pups
>
> Yes, we are the wagon burners
> We'll play a song for you
> Or we'll burn your fuckin' wagons
> Until we get a brew.

In the afternoons I drink beer in Silly Al's and argue about nomadism with a German vendor of lapis lazuli jewelry. In light of the drug laws and a nagging suspicion that some of his stories might be true I will call him by his first name: Charles. He wears a red beret, a luxuriant mustache and a great deal of lapis lazuli jewelry. He claims to have been Bob Dylan's road manager in the 1960s, a photojournalist for German magazines, an international drug smuggler, an LSD chemist who still cooks up from time to time, for himself and a select clientele who will settle for nothing but the very best. All I can tell you for certain is that he is intelligent, well educated and well traveled, and running short of money. And his pomposity is so unwavering and extreme that it achieves a kind of magnificence.

He cannot believe I am including the RVers in a book about nomads. It makes him pound his fists on the bar and denounce me as a fucking idiot. "They are not true nomads! I am the true nomad! I have traveled all over the world, to India, Thailand, Morocco, to Afghanistan, where I first discovered the la-*peeez*, the most powerful of all stones. If you say to me, okay, tomorrow we drive to the Yukon, the salmon fishing is great right now, I say let's go. We leave in the morning. If I have no money, I sell my jewelry on the road. These RVers are traveling with a safety net. Take away their social security checks and the RV rolls to a halt. They are not truly free."

I make my counter-arguments. They have no fixed abode, they move with the seasons, there are probably a million of them, maybe three million. How can I ignore them? Their social security checks are as dependable as the full moon every month, so why blame them for using this resource, and would he not do the same? I delve into the semantic hell surrounding the word "nomad." I suggest that he and I are better described as travelers. True nomads exist within tightly knit groups. They are not necessarily looking for adventure. They follow a reliable, predictable migration pattern, which best ensures survival and does not cross oceans in search of new experiences.

I push the point further, partly in the hope of provoking another outburst, and partly because I think it is true, in a perverse, metaphorical sense. Like it or not, the RVers are the dominant nomads in modern America, as the Comanche and Sioux were the dominant nomads in the nineteenth century. The RV has replaced the tepee as the symbol of American nomadism and is obliquely descended from the same tradition.

That gets a big guffaw. "Bah, you understand nothing. The nomad must be free. He must be the master of his destiny. These RVers, these little old ladies, *come on*."

★   ★   ★

Marie Williamson has moved north a few miles, to a WINS rally on the far desert fringes of the Quartzsite gathering. There are about two hundred RVs parked around the central fire-pit, with an inner circle of two hundred lawn chairs. Marie is welcomed with big, beaming smiles and enthusiastic hugs. Some of the people she knows, from recent rallies at casino parking lots in Nevada, a campground in Death Valley, an RV park in Yuma, and "The Slabs," a derelict air force base in the Mojave Desert that is taken over by some hundred thousand RVers every winter. Others she has never seen before, but she hugs them back just the same. The WINS have determined that hugging is what you miss most as an RVing single, and consequently they have made it a written requirement in their protocols.

The daily schedule is displayed on a board by the fire-pit. It begins at 7:30 in the morning with a communal "Sunrise Walk," then returns to camp for "Coffee and Hugs" at 8:30, then out again for "Doggie Walk" at 9:00. And so on throughout the day, with each new activity announced by someone blowing on a whistle—"rockhounding" expeditions to look for minerals and gemstones in the desert, "bring your own topping" potato bakes and potluck suppers. There are daily discussion circles, covering such topics as where to get free coupons for casinos or cheap insurance for driving into Mexico, how to avoid price-gouging RV mechanics and what to do if you have a heart attack on the road. At 7:30 in the evening there is a mass convoy, in carpools with designated drivers, to Silly Al's for country and western dancing. Since the men are outnumbered they are required to make sure that every woman gets at least one dance.

One is struck by their energy and enthusiasm for life, and their practical, no-nonsense attitude toward death. When it happens, it happens, and better sudden than protracted. In the meantime they are busy cramming as much living as possible into every day. It is an article of faith among nomadic retirees that the road has rejuvenating properties, and by their behavior and demeanor they make a strong case. "One thing I've discovered is that seniors who travel tend to live longer than the ones that stay home and sit in their rocking chairs," says Marie. "Every day on the road is an adventure. You're constantly meeting new challenges, having new experiences, meeting new people, and solving problems. When I think about going back to the sedentary life, the same humdrum routine every day, a little piece of me starts to die."

The biggest challenge of the RV lifestyle, as with most forms of modern nomadism, lies in the arena of romance. It is harder to make relationships work on the road. It requires higher levels of compatibility, or a greater willingness to compromise or, as Marie suggests, an unusual degree of love and lust. Even the largest RVs, forty-five feet long and eighteen feet high, which look so gigantic on the highways, can feel very small and cramped on the inside, especially if you are used to sharing a house of equivalent value.

It is difficult for nomadic couples to find periods of solitude from each other, or live divergent lives, and this makes it easier to get on each other's nerves. The lifestyle affords plentiful opportunities for arguments, over whose belongings or purchases are taking up unnecessary space, and how long to stay in a place, and where to go next. Full-time RVing puts marriages to the test and soon finds out the weak ones, and it works against lasting relationships among the singles, many of whom have grown accustomed to their independence. (Another dubious statistic: between 13 and 18 percent of RVers are estimated to be single.)

Because we have talked so much about love, sex and relationships, Marie is concerned that I have misunderstood her motivations and priorities. If the right man should happen to come along, and demonstrate his commitment with a proposal of marriage, she *might* consider taking him on board. But she is not looking for a man, and is certainly not desperate for one.

The feelings never go away: the desire to attract and hold a man, to be loved and cherished and intimate with a man. Marie still finds herself fretting over what to wear when she goes out dancing, even though she usually ends up in Wranglers, sneakers or cowboy boots and a plaid shirt. She still wonders who will ask her to dance, and what it will feel like in his arms. She still develops crushes from time to time, and sometimes she catches herself flirting in advance of any conscious decision to begin flirting.

At the same time she is a practical woman, and she has come to the conclusion that she is probably better off without a man. She has grown accustomed to following her whims, setting her own schedule and changing it when she feels like it. She relishes the independence of her new life and looks back at her marriage as a long servitude by comparison, "thirty-two years of looking after a man" that ended in pain and acrimony. Like the single men whom Joy Lane described, she is wary about putting herself in a position where she could be hurt like that again. Marie gets lonely from time to time, but her happiest moments are spent alone: packed-up, hitched-up and ready to go, with a long, straight highway ahead of her. Every time she leaves a place she cues up the same Willie Nelson song on her tape deck: "On the road again/Just can't wait to get on the road again."

She winters on the WINS circuit, making short hops around the Southwestern deserts, and then launches out on her own for Alaska, driving five or six hundred miles a day. These long, solo spring migrations set her apart from most RVers, male or female, married or single. The usual pattern is to move in small increments around the country, covering maybe two hundred miles a month, moving gradually north with the summer and south in winter, and remaining within the same group of people. "It gets too samey and regimented for me after a while," she says. "I start feeling hemmed in. My key fingers get itchy."

Sitting next to her at a WINS discussion circle, I am called on to stand up, introduce myself and state my business. I say my piece and conclude with a question: "Why do you live on the road?"

There is talk of freedom, independence, adventure and then, like good nomads, they respond with the flip-side of the question and start attacking the sedentary.

"Why would anyone want to sit in an armchair for the rest of their life?"

"You try to explain to them what they're missing out on, but they just don't get it."

"A bunch of old sticks in the mud," contributes Marie.

I offer up Satanta's comment from Medicine Lodge in 1867, "When we settle down, we grow pale and die," and there is a chorus of agreement. Not only do they consider themselves more vigorous than the armchair brigade, but when you're nearing seventy, and living full-time on the road, settlement is inextricably linked with death. It means the end of independence, the curtailment of freedom, a maudlin life-change known as "hanging up the keys." It conjures up the prospect of nursing homes, hospital beds, the inability to travel that precedes the grave. One cheery old gentleman says he would rather die in the bedroom of his RV, by way of a Viagra-induced heart attack, "in the saddle," as they say—a notion that does not go down well with the assembled women.

The great nomad encampment is starting to disperse. Every day you see more and more RVs stacked up behind the interstate ramps; more and more tramps standing there with their thumbs out and not getting a ride. Chad and Tiffany are packing up their van, bound for the gem and mineral show in Tucson, and the nightly tramp party in the grove of tamarisk trees adjoining it, four blocks from my house. Marie Williamson is in a state of high anticipation, and not just at the prospect of getting on the road again. A certain cowboy from Montana has called her message center and announced that he is on his way to meet her in Tucson. Something about the way she talks about him—coy, excited, giggly—leads me to tease her, "But Marie, I thought you were a pillar of virtue. I thought you didn't believe in sex without marriage. I thought you didn't want that kind of reputation."

"Oh, we've known each other for years," she says. "Eleven years, as a matter of fact. It's not like jumping into bed with some tepee-creeper. It's a completely different thing."

I take the long way home, craving silence and desert solitude. In the new way of doing things I call up Gale first and ask her how she feels about it. In the new way of doing things she tells me to go ahead, with no sign of annoyance or disappointment in her voice that I can discern. She does not say the dread word, "Fine!" Like so many women I have known, she uses this word in its passive-aggressive sense, as in, "Fine! Do whatever you like. I don't care."

Now that my love and commitment have been solidly established, I don't hear that any more. She has come to accept my
wandering in much the same way that I do. It is something to
be worked around, a necessary, if sometimes inconvenient, precon-
dition to my happiness. She jokes that I am on some kind of
lunar cycle, similar to her own. Three weeks into it I get tetchy,
out of sorts with myself and irritable with others, and sometimes—let us be frank—insufferable to be around. By the time
twenty-eight days are up I have left and begun a new cycle.

An hour's drive south from Quartzsite is the beginning of a
place known to its aficionados (we are small in number and very
few of us are female) as the Big Empty—three million acres
without a paved road or an occupied building, divided up on the
maps into the Cabeza Prieta Wildlife Refuge, the Barry M.
Goldwater Air Force Range and the western half of Organ Pipe
Cactus National Monument. Further south, across the Mexican
border and one paved road, it continues into the volcanic Pinacate
desert, an area of black rock and craters where the astronauts
trained for the moon, and the dunes of the Gran Desierto, the
largest sand sea in the Americas. There are bigger stretches of
desert in the world, but none of them is as ecologically intact,
or in more urgent need of preservation.

Gale doesn't share my enthusiasm for this parched enormity
of sand, rock, scrub and cactus. She was born and raised in the
Arizona desert (unlike most aficionados of the Big Empty) and
she is attracted to its oases: places of greenery, shade and water.
Out here there are no springs or rivers, and all the streams are
ephemeral. They roar into life after a downpour and dissolve into
the sands, and some years the rains never come.

There is water here. In certain places, far-flung and undetectable
unless you know where they are, or study the flight of birds, the
sparse rainfall collects in natural rock cisterns known as *tinajas*,
Spanish for "tanks," or earthenware jars of water. I make camp
by the most dependable of these *tinajas*. The others are prone to
evaporating away in dry periods, but there is always water to be
found at Tinajas Altas, assuming that you arrive here with the
strength to climb. Tinajas Altas: High Tanks, a series of pools caught

in a steeply descending defile, in a low, rocky, honeycombed mountain range that looks like a pile of pelvic bones.

It has rained this winter and there is water in the lowest tank. The water is covered in scum, algae and insects, and this is a good sign. If you come across water in the desert and the insects aren't drinking it, neither should you. Up by the highest tank, desert bighorn sheep are silhouetted against the sunset—such proud, actorly creatures. The rams, in particular, love to strike dramatic poses in high places with magnificent backdrops that show off their curling horns to full advantage. And then, with an air of insouciance, they lead their harems through a series of death-defying bounds, from one precarious ledge to the next, down an almost vertical cliff face. How low the domestic sheep has fallen. Some breeds cannot even give birth without human assistance.

In dry spells the scummy waters of the lowest tank evaporate down to sand, and it requires a tricky and energetic climb to get to the higher tanks, some of which always contain water. The sixty graves that used to surround Tinajas Altas, and are now mostly vandalized and gone, marked the deaths of those who arrived here too weak to make the climb and died of thirst. This is the worst way to go that I can imagine, despite the desert setting. There are journal accounts of people scrabbling at the rockface until they wore their fingers down to the bone, knowing that water was fifteen feet above them.

What were they doing out here in the first place? Many of them were argonauts, trying to reach the California goldfields in 1849. They risked the terrible trail across these deserts—El Camino del Diablo, The Highway of the Devil—to avoid the Apaches to the north, who were raiding along the Gila River. The trail was littered with the bones of dead horses, oxen and other livestock. A macabre custom developed. People would lift up their dead, stiffened animals until they were standing on all fours again and leave them there as signposts, until the wind and the scavengers worked off the meat and hide and the skeleton collapsed. The approach to Tinajas Altas, in 1861, was a "long avenue between rows of mummified cattle, horses, and sheep."

Here is a sight that never ceases to amaze me. Around the lowest pool at Tinajas Altas there are grinding holes worn down into the rocks. Dressed in rabbit-hide skirts and sandals, bare to the waist, the women of the Sand Papago bands would pulverize the ripened seed pods of mesquite trees in these holes. They made a kind of flour, mixed it with water from the *tinajas*, and laid out the paste to dry on the rocks, forming a kind of bread, sweet to the taste. To be accompanied, perhaps, by toasted caterpillars, moth larvae or rats. Maybe a jackrabbit, run down until it collapsed from exhaustion, or if the hunters' medicine was strong, an elusive bighorn sheep.

I have read the sparse literature in its entirety. I know how they survived out here, in one of the hottest, driest, harshest environments in the world, but it required a level of toughness and resourcefulness that I find unimaginable. There were never more than five hundred Sand Papagos (known to themselves as the Hiaced O'Oodham), and perhaps as few as two hundred, but they lived in these deserts, without interruption, for thousands of years, moving from one *tinaja* to the next, hunting and gathering, covering immense distances on foot. When Spanish explorers, and later Mexicans and Anglos, told them that they lived a poor and miserable life in a godforsaken hell not meant for human beings, they scorned the idea, and said they lived well.

Graves and grinding holes: monuments to two different strands of the wandering tradition. The linear migrations of the argonauts, born of restlessness and dreams of fortune in a new land to the west. And the circular wanderings of the Sand Papago, a people so finely tuned to the meager shifting resources of their homeland that they regarded it as a place of bounty that supplied everything necessary for life.

They ate a lot of roots, seeds, cactus fruit, grubs, rodents, reptiles and insects. When the moon called up high tides in the Gulf of California and swept fish into the coastal shallows and rock pools they speared them with the tailbones of the barbed stingray. They collected clams and other shellfish, salt and colored seashells for trade. They hunted sea lions, made sandals from their hides, and then went back into the deserts to harvest whichever plant had come into season, or drink from some *tinaja* filled by a distant storm and hunt the animals attracted by the water.

As a freelance writer who loves to wander in their former homeland (until I run out of supermarket food or get low on water) there is one facet of Sand Papago culture that intrigues me above all else. As they lay sleeping in the desert—under trees, out in the open or in "sleeping circles" of rocks, stacked up to keep out the wind—stories and songs came to them in dreams, which they converted into a commodity with economic value in the marketplace. They would show up at the Cocopa villages on the Colorado River and trade these songs and stories for food, pottery and other items. The Cocopa thought that the dreams of the Sand Papago were valuable because of their spiritual power. None of the songs or stories has survived, but who knows? Maybe the Cocopa were right. All the world's major religions were dreamed up by desert wanderers, which is why they focus on deities who live in the sky.

There is another reason why I have been reading up on the Sand Papago. Perhaps a scholar somewhere can produce an obscure band in the wilds of Nevada, but I have seen it written in several places that the Sand Papago were the last free-roaming Indians in the lower forty-eight states. They were reduced and disrupted in the mid-nineteenth century, primarily by an attack of yellow fever in 1851, but some of them were still out here in the 1890s, robbing and killing travelers on the Devil's Highway. They had never been a kind and gentle people toward outsiders and intruders. Bernard Fontana, the leading authority, describes them as "a tough and quarrelsome lot," and Carl Lumholtz, the intrepid and fair-minded Norwegian traveler who hired some Sand Papago guides in the early twentieth century, said they were, or had been, "rapacious and probably merciless to strangers, whether Indian or Mexican."

The last of them, a hermit named Juan Caravajales, whose wife had left him because she couldn't take the isolation, came in from the Pinacate Desert in 1912 and joined the remnants of his tribe in the settlements on the Gila River, where they had taken up farming and paid labor. Why did they hold out for so long? Mainly because they were able to. The Big Empty was considered a worthless, diabolical wasteland by everyone else, which is why it remains

so unspoiled today—we have not found a way to wrest a profit
from it. But for the Sand Papago it was their homeland, filled
with sacred sites. They thought wandering the desert was how
they were meant to live, and so they clung to the old life for as
long as possible. It was how they defined themselves as a people.
"We don't stay in one place," said one of their elders, interviewed
in the 1980s. "We are the Sand Indians originated out of the sand
to roam on top of it."

My desert wanderings are governed by entirely different reasons,
which I don't fully understand. I cannot claim survival require-
ments or cultural imperatives. To the east of Tinajas Altas is the
Lechuguilla Desert, a wide, flat pan of sand and scrub that leads
to the next mountain range and the next *tinaja*. Why do I feel
compelled to walk the seventeen miles across it, fill up my canteen
and walk back again? I have given up trying to explain these
things in conversation. Some people think it must be something
to do with machismo—conquering fears or adversity—but this
is not it at all. It is a humbling experience, a form of surrender,
a stripping away of the ego, a blooming of the senses.

To a fellow desert rat, the attraction is understood, and so is
the impossibility of capturing it in words. We talk instead about
graves and grinding holes, how many miles to the next *tinaja*, the
weather, the history, the geography, skirting around the thing itself,
because language is a poor tool for describing nothingness and
space. There have been some valiant attempts—Edward Abbey on
the American Southwest, Paul Bowles writing about the Sahara,
Wilfred Thesiger in *Arabian Sands*—but the literature of deserts
is essentially a failure. One becomes familiar with a grasping tone,
a tacit admission of defeat (often signposted by flinging more and
more purple prose at the problem, like Everett Ruess), and herein
lies the appeal of deserts for those who love them. They defy our
language, written and visual. They leave our photographers,
painters and cinematographers scratching at the surface of what
is really there.

Why are some people attracted to deserts and others indif-
ferent toward them or repelled? Why are some people attracted

to mountains and others to beaches or oceans? Why do some people feel an affinity for the outdoors while others are drawn toward cities? There is no way to examine a person's background, cultural or genetic, and predict these things with any authority. Some people feel happiest and most alive in familiar environments. Others are attracted to the opposite of the familiar. Siblings often have completely different tastes.

Why do some people feel compelled to wander? In the first chapter I mentioned Bruce Chatwin's theory that human beings are a migratory species, genetically hard-wired for travel during our long evolution as wandering hunter-gatherers, and that all the ills and miseries of our societies stem from the repression of this basic human instinct. I have tried hard to believe in this theory and come up short. The game is always receding, edible plants come into season at different times in different places. Travel is certainly necessary for survival among hunter-gatherers, a task that everyone has to perform, but that does not necessarily prove that the urge for travel became instinctual. Did the Sand Papago resist settlement because they were in tune with their instincts, or because they were culturally conservative and happy enough with life as they knew it?

Chatwin's theory has an elegant symmetry, and it is certainly curious that all human babies are calmed by the rhythm of motion, as they are by music, but it does not answer the question that nomads are always asking: why do so many people prefer to stay in one place? The sedentary are not all discontented and repressed. They are not all weak, foolish dupes who have traded their freedom for security, as nomads would have us believe. Some people simply lack the urge to travel, and, given a free choice, they are perfectly happy and content with the sedentary life.

I read the other day about some ten-thousand-year-old bones that were dug up in Scotland—a country that furnished so many restless wanderers to North America in the nineteenth century. The scientists DNA-tested the bones and the inhabitants of the nearest village and found that many of the latter were direct descendants. Presumably, the ten-thousand-year-old corpse had many other descendants who spread his lineage further afield, but the findings indicate an extraordinary lack of wanderlust in these village clanfolk, a striking absence of anything resembling a migratory instinct.

I think wanderlust is simply a human personality trait, one of many lying in the reservoir of our genes, comparable to greed or generosity, caution or recklessness, and subservient to the influence of culture. It is called forth more frequently in societies with a tradition of wandering and restlessness, and in places where it is easy to live a mobile life. Restless parents tend to bequeath restless children, but not all of their offspring will manifest the personality type. Likewise, wanderers are born into families that have lived in the same place for generations. It is not an instinct, it is not a psychiatric disorder, it is not a disease.

"When all is said and done, there are two types of men: those who stay at home and those who do not." I seldom find myself agreeing with Rudyard Kipling, but if we take Marie Williamson as a cue, and substitute "people" for "men," I have reached the same flat conclusion.

At this point in the narrative, I am supposed to wander off into the sunset. That was my plan: three days with a backpack over the sand dunes of the Gran Desierto, the emptiest quarter of the Big Empty. Instead, I find myself pulled in the opposite direction, east toward Tucson, the comforts of home and the woman I love, which have also become necessary to my happiness.

In closing, I would like to thank the federal government and the hard-working agents of the Immigration and Naturalization Service. Fear of deportation overcame deeper fears and prejudices and led to a wedding that should have taken place years ago.

SELECTED
BIBLIOGRAPHY

Abbott, E. C., and Smith, Helena Huntington, *We Pointed Them North: Recollections of a Cowpuncher*, Norman, University of Oklahoma, 1955

Basso, Keith H. (ed.), *Western Apache Raiding and Warfare*, Tucson, University of Arizona Press, 1993

Bell, Fillman, *The Quitobaquito Cemetery and its History*, Tucson, Western Archaeological Center, National Park Service, 1980

Bey, Hakim, *T.A.Z.: The Temporary Autonomous Zone, Ontological Anarchy, Poetic Terrorism,* Brooklyn, Autonomedia, 1991

Brown, George Willard (ed.), *Desert Biology*, New York, Academic Press, 1974

Cabeza de Vaca, Alvar Nuñez, *Adventures in the Unknown Interior of America*, Albuquerque, University of New Mexico Press, 1997

Castañeda, Pedro de, et al., *The Journey of Coronado*, New York, Dover, 1990

Chatwin, Bruce, *The Songlines*, New York, Viking Penguin, 1987

—— *What Am I Doing Here*, New York, Viking Penguin, 1989

—— *Anatomy of Restlessness*, New York, Viking Penguin, 1996

Counts, D. A., and Counts, D. R., *Over the Next Hill: An Ethnography of RVing Seniors in North America*, Peterborough, Ontario, Broadview Press, 1996

Deleuze, G., and Guattari, F., *A Thousand Plateaus: Capitalism and Schizophrenia*, Minneapolis, University of Minnesota Press, 1987

Deloria, Vine, *Custer Died for Your Sins*, Norman, University of Oklahoma, 1988

Denhardt, Robert M., *The Horse of the Americas*, Norman, University of Oklahoma Press, 1975

De Voto, Bernard, *Across the Wide Missouri*, Boston, Houghton Mifflin, 1947

—— *The Course of Empire*, Lincoln, University of Nebraska Press, 1952

Dobie, J. Frank, *The Mustangs*, Boston, Little, Brown, 1952

—— *The Longhorns*, New York, Grosset & Dunlap, 1941

Faragher, John Mack, *Daniel Boone: The Life and Legend of an American Pioneer*, New York, Henry Holt, 1993

Fehrenbach, T. R., *Comanches: The Destruction of a People*, New York, Da Capo Press, 1994

Ferris, Warren, *Life in the Rocky Mountains*, Denver, Old West Publishing Company, 1940

Fischer, David Hackett, *Albion's Seed*, Oxford, Oxford University Press, 1989

Foster, Morris W., *Being Comanche*, Tucson, University of Arizona Press, 1991

Garrard, Lewis H., *Wah-to-yah and the Taos Trail*, Norman, University of Oklahoma Press, 1966

Gilbert, Bil, *Westering Man: The Life of Joseph Walker*, Norman, University of Oklahoma Press, 1983

Hayden, Julian, *Sierra Pinacate*, Tucson, University of Arizona Press, 1998

Khazanov, A. M., *Nomads and the Outside World*, Madison, University of Wisconsin Press, 1994

Leonard, Zenas, *Adventures of a Mountain Man*, Lincoln, University of Nebraska Press, 1978

Maguire, James H., Wild, Peter, and Barclay, Donald A. (eds.), *A Rendezvous Reader: Tall, Tangled, and True Tales of the Mountain Men, 1805–1850*, Salt Lake City, University of Utah Press, 1997

Morgan, David, *The Mongols*, New York, Blackwell, 1986

Niman, Michael I., *People of the Rainbow: A Nomadic Utopia*, Knoxville, University of Tennessee Press, 1997

Olsen, Paul A., *The Struggle for the Land*, Lincoln, University of Nebraska, 1990

Olson, Charles, *Call Me Ishmael*, New York, Reynal & Hitchcock, 1947

Onon, Urgunge, *The Secret History of the Mongols*, Richmond, Curzon, 2000

Roberts, David, *Once They Moved Like the Wind: Cochise, Geronimo, and the Apache Wars*, New York, Simon & Schuster, 1994

Rusho, W. L., *Everett Ruess: A Vagabond for Beauty*, Salt Lake City, Peregrine Smith, 1983

Ruxton, George Frederick, *Life in the Far West*, Norman, University of Oklahoma Press, 1951

Salzman, Philip Carl, *When Nomads Settle*, New York, Praeger, 1980

Sandoz, Mari, *The Buffalo Hunters*, Lincoln, University of Nebraska Press, 1954

—— *The Cattlemen*, Lincoln, University of Nebraska Press, 1958

—— *The Beaver Men*, Lincoln, University of Nebraska Press, 1964

Stegner, Wallace, *Where the Bluebird Sings to the Lemonade Springs*, New York, Penguin, 1993

Thistlethwaite, Frank, *The Great Experiment*, Cambridge, Cambridge University Press, 1955

Turner, Frederick, *Beyond Geography: The Western Spirit Against the Wilderness*, New Brunswick, Rutgers University Press, 1994

Wallace, E., and Hoebel, E. A., *The Comanches: Lords of the South Plains*, Norman, University of Oklahoma Press, 1986

Webb, Walter Prescott, *The Great Plains*, Boston, Houghton Mifflin, 1936

Westermeier, Clifford, *Man, Beast, Dust*, Denver, World Press, 1948